Refuge in
the Lord

Lawrence J. McAndrews

Refuge in the Lord

CATHOLICS,

PRESIDENTS &

THE POLITICS OF

IMMIGRATION,

1981–2013

The Catholic University of America Press
Washington, D.C.

Library of Congress Cataloging-in-Publication Data
McAndrews, Lawrence J. (Lawrence John)
Refuge in the Lord : Catholics, presidents, and the politics
of immigration, 1981–2013 / Lawrence J. McAndrews.
pages cm
Includes bibliographical references and index.
ISBN 978-0-8132-2779-5 (paperback : alkaline paper)
1. United States—Emigration and immigration—
Government policy—History—20th century.
2. United States—Emigration and immigration—
Government policy—History—21st century.   3. United
States—Emigration and immigration—Religious
aspects—History.   4. Presidents—United States—
History—20th century.   5. Presidents—United
States—History—21st century.   6. Catholics—
Political activity—United States—History.   7. Religion
and politics—United States—History.   8. Church and
state—United States—History.   9. United States—
Politics and government—1981–1989.   10. United States—
Politics and government—1989–   I. Title.
JV6483.M3345 2015
325.73—dc23   2015016879

To My Students

Contents

Acknowledgments

I AM GRATEFUL to Brittany Young, Krista Perine, Nancy Halsey, and all of the archivists who helped me to research and prepare this manuscript. Special thanks to the readers of this manuscript, the editorial committee, and director Trevor Lipscombe, for recommending this manuscript for publication by the Catholic University of America Press.

Preface

AS AN AMERICAN AND A CATHOLIC, I have long been intrigued by the relationships between my government and my church. As a presidential historian, I have devoted much of my scholarship to the interactions between American presidents and Catholic leaders. Two of my books focused on American education policy and politics, in which Catholics, led by their bishops, have played a prominent role. A third book studied the influence of Catholics, led by their bishops, on matters of social justice, war and peace, and life and death.

While I was finishing this third book, the topic of immigration reform was moving to the front and center of presidential politics. Since immigration has been an integral part of the American Catholic story, it seemed a natural candidate for my next research topic. As in my previous work, I sought to uncover the impact of Catholic voices on the immigration debate.

What particularly fascinates me about American Catholics is that they defy easy ideological identification. Conservative Republicans have cheered the church power structure's allegiance to federal aid for Catholic schools and resistance to federal funding of abortion. Liberal Democrats have applauded the hierarchy's aversion to large federal defense budgets and its advocacy of generous federal social expenditures. Meanwhile, the Catholic rank and file in recent times have constituted a "swing vote," feverishly courted by both major parties.

While they have been forthright in taking their stands on pressing political issues, Catholic leaders have not always been effective in helping to convert their positions into American policy. They have largely failed in their attempts to obtain federal aid for their schools but have mainly succeeded in their mission of helping to prevent federal funding of abortion. They have alternately failed and succeeded in their efforts to help reduce defense budgets and increase social spending.

My concern in this book, as in the others, is not whether I share the political positions of these Catholic leaders. It is whether they are being rigid or reasonable, advancing or inhibiting their cause, abetting or undermining the presidents, and attracting or alienating their fellow Catholics. Through my research, I would discover that in the politics of immigration from 1981 to 2013, Catholic leaders and American presidents frequently found areas of agreement. Yet in part because of the way in which these Catholics pursued their disagreements, the problems festered and the presidents failed.

Refuge in the Lord

Introduction

It is better to take refuge in the Lord than to rely on human beings,
better to take refuge in the Lord than to rely on Princes.

Psalm 118

IMMIGRATION HAS LONG DEFINED AMERICANS, but it has also divided them. In the last three decades, as American presidents have sought to fix the nation's immigration system, it has only become more broken. With no credible resolution on the horizon, American Catholic leaders have tried to make the best of a bad situation. In so doing, however, they have found themselves at times challenging their presidents and unsettling their followers.

In vigorously seeking a solution to the country's immigration conundrum, the American bishops and other Catholic immigration advocates have too often exacerbated the problem. While accurately indicting American "princes" for their inability to construct workable compromises on immigration issues, these Catholics exhibited their own unhealthy intransigence as they took "refuge in the Lord." By adopting unrealistic positions in the name of religion, they too often impeded sensible accommodations in the realm of politics. The failure of immigration reform, therefore, has been the responsibility of church as well as state.

There is no shortage of books on American immigration policy. Among them are Elizabeth Rolph, *Immigration Policies: Legacy From the 1980's and Issues from the 1990's;* Saskia Sassen, *Losing Control? Sovereignty in an Age of Globalization;* Frank Bean, *At the Crossroads: Mexico and U.S. Immigration Policy;* Peter Schuck, *Citizens, Strangers, and In-Betweens;* James Gimpel and James Edwards, *The Congressional*

Politics of Immigration Reform; Debra DeLaet, U.S. Immigration Policy in the Age of Rights; Nicolas Laham, Ronald Reagan and the Politics of Immigration; Cheryl Shanks, The Politics of American Sovereignty; Hugh Davis Graham, Collision Course: The Strange Convergence of Affirmative Action and Immigration Policy in America; Roger Daniels, Guarding the Golden Door: American Immigration Policy and Immigration Since 1882; Mae Ngai, Impossible Subjects: Illegal Aliens and the Making of Modern America; Marc Rosenblum, The Transnational Politics of U.S. Immigration Policy; Otis Graham, Immigration Reform and America's Unchosen Future; Kathleen Arnold, Immigration after 1996: The Shifting Ground of Political Inclusion, and Philip Kretsedemas, The Immigration Crucible: Transforming Race, Nation, and the Limits of the Law.[1]

There are several studies of Catholic teaching on immigration. Felix Podimattam's The Struggle for Justice and Responsible Disobedience; Daniel Groody's Border of Death, Valley of Life; Gioacchino Campese and Pietro Ciallella's Migration, Religious Experience, and Globalization; David Badillo's Latinos and the New Immigrant Church; Daniel Groody and Gioacchino Campese's A Promised Land: A Perilous Journey; Patrick Bascio's On the Immorality of Illegal Immigration; Donald Kerwin's And You Welcomed Me: Migration and Catholic Social Teaching, Ben Daniel's Neighbor, Timothy Matovina's Latino Catholicism, and Todd Scribner and Kevin Appleby's On "Strangers No Longer" are recent treatments of this topic. Papal encyclicals and bishops' statements and pastoral letters have also shed light on the subject.[2]

This study is the first effort to connect the roles of church and state, by examining the interactions between the presidents who have executed American immigration policy and the Catholics who have endorsed, implemented, opposed, and obstructed it. This relationship has been alternately cooperative and combative. But it has always been vital. Many of the recent immigrants to the United States have been Latinos. And most of these Latinos have been Catholics. So neither presidents casting for votes nor prelates searching for souls should dare overlook them.

Catholics and Immigration

The story of American Catholics is one of an immigrant church in an immigrant nation. From 1820 to 1920, over thirty million newcomers, mostly European and heavily Catholic, arrived in the United States. By the turn of the twentieth century the foreign-born comprised 15 percent of the nation's population, and Catholics were 75 percent of the foreign-born. From 1880 to 1926, the U.S. Catholic population increased from 7.34 to 18.6 million.[3]

These newest Americans were not always welcome. Protestants burned Catholic churches in 1844 in Philadelphia to prevent the city's public schools from adopting the Catholic Bible. The American, or "Know-Nothing," Party formed in 1850 to preclude Catholics from holding public office. And Catholics were among the targets of the Ku Klux Klan, founded in 1866 in Pulaski, Tennessee to advance white Protestant supremacy. Mexican Catholics who became Americans when their country lost a war and much of its territory in 1848 would endure discrimination at school, at work, and at the polls long after that.

Shunned by mainstream society, many American Catholics turned inward, creating their own neighborhoods, churches, and schools. In August 1917, 115 delegates from sixty-eight dioceses and twenty-eight national organizations met at the Catholic University of America in Washington, D.C. "to devise a plan of organization throughout the United States to promote the spiritual and material welfare of the United States troops at home and abroad and to study, coordinate, unify, and put into operation all Catholic activities incidental to the war." In November, this organization became the National Catholic War Council.

Two years later, World War I had ended but the work of the council had not. The bishops renamed the organization the National Catholic Welfare Council, which included a seven-member administrative committee chosen by the bishops and a General Secretary selected by the Administrative Committee. In 1920, the National Catholic Welfare Council established an immigration bureau to dispense money and counsel to arriving immigrants. In 1922, the Holy See recognized the council, which then became the National Catholic Welfare Conference (NCWC).[4]

In 1923, the National Catholic Rural Life Conference (NCRLC) grew out of the NCWC's Rural Life Bureau in order to provide spiritual guidance, educational assistance, and political support for rural dwellers. With the blessing of his fellow prelates, Archbishop Robert Lucey of San Antonio in 1945 formed the Bishops' Committee for the Spanish Speaking. In 1953, the Immigration Bureau became the Immigration Department, and in 1965 it became the Office of Migration and Refugee Services, in charge of refugee resettlement, immigrant services, and public advocacy on immigration matters. In 1966, the NCWC split in two—the National Conference of Catholic Bishops (NCCB) would be in charge of canonical matters, and the United States Catholic Conference (USCC) would deal with civil issues. Upon Archbishop Lucey's retirement in 1969, the Bishops' Committee for the Spanish Speaking formally joined the USCC as the Bishops' Committee for Hispanic Affairs. In 2001, the NCCB and USCC became one, the United States Conference of Catholic Bishops (USCCB). In 2007, the Secretariat for Hispanic Affairs became part of the Secretariat for Cultural Diversity in the Church.[5]

Presidents and Immigration

The United States government, which had opened its doors to virtually all comers during the country's first tumultuous century, began to close them in 1882. That year, Republican president Chester Arthur signed the Chinese Exclusion Act, which imposed a ten-year halt to the importation of Chinese workers. The law also mandated that Chinese nonlaborers obtain certification from their country's government before emigrating to the United States. Very few Chinese received this permission, however, because of the statute's definition of workers as "skilled and unskilled laborers and Chinese employed in mining." The Geary Act extended this act for ten more years in 1892, and it became permanent in 1902.[6]

Infected by the nativism which accompanied the country's participation in World War I, Congress, over Democratic president Woodrow Wilson's veto, enacted the Immigration Act of 1917. The law prohibited the immigration of illiterate persons and those with mental health problems, while further restricting the admission of Asians and expanding the category of aliens subject to deportation. Following the war, Republican president Warren Harding signed the Immigration Quota Act of 1921, which established an annual immigration quota of 3 percent of each nationality of foreign-born persons residing in the U.S. in 1910. Three years later, Republican president Calvin Coolidge signed the Immigration Act of 1924, which reduced the 1921 quotas to 2 percent, while excluding Japanese and Korean immigrants. Although the League of Nations had devised a legal definition of "refugee" to distinguish those (such as Armenians and Russians) needing special humanitarian assistance from other immigrants, the U.S. quotas made no such distinction. By the time Congress and Republican president Herbert Hoover had extended the 1924 law in 1929, immigration had dipped to half of the 1920 total. In 1930, Hoover expanded the term "likely to become a public charge (LPC)," which had been part of U.S. immigration law since 1891, to include those who were unlikely to find a job.

Between 1933 and 1944, the United States under Democratic president Franklin Roosevelt accepted about 250,000 refugees, primarily Jews fleeing the Holocaust, but, due in large part to a liberal interpretation of the LPC provision, the country filled only 40 percent of its quota for German immigrants. On the eve of U.S. entrance into World War II, Roosevelt also instituted a temporary asylum program to admit those endangered by the growing war in Europe. In 1942 Roosevelt responded to the country's need for agricultural labor during World War II by issuing an executive order which established the *bracero* program. The directive authorized a series of short-term contracts between American growers and Mexican workers. In 1943, Roosevelt revoked the Geary Act's exclusion of Chinese immigrants, as a gesture to the United States' wartime ally.

In 1951, Democratic president Harry Truman refused to sign the United Nations Convention Relating to the Status of Refugees, which defined a refugee as someone with a "well-founded fear of being persecuted for reasons of race, religion, nationality, [or] membership of a particular social group or political opinion," even though it did not require any signatory to admit refugees. The Immigration and Nationality Act of 1952, which Congress passed over Truman's veto, revised the 1924 quota scheme to one-sixth of 1 percent of the number of inhabitants from each country in the continental United States in 1920, and granted the attorney general "parole" authority under which he could temporarily admit persons if it served the "public interest"—a phrase which for the next three decades largely opened the door to refugees from communist countries while closing it on almost everyone else. The 1952 law also removed race and gender distinctions from immigration decisions. The following year, Truman signed the Refugee Relief Act, which permitted exceptions to immigration quotas for those "escapees" who were fleeing communist or Middle Eastern countries.

Ignited by the inclusiveness of the civil rights movement and the competitiveness of the Cold War, the federal government under Democratic president Lyndon Johnson reversed the quotas of the earlier legislation with the Immigration and Nationality Act of 1965. The new law established a seven-category preference system which primarily valued family reunification and secondarily valued skills needed in the United States. It doubled the number of immigrants accepted into the United States, while placing no limits on the admission of the spouses, children, and parents of U.S. citizens. It welcomed as many as 170,000 immigrants from the eastern hemisphere (with no more than twenty thousand from each country) as well as 120,000 from the western hemisphere every year.[7]

Since the law attached no quotas to its family reunification provisions, annual legal immigration numbers rose by over 100,000 by 1975, and continued to rise into the 1990s. Between 1960 and 1964, an average of 800,000 legal immigrants each year had been Canadian or European, 485,000 Latin American, and 144,000 Asian. From 1975 to 1979, only 429,000 legal immigrants arrived annually from Canada and Europe, but 992,000 came from Latin America and 918,000 from Asia. The law's liberal family reunification guidelines, coming on the heels of the abolition of the *bracero* temporary worker program in 1964, unintentionally encouraged a wave of illegal immigration and the demand to stop it.[8]

So in 1986 the federal government under Republican president Ronald Reagan instituted the Immigration Reform and Control Act. This measure granted amnesty to those irregular aliens already in the United States, and punished employers who sought to hire more. Republican president George H. W. Bush signed the Immigration Act of 1990, which raised immigration limits while modifying the reasons for exclusion and deportation, and extending protected status to aliens from selected countries. Democratic president Bill Clinton enacted the Illegal Immigration Reform and Immigrant Responsibility Act of 1996, which strengthened border enforcement, combated alien smuggling and document fraud, and further revised the basis for exclusion and deportation.[9]

In the wake of the September 11, 2001, attacks, President George W. Bush conducted a coordinated military, diplomatic, intelligence, and economic effort to deny entry into the country by persons deemed national security risks. The House of Representatives passed the Border Protection, Antiterrorism, and Illegal Immigration Control Act of 2005, which mandated increased border security, while the Senate passed the Comprehensive Immigration

Reform Act of 2006, which coupled border enforcement with a five-year path to citizenship for unauthorized aliens. But the failure to reconcile the two versions helped prevent Bush, who was more sympathetic to the Senate approach, from signing a new, more restrictive bill into law.

Democratic president Barack Obama took his turn at solving the immigration riddle in 2010 by endorsing the Development, Relief, and Education for Alien Minds (DREAM) Act, which would have offered a path to citizenship for the foreign-born children of unauthorized aliens who attend college or serve in the military. After the measure failed on Capitol Hill, the president in 2012 issued an executive order granting temporary legal residence, though not citizenship, to all children of irregular immigrants thirty years old or younger who had arrived in the United States before they turned sixteen. In 2013, after winning reelection with the votes of close to three-quarters of Asian-Americans and Latinos, Obama embraced a comprehensive immigration reform measure which, despite its bipartisan origins, passed the Senate with mostly Democratic support, only to die in the more restrictionist, mostly Republican House of Representatives.[10]

Meanwhile, the illegal immigration problem remained unresolved. The annual arrival of about 800,000 undocumented aliens (300,000 of whom were deported) had raised their number to over 12 million by 2008, adding a population whose growth rate exceeded those of native-born citizens and legal immigrants. Most of the newcomers were from Mexico and Central America, and, like those who had flocked to American shores a century earlier, most of them were Catholic.[11]

The Catholics Respond to the Presidents

The Roman Catholic Church had been addressing immigration long before the issue confronted U.S. presidents. The first source of

Catholic social teaching on immigration is the Bible. The expulsion of Adam and Eve from the Garden of Eden, the exile of Cain following the murder of his brother Abel, the exhortation to Noah to travel in an ark, and the exodus of Moses and the Israelites from slavery in Egypt to freedom in Zion are among the immigration stories which permeate the Old Testament. "When an alien resides with you in your land, you shall not oppress the alien," God instructs in the Book of Leviticus. "The alien who resides with you shall be to you as the citizen among you; you shall love the alien as yourself."[12]

Immigration infuses the telling of the New Testament as well. Jesus is born to migrant parents who journeyed from Nazareth to Bethlehem. The Christ child's first visitors are Magi who have carried their gifts across political borders. Many of Jesus' parables, including the tale of the Good Samaritan, prescribe hospitality to strangers. At the Last Judgment, according to the evangelist Matthew, "the just" will testify to God that "when did we see thee a stranger, and took thee in." During the end times, the City of Man will yield to the City of God, where everyone is an immigrant. "Its gates will never be shut by day, and there will be no night there," writes the evangelist John. "People will bring into it the glory and honor of the nation."[13]

Catholic social teaching has built upon this Biblical foundation. Modern Catholic concepts of "social justice" trace their origins to the thirteenth-century writings of St. Thomas Aquinas, who defined "general justice" as the pursuit of the "common good." To this first principle he would add "distributive justice," which dictated the "subsidiarity" of society, and "commutative justice," which required the "solidarity" of society, in this quest for the common good. Pope Leo XIII, in his 1891 encyclical *Rerum Novarum* (Of New Things); Pope Pius XI, in his 1931 encyclical *Quadragesimo Anno* (The Fortieth Year); and Pope John XXIII, in his 1963 encyclical *Mater et Magister* (Mother and Teacher), adapted these themes to the modern era.[14]

Under this broad rubric of Catholic social teaching the church has specifically addressed immigration. "We find in most countries, cities, and dioceses people of diverse languages who, though bound by one faith, have varied rights and customs," the church hierarchy observed at the Fifth Lateran Council in Rome in 1215. "Therefore we strictly enjoin that the Bishops of these cities or dioceses provide the proper men, who will celebrate the Liturgical Functions according to their rite and language." Over seven centuries later, President Truman appointed one of these "proper men," Archbishop Lucey, to his advisory panel on the *bracero* program. During the panel's public hearings in 1950, Rev. Theodore Radthe of the Bishops' Committee for the Spanish Speaking testified against the oppressive conditions under which the *braceros* labored.[15]

In the 1952 apostolic constitution *Exsul Familia* (Refugee Family), Pope Pius XII depicted the "emigre Holy Family of Nazareth, fleeing into Egypt," as "the archetype of every refugee family." The church particularly feared that those persons displaced during the aftermath of the Second World War might fall under atheistic communist rule, as the Iron Curtain descended on Europe. The United States Catholic bishops therefore opposed that year's restrictive immigration law, with Rev. William Gibbons of the National Catholic Rural Life Conference testifying in Congress in favor of higher ceilings for immigration from heavily Catholic eastern and southern Europe. In 1958, Catholic Democratic senator John F. Kennedy echoed the principles of his church in the book *A Nation of Immigrants,* in which he espoused the replacement of the 1924 national origins quotas with the admission of more immigrants based on their skills and the reunification of their families. These tenets would become the foundation for President Kennedy's immigration reform proposal in 1963.[16]

In "Christus Dominus" (Christ the Lord), the Second Vatican Council (1962–1965) urged the world's bishops to minister to the needs of those who "are not adequately cared for by the ordinary pastoral ministry of the parochial clergy or not entirely deprived of it," especially "the many migrants, exiles, and refugees." In his encyclical *Pacem in Terris* (Peace on Earth) in 1963, Pope John XXIII posited that "among man's personal rights we must include his right to enter a country in which he hopes to be able to provide more fittingly for himself and his dependents." The Jesuit periodical *America* thus editorialized in favor of Kennedy's proposal. "*In Pacem in Terris*," the editors wrote in August 1963, "John XXIII taught that the state has a grave and moral obligation to accept immigrants who have a reasonable hope of providing a better future for themselves and their families." Two years later, the National Catholic Welfare Conference aggressively lobbied for the Immigration and Nationality Act, the fulfillment of the two Johns' Catholic vision. Every Catholic senator, and all but three Catholic representatives, followed their church's lead in voting for the law, which President Johnson signed in New York on October 3, 1965, the day before Pope Paul VI's arrival there.[17]

In his *Instructions in the Pastoral Care of People Who Migrate* in 1967, Pope Paul VI noted that "migrating people carry with them their own mentality, their own language, their own culture, their own religion. All of these things are parts of a certain spiritual heritage of opinions, traditions and culture [to be] prized highly everywhere." In 1973 and 1974, in support of such "migrating people," the NCRLC joined the United States Catholic Conference in endorsing boycotts of grapes and lettuce in support of collective bargaining rights for largely Mexican-American farm workers in the United States.[18]

In his 1981 encyclical *In Laborem Exercens* (Of Human Work), Pope John Paul II maintained that every person has the right to work, and if that right becomes exclusive, to seek employment elsewhere. "The more prosperous nations are obliged, to the extent that they are able, to welcome the foreigner in search of the security and the means of livelihood which he cannot find in his own country of origin. Public Authorities should see to it that the natural right is respected that places a guest under the protection of those who receive him," the *Catechism of the Catholic Church* stipulated in 1994.[19]

In "One Family Under God" in 1995, the American Catholic bishops established five principles underlying their immigration position: "First, persons fleeing persecution have a special standing and thus require special consideration as emigrants. Second, workers have a right to live and work without exploitation. Third, family reunification remains an appropriate basis for just immigration policy. Fourth, every effort should be made to encourage and enable highly skilled and educated persons to remain in or return to their homelands. Fifth, efforts to stem migration that do not effectively address its root causes are not only ineffectual, but permit the continuation of the political, social, and economic inequalities that cause it."[20]

In their pastoral "Strangers No Longer: Together on the Journey of Hope," the American and Mexican bishops in 2003 urged adoption of principles in both countries, including comprehensive U.S. immigration reform, that would entail "earned legalization, a future worker program, family-based immigration reform, restoration of due process rights, addressing root causes of migration, and enforcement measures" which target "criminal aliens," impose "proportional" penalties, prioritize family reunification, and protect "vulnerable populations." The next year's *Adult Catechism of the Catholic Church* asserted that "the more prosperous nations are obliged to the extent that they are able" to admit the foreign-born. The catechism permitted parents who have little to take food from those who have much if that is the only way to feed their children. "There is no theft if consent can be presumed," the document contended, "or if refusal is contrary to reason and the universal destination of goods."[21]

In elevating the dignity of the migrant minority above the laws of the native-born majority, the official Catholic stand on immigration would cause the church, under certain conditions, to advocate intentional circumvention of, or resistance to, certain laws. "Catholic Social Teaching is a divine calling to recognize our common 'sacred dignity,'" Catholic scholars Olivia Ruiz Marrujo and Alberto López Pulido wrote in 2010, quoting Moisés Sandoval, long-time editor of *Maryknoll Magazine*, " that moves us to actively work toward the development of our inherent rights as humans, regardless of legal status, to be full participants in our society."[22]

To many Americans, including many Catholics, such a stance was untenable on legal and moral grounds. "It is not a pleasant task for a priest to take a position that is not shared by the hierarchy of his Church," Rev. Patrick Bascio conceded in 2009. "The Christian Church currently favors an immigration policy that assists those who violate our laws rather than enter the legal process that leads to legal immigration," Father Bascio lamented. "The Christian Church, in some quarters, actually recommends to ministers and priests that they break the law by helping illegals that break the law," most notably by establishing churches as havens from immigration enforcement.[23]

The church had long since championed respect for civil law, according to those who side with Father Bascio. They quote St. Paul's controversial passage, "Let every person be subject to the governing authorities, for there is no authority except for God, and those authorities that exist have been instituted by God." The first pope, St. Peter, proclaimed that "for the Lord's sake, accept the authority of every human institution, whether of emperor as supreme, or of governors, as sent by him to punish those who do wrong and to praise those who do right."[24]

According to this view, "those who do right" were the millions of legal and would-be legal immigrants who patiently and painfully waited their turn to enter the United States through the proper channels, and those foreign-born and native-born persons lawfully residing in the United States whose livelihoods were under siege by the army of the undocumented. "Political authorities, for the sake of the common good for which they are responsible, may make the right to immigrate subject to various juridical conditions, especially with regard to the immigrants' duties toward their country of adoption," the 1994 edition of the *Catholic Catechism* provided. "Immigrants are obliged to respect with gratitude the material and spiritual heritage of the country that receives them, to obey its laws and to assist in carrying civic burdens."[25]

And many contemporary Catholic admissionists have stopped short of promoting open borders, because neither the church nor the country could grapple with the result. "Even though most illegal immigrants are Catholics from Mexico and Central America," immigration attorney William Chip wrote in 2008, "the Catholic Church does not provide them a free education in Catholic schools, or free treatment in Catholic hospitals, for the simple reason that the Church could not afford to keep such promises." Theodore Cardinal McCarrick of Washington, D.C., a leading spokesperson for the hierarchy's pro-immigration stance, admitted as much in a 2006 interview with the Catholic conservative website Beliefnet. What Cardinal McCarrick did not acknowledge, however, was that local and state governments could not easily finance such services either. While Catholic admissionists claim a net economic benefit for illegal immigration, a 2009 Pew Hispanic Center study concluded that unauthorized entrants were costing California up to 6 billion dollars, and Arizona as much as 1.3 billion dollars per year. Yet by law these states had to serve them.[26]

And when Catholic schools did admit undocumented students, they did not always adequately care for them. A 2010 Ford Foundation study of the nation's twenty-eight Jesuit colleges and universities by member schools Fairfield University, Santa Clara University, and Loyola University of Chicago discovered that while 76 percent of the administrators, faculty, and immigrant students whom the researchers interviewed believed that "enrolling and supporting undocumented students fits the mission of their institution," only

60 percent were aware of any campus programs to support them (even if those programs existed).[27]

Advocates of the church's teaching had ready answers for both the legal and moral arguments against illegal immigration. While there was an honorable tradition of Catholic adherence to civil laws, there was also a long list of martyrs and saints who had defied the authorities, including Jesus himself. "In the Old Testament, temple laws, kinship, and priesthood were divine institutions," Joseph Ratzinger, then a theologian and later Pope Benedict XVI, wrote in 1965. "Still, the Church criticized them." When rebuked for picking grain and healing a man on the Sabbath, Jesus replied, "The Sabbath is made for man, not man for Sabbath."[28]

According to church doctrine, such "responsible disobedience" needed to meet eight criteria. It must be spiritually sound, it must accept punishment by civil authorities, it must accompany adherence to one's other moral and legal obligations, it must not harm others, it must attempt to persuade rather than persecute those who disagree, it must derive from reason rather than emotion, it must arrive only as a last resort after one has exhausted all legal remedies, and it should occur only if the good it inspires outweighs the evil it inflicts.[29]

To the moral objection that the undocumented unjustly "jump the line" in front of legal immigrants, Fordham University law professor Eduardo Moisés Penalver likens them to early nineteenth-century squatters in the American West, while St. Louis University philosopher Rev. John Kavanaugh compares them to famous dissidents such as Elizabeth Cady Stanton and Martin Luther King, Jr., who broke the law in the name of a higher cause. Immigration attorney Michael Scaperlanda adds that far from undermining the American economy, undocumented immigrants invigorate it with higher rates of labor force participation, lower rates of unemployment, and lower rates of incarceration than natives with similar levels of education.[30]

A 2012 Cato Institute study by Daniel Griswold bolsters these Catholic immigration proponents. "Low-skilled immigrants do impose a net cost on government, in particular on the state and local level," Griswold determines, "but those costs ... are offset by broader benefits to the overall economy." He cites a Texas comptroller's report which found that while the state's undocumented population consumed $2.6 billion worth of services, it added $17.7 billion to the state's economy. Griswold notes that since the 1996 welfare reform law, while noncitizens in the United States receive emergency health care and their children have access to public education, they do not qualify for such federal benefits as Food Stamps, Medicaid, and the State Children's Health Insurance Program.[31]

The U.S. Catholic bishops add that for most of the undocumented, there is no "line" to jump. Immigrants can enter the country in three ways: by family reunification, by seeking political asylum, and through sponsorship by an American employer. Yet it can take between five and twenty years to implement the first; most of the undocumented are economic, not political refugees; and there are only five thousand "green cards" available for the hundreds of thousands of low-skilled workers who enter the United States each year. To obtain an H2A visa in order to hire a temporary worker, a farmer has to apply two and one-half months in advance, pay fees, fill out papers, and arrange an interview with the worker by the State Department. As a result, even though there are no limits on the number of H2A visas, the federal government issued only 65,000 in 2012. "The Catholic Church believes that immigrants should come to the United States lawfully," the bishops maintain, "but it also understands that the current immigration legal framework does not adequately reunify families and is non-responsive to our country's need for labor."[32]

So to Catholic immigration proponents, undocumented immigrants were not transgressors to be prosecuted for breaking legitimate civil laws. They were workers to be assisted in providing for their families, even if that meant disregarding legitimate civil laws. "The assumption that violating immigration law makes people criminals places immigration violations in the same category as burglary, assault, rape, and murder," Mia Crosswaite, legislative liaison for the Diocese of Boise and Catholic Charities of Idaho, asserted in 2003. "A better understanding sees them as administrative transgressions, such as failing to renew your license plate or register for Selective Service."[33]

Between 1981 and 2013, these Catholic immigration interests could justifiably point to their willingness to negotiate on matters such as specific numbers of visas and timelines for legalization, their acceptance of some enforcement measures, and their support for some incremental legislation that fell short of comprehensive reform. They could persuasively argue that by clinging to their hard-line stances, they at times drew concessions from legislators and helped alter the course of legislation. They could credibly maintain that even had they been more conciliatory in their dealings with Congress and the White House, they could not have overcome the dysfunction which increasingly afflicted both political parties. And they could accurately observe that while their immigration positions were discomforting to many of their fellow Catholics, such ruptures were hardly new to a church which had long divided over issues of social justice, war and peace, and life and death.

This study nevertheless will demonstrate that the recalcitrance of Catholic immigration advocates too often undercut their campaign for comprehensive immigration reform, as they contributed to an atmosphere which the *International Herald Tribune* aptly described as "two groups yelling across a void." The realities that these Catholics were only one group of players on a larger stage, and that their adversaries could be even more obstinate in their political postures, did not relieve them of their portion of the responsibility for the mostly unfavorable outcomes for their objectives between 1981 and 2013. The following pages show that in their often unwavering quest to welcome strangers across lax borders and at unregulated workplaces, to procure citizenship for the undocumented, and to ensure ever higher levels of refugees and legal immigrants, American Catholic immigration advocates frequently antagonized the presidents whose goals they largely shared, and ultimately disappointed the immigrants they so badly wanted to help.[34]

1. Ronald Reagan
1981–1989

FOR RONALD REAGAN, immigration was institutional. Though he had been a border-state governor who had reached out to Mexican-Americans, Reagan may never have addressed immigration reform if his predecessor, Democrat Jimmy Carter, hadn't. In 1978, Carter had created the Select Commission on Immigration and Refugee Policy, and had appointed University of Notre Dame president Rev. Theodore Hesburgh to chair it. Thus would the first major reform since the passage of the Immigration and Nationality Act of 1965 become in large measure a collaborative effort between a Republican president who had inherited the task and a Catholic priest who relished it. The enactment of the Immigration Reform and Control Act of 1986 would be a victory for both. But its implementation would be a victory for neither.

Catholic immigration advocates opposed President Reagan through most of the battles over refugees and immigration reform. On refugees, these interests received little of what they sought. On immigration reform, they obtained virtually all of what they wanted. By the end of the Reagan administration, they had helped certify that the country's immigration imbroglio was far from over.

Refugees under Carter

In 1968, the United States signed the United Nations Protocol Relating to the Status of Refugees, which mandated that governments protect refugees who fled their countries of origin because of a "well-founded fear of being persecuted for reasons of race, religion, nationality, political opinion, or membership in a particular social group." Presidents Lyndon Johnson, Richard Nixon, and Gerald Ford nevertheless continued to tailor U.S. refugee policy to Cold War concerns, admitting refugees from communist countries while turning away those fleeing anti-communist governments.

To try to bring order out of the chaos of refugee resettlement, President Carter in 1979 issued an executive order establishing the Office of Coordinator of Refugee Affairs in the State Department. The next year Congress passed and Carter signed the Refugee Act, which institutionalized the coordinator's office and added the Office of Refugee Resettlement (ORR) within the Department of Health and Human Services, with the mandate to embark on an overall strategy for refugee resettlement to replace the *ad hoc* approach to refugee admission which had existed since 1945. The law removed refugees from the immigration preference system, established 50,000 as the "normal" annual maximum of refugees, prescribed annual consultations of Congress by the president regarding numbers of refugees and emergency procedures, and imposed an annual ceiling of 270,000 nonrefugee immigrants from around the world. It offered a process of adjustment to regular status for refugees after one year of residence in the U.S. The Refugee Act also broadened the definition of "refugee" to include "any person who is unable or unwilling to return to [his] country because of persecution, on account of race, nationality, membership in a particular social group, or political opinion."[1]

The American Catholic bishops welcomed the new definition of a refugee. In March 1976, Archbishop Robert Sanchez of Santa Fe had testified before the Senate Judiciary Committee in favor of the adoption of the definition in the United Nations Protocol on Refugees, which was "any person who is outside their country of origin and unable or unwilling to return there or to avail themselves of its protection on account of a well-founded fear of persecution for reasons of race, religion, nationality, membership in a particular group, or political opinion." A week after Carter's election in November 1976, the bishops issued a "Resolution on the Pastoral Concern of the Church for Peoples on the Move," in which they urged a new definition of a refugee to better "provide a haven for oppressed people from any part of the world regardless of their race, religion, color, and creed." The prelates were also among the distinct minority of Americans (19 percent in a September 1979 Roper poll) who agreed with Carter's doubling of the admission of Indochinese refugees to 168,000 per year.[2]

The bishops also welcomed the mostly Catholic Haitian and Cuban exiles who entered the United States in 1980. From April to October, when the latest wave of Cubans boarded their ramshackle rafts bound for freedom 110 miles to the north, Cuban dictator Fidel Castro did not only allow the boats to sail. He helped to fill them. Of the 125,000 exiles who had disembarked from Mariel, twenty-seven miles west of Havana, about ten thousand left asylums and prisons. Seven of ten would settle in Miami's Dade County, where within a year most were on food stamps and about half were living below the poverty line.

Within a year, these Cuban exiles were also seven times more likely than other U.S. residents to commit suicide, half were out of work, and few spoke English. The worst of the bunch were at Fort Chafee, Arkansas, where, when not awaiting a sponsor and an asylum hearing, they were fomenting riots. "I never expected to leave one prison to come to another," Alberto Castillo Roselli, holed up in an Atlanta penitentiary, spoke for many of his fellow *Marielitos*.[3]

In addition to this latest influx of Cubans, emigrants from neighboring Haiti continued to flee the poverty and repression there. The Carter administration claimed that the Haitians did not fit even the Refugee Act's generous definition, because they were primarily seeking employment, not fleeing oppression. But federal judge James Lawrence King rejected the administration's distinction, arguing instead that the economic conditions in Haiti were direct consequences of Jean-Claude "Baby Doc" Duvalier's conspicuous kleptocracy. The U.S. Catholic bishops agreed, urging the president in March 1980 to "grant asylum and permanent residence to the boat people of both Cuba and Haiti who are seeking asylum and safety on our southern shores."[4]

The Carter administration shared the bishops' critique but not their conclusion. Rather than continue to identify the Cubans as political refugees and the Haitians as economic migrants, the administration decided to treat them the same, as "Cuban-Haitian Entrants." Under this new status, exiles from both countries could remain in the United States and be eligible for Supplemental Security Income and medical and emergency assistance. The federal government would reimburse the states for three-quarters of these costs.

The congressional delegation from Florida, which was bearing the brunt of the influx, then successfully amended the Refugee Educational Assistance Act to grant the Cubans and Haitians benefits equal to those received by refugees, and compelled the federal government to repay the states fully for the costs of such aid. This dire situation would soon become Ronald Reagan's responsibility.[5]

Refugees under Reagan

"It is my hope that some segment of the Transition Committee will have the opportunity to review our refugee resettlement and assistance programs," United States Catholic Conference Director of Migration and Refugee Services Rev. John McCarthy wrote Republican National Committee Chairman William Casey two weeks after Reagan's election in November 1980, "which are now a mess." McCarthy deplored the federal government's transformation of a formerly nongovernmental endeavor into a "total disaster." McCarthy explained that too many refugees had become overly dependent on public assistance. "It must seem strange that I, the Director of the world's largest agency in the refugee field, should be writing a letter of this type," Father McCarthy confessed, "but I honestly believe our refugee resettlement is a textbook example of where a program can be improved by reduced funding."[6]

The bishops' uncharacteristic plea for less public money was a pleasant surprise in the new fiscally conservative White House. In March, Reagan established his Task Force on Immigration and Refugee Policy, chaired by Attorney General William French Smith and including the secretaries of State, Defense, Education, Labor, Health and Human Services, and Transportation; and the director of the Federal Emergency Management Agency, as well as White House aide Frank Hodsoll. As if to address Father McCarthy's concern, the secretary of the treasury and the director of the Office of Management and Budget would also be members of the task force.[7]

Three months later Mother Teresa, the saintly nun from Calcutta, visited the slums of Miami, where she opened a halfway house for the impoverished, many of whom were Cuban or Haitian. "God must have chosen you for something special," she said in a speech to the more fortunate residents of Miami, "because at your gates hundreds of people have come, and you have not shut your doors."[8]

The Hesburgh Commission would not shut America's doors to refugees, or to their Catholic mouthpieces. Over the course of its deliberations it heard from numerous church spokespersons. Terry Abelese of the Indochinese Services Office of Catholic Social Services for the Diocese of Harrisburg called for more government help for Southeast Asian refugees. C. C. Sweeney of the Catholic Resettlement Group pressed for more federal funds and greater federal coordination to expedite family reunification of refugees. Rev. Michael Haddad, Director of the United States Catholic Conference Resettlement Office for the Archdiocese of New Orleans, requested that the federal government provide health care to all refugees (regardless of their ability to pay) during their first year in the country. Sharon Rodi of Associated Catholic Charities urged a "better bilingual health system" and criticized the "meager amount of funding" from the federal government for education services for refugees. Diane Brede, director of Refugee Services for Catholic Social Services of San Francisco, lobbied for "equity related to services among refugees, immigrants, and citizens."

Rev. Rafael Mellan, himself a refugee who had escaped Cuba in 1962, testified for the Citizens Committee on Immigration, and Sister Thomasette Pittari spoke for the Latin American Apostolate, in favor of more liberal family reunification guidelines. Rev. Cuchulain Moriarty of the Social Justice Commission of the Archdiocese of San Francisco denounced the federal government's inconsistency in accepting refugees from left-wing Cuba but not right-wing Haiti, and welcoming refugees at seaports and airports but not on land. Sister Margaret Phelan of the Catholic Social Services refugee program in San Francisco advocated recognition of Cuban, Haitian, Iranian, Salvadoran, and Nicaraguan exiles as refugees fleeing a "well-founded fear of persecution," and championed the admission of "any of these refugees who appear at our borders."

Speaking for the bishops, Lydia Savokya, Director of the United States Catholic Conference Office of Migration and Refugee Services, proposed a reorganization of the management of the Immigration and Customs Service. "The fact that the Service can no longer cope effectively," she said, "is a clear indication that the number of persons seeking admission to the United States greatly exceeds the number admissible under current legislation."[9]

The Commission was listening to these Catholic voices. Although its March 1981 report recommended a ceiling of 50,000 refugees per year, it also accepted the 1980 Refugee Act's new definition. It acknowledged "changes that are needed in the areas of cash and medical assistance programs, strategies for resettlement, [and] programs to promote refugee self-sufficiency." With an eye to Cuba, Haiti, and Central America, it also advised that "the U.S. allocation of refugee numbers include both geographic considerations and specific refugee characteristics." It called for a streamlining of government refugee programs to promote efficiency and equity. But it did not specifically address Cuban and Haitian cases.[10]

A month later, Attorney General Smith presented the recommendations of the administration task force to the House and Senate Immigration Subcommittees, chaired by Catholic Democratic representative Romano Mazzoli of Kentucky and Republican senator Alan Simpson of Wyoming. The report called for legislation to allow Cubans and Haitians who arrived before October 10, 1980, to apply for permanent resident status after living in the United States for two years; to repeal the 1966 Cuban Adjustment Act (which established a special program for Cubans separate from other refugees); and to continue to house Cuban mental patients and criminals in federal facilities until they could return to Cuba. The task force also proposed legislation to streamline the asylum process, Coast Guard interdiction of vessels transporting undocumented aliens to the United States, and international negotiations to resettle Haitians in other countries and to prevent more from departing for the U.S.[11]

"We shall strive to distribute fairly, among various localities of this country, the impacts of our national immigration and refugee policy," President Reagan promised in introducing the task force report. "We shall seek new ways to integrate refugees into our society without nurturing their dependence on welfare. Finally, we recognize that immigrant and refugee problems require international solutions."[12]

If there were solutions at all. . . . "We have lost control of our borders," Attorney General Smith lamented in his presentation to the Simpson and Mazzoli panels. Even the bishops had to admit the truth of that statement. The stream of newcomers was making "the American and Christian response extremely difficult in the state of Florida," that state's Catholic bishops confessed in their October pastoral, as "even the American Catholic begins to see in the entrant or refugee not Christ, but the enemy."[13]

The bishops nonetheless pressed on. Since 1975 the USCC had aided almost half the refugees admitted to the U.S., and in 1981 it would resettle 58,000 refugees. The USCC thus appeared on a May 1981 White House list of "key contacts for refugee issues," and Donald Hohl, associate director of the USCC Office of Migration and Refugee Services, attended a meeting of voluntary agencies chaired by the administration's Kathy Collins in June. Auxiliary Bishop Anthony Bevilacqua of Brooklyn, chairman of the United States Catholic Conference Committee on Migration and Tourism, told the Mazzoli Subcommittee in October that his church's traditional role "as a haven for the oppressed" compelled the bishops to endorse an appeals process for applicants denied asylum and resettlement assistance for long-term detainees. And he repudiated the Reagan task force's call for interception of boats on the way to the United States as a "clearly evident . . . violation of individual human rights and danger to human life" and a potential "violation of international law." Rejecting the comparison between "contraband cargo" and "human beings implicit in the Reagan proposal," Bevilacqua asked, "Are we to equate material goods with human life?"[14]

The bishops continued their refugee advocacy in 1982. "In the limited period of its existence we have found the provisions of the Refugee Act of 1980 related to definition, numbers, flexibility, and congressional oversight to be working quite satisfactorily," Hohl testified for the USCC before the Simpson Subcommittee in January. Briefly reviewing the history of federal policy toward immigrants, Hohl defended "an established ceiling for refugees separate from that of 'normal' immigration," adding that "the fate of refugees and the reunification of families should be linked together."[15]

In March, Senator Simpson and Representative Mazzoli introduced their immigration reform legislation, which would give temporary legal status to those aliens in the country since January 1, 1980, and to Cubans and Haitians who arrived before October 10, 1980. These refugees could receive permanent status within two years and citizenship within five years. The Simpson-Mazzoli bill would also afford more legal rights, including the right to an attorney, to those Haitians seeking asylum.[16]

"This is a major step forward," said Bishop Bevilacqua, conveying the American hierarchy's reaction to the Simpson-Mazzoli refugee plan. "If the section of these proposals on asylum has a weakness," the bishop hedged, "it is in its failure to clearly specify the rule of review of any denied application. Only by review of negative decisions by a panel of the [proposed] United States Immigration Board can we preserve this new system from capricious and arbitrary decisions. While review seems to be called for, it is not clearly spelled out."[17]

Under the version of the Simpson bill which emerged from the full committee, the attorney general would choose the members of the new Immigration Board. In a letter to all senators, USCC General Secretary Monsignor Daniel Hoye urged them to amend the legislation to require the "advice and consent of the Senate" in the appointment process.[18]

They would not. By August, when the Senate easily passed the Simpson bill, the attorney general had retained his unilateral authority to appoint the board members and immigration judges. The board nevertheless had secured, as the USCC had sought, "an increase in training, an increase in stature, and increased independence," with the "authority to review appealed asylum applications denied by immigration judges."[19]

The House Judiciary Committee would also address the bishops' concerns about the process of selection for the Immigration Board. The Mazzoli bill reported by the panel in September would, according to the USCC, provide for a United States Immigration Board "appointed by the president by and with the advice and consent of the Senate," and which would "function as an independent agency in the Department of Justice with the authority to review most decisions of the Administrative Law Judges."[20]

This action did not satisfy the bishops. They now called for the advice and consent of the Senate *following* the president's appointment of immigration judges. They also feared that the full House would follow the lead of the Hesburgh Commission and add a ceiling on the number of refugees accepted into the country every year. "The admission to the United States of refugees must not be so strictly constrained," Monsignor Hoye wrote to all the representatives in September, "that the country cannot make an immediate response to refugee situations as they occur."[21]

To the relief of Catholic immigration proponents, the House would not vote for a refugee cap. In fact, it would not vote at all. At 3:30 on Saturday afternoon, December 18, the House stopped debating the Mazzoli bill and went home for Christmas.[22]

The New Year opened with the bishops and the president still on the same side, backing the Simpson and Mazzoli bills despite reservations held by both. But in July 1983, when the House Judiciary Committee amended the Mazzoli bill to move Reagan's Executive Office for Immigration Review outside the Justice Department as an independent entity, and granted the right to an attorney to all asylum seekers, the bishops had intensified their support for the legislation, while the president had abandoned his.[23]

The split between the bishops and president widened as refugee admissions declined. When Reagan took office in January 1981, the U.S. was admitting 159,252 refugees per year. By fiscal year 1985, the number was down to 70,000, only about 5 percent of the total annual migrant population.[24]

It would take over three more boisterous years to enact Simpson and Mazzoli's Immigration and Control Act of 1986, with the president back on board and the bishops barely hanging in there. The final version failed to address the overall refugee situation, narrowing its focus to Cuban and Haitian arrivals.[25]

Cuban and Haitian Refugees under Reagan

"What should be the status of Cubans and Haitians who arrived in Florida in large numbers recently and whose status expires July 15, 1981?" a Reagan administration issue paper asked as the new president took office. The document explained that the Carter administration had permitted Cuban and Haitian refugees to remain in the country until July 15 under the parole power of the attorney general. In the meantime, Congress was to pass new legislation to determine their fate.[26]

"Everyone knows Cubans will be here [a] long time," Reagan aide Kathy Collins observed in her notes on the June 1981 meeting of voluntary resettlement agencies, including the USCC, called to discuss these alternatives, "but not Haitian[s]." The group went on to discuss the "lack of equality [of federal policy] between Haitians and Cubans."[27]

By July 1981 the administration had adopted its approach. It would propose legislation to repeal the 1966 Cuban Adjustment Act and "to authorize Cubans and Haitians who arrived before October 1980 to apply for permanent resident status after residing here two years, but maintain in custody criminals, mentally ill, and others who cannot be released into the community pending their repatriation to Cuba; to prevent the transport of illegal aliens to the United States, particularly during a mass exodus; to reform and expedite exclusion proceedings; to provide for holding status and emergency budgetary authority for future mass influxes; to pursue international negotiations to restrain Haitian illegal immigration (while providing resettlement opportunities in other countries) to discourage third countries from serving as conduits for illegal immigration; to return to Cuba the Cuban criminals, mentally ill, and anti-social [being held at Fort Chafee, Arkansas]; to interdict Haitian vessels on the high seas suspected of attempting to violate U.S. laws and negotiate an agreement with Haiti whereby we could do this on their behalf." The administration also replaced the Carter policy of paroling aliens seeking asylum with the requirement of detaining aliens seeking asylum. Immigration and Naturalization Service deputy commissioner Alan Nelson estimated that as many as 35,000 Haitians then in the United States illegally would be eligible to apply for legalization.[28]

In October, thirty-three Haitian exiles drowned when their boat capsized off the Florida coast. In a March 1982 meeting with Vice President George Bush, Baptist civil rights leader Rev. Jesse Jackson conveyed the offer of the U.S. Catholic bishops to absorb all Haitian detainees currently in the United States into their parishes. Vice President Bush then passed the bishops' offer on to National Security Advisor William Clark, a Catholic. "I was not aware of the Catholic Conference of Bishops' offer," Bush wrote Clark after his meeting with Jackson, "and I am wondering if it has any ingredients for a solution to this very difficult problem."[29]

It would not. "Deterring illegal entry by Haitians appears to be working better because of a number of factors, including our actions here and our agreement with Haiti on interdicting undocumented aliens on the high seas," Clark replied to Bush. Clark therefore concurred with the Departments of State and Justice that "releasing detainees now would likely detract from our efforts to deter such entry." The State Department nonetheless planned to "continue a dialogue" with the bishops on the administration's Haitian refugee policies.[30]

New INS commissioner Alan Nelson preferred a monologue. "It has been INS experience that nearly sixty percent of Haitians paroled in Miami failed to appear when called for exclusion hearings," Nelson wrote two days after Clark's response to Bush. "The offer of the U.S. Catholic Conference to resettle the Haitians already in detention," Nelson wrote two weeks after the Bush-Clark exchange, "is not feasible."[31]

Neither was the status quo. Two months later Attorney General

Smith decided to "consider for parole for humanitarian reasons undocumented aliens from Haiti who have counsel and have not been found excludable from the U.S." To the chagrin of the bishops and other Catholic refugee advocates, however, the administration's interdiction policy would remain in place.[32]

To the relief of these refugee supporters, however, President Reagan announced a Caribbean Basin Initiative of aid and trade to help Haiti and its neighbors rebuild their economies and retain their populations. Archbishop John Roach of St. Paul, president of the USCC, wrote to President Reagan in April to salute this "welcome step to focus U.S. attention on the issues of poverty and human needs in the Caribbean region."[33]

But the president still had not met with the archbishop. The USCC's "oft-voiced anti-Administration positions are the result of an extremely liberal bureaucracy," and "the USCC is not necessarily representative of American Catholics or even American bishops," White House aide Elizabeth Dole wrote Reagan on the eve of the November 1982 congressional elections. She nevertheless advocated that "on issues of mutual concern," there should be "a series of meetings with key Administration leaders and selected members of the Catholic hierarchy" to "enlist support or at least minimize their opposition."[34]

President Reagan met with Archbishop Roach later that month. "Many great questions of public policy face the country today," read the president's invitation to the archbishop. "And you have my best wishes in bringing the insights of the Christian tradition to bear on them."[35]

The refugee problem was one of those great questions. In 1983 the Eleventh U.S. Circuit Court of Appeals agreed with U.S. District Judge Eugene Spellman of Miami (and the U.S. Catholic bishops) in striking down the Reagan administration's substitution of detention for parole in Haitian refugee camps. The administration appealed the decision, and the policy continued. The same year U.S.

District Court Judge Marvin Shoob ruled the *Marielitos'* indefinite detention an unconstitutional abridgment of their rights to due process. Then a higher court overruled him, asserting that giving these exiles due process would preclude the United States from securing its borders.[36]

In a 1984 treaty with the U.S., Fidel Castro promised to take back 2,700 "undesirables" among the 125,000 émigrés whom he unloaded on American shores in the 1980 boatlift. In return, President Reagan pledged to admit up to 20,000 Cubans annually through the usual immigration channels, as well as 3,000 political prisoners and their families. In October 1984, Castro told a delegation of American Catholic bishops that he would begin releasing political prisoners, seventy-five of whom would soon be on their way to the U.S. A few months later, he vowed to French explorer Jacques Cousteau that he would be sending twenty-six more.[37]

But by May 1985, after blaming the Reagan administration for inflicting Radio Marti broadcasts upon his country, Castro reneged on his end of the treaty. So Reagan pledged to do the same. The administration declared that it would admit only long-term political prisoners whom Castro had previously released. By processing these cases individually, however, the administration was taking too long to avoid criticism from Cuban-American leaders and American Catholic bishops.

In August 1986, Reagan further punished Castro by prohibiting Cuban immigration through third countries. Reagan charged that Castro was "extorting up to $30,000 per exile" in allowing this third-country emigration.[38]

In September, the administration finally agreed to admit fifty-four of the seventy-five prisoners identified by the bishops in their visit to Cuba (eighteen did not want to leave, and three were either ill or deceased). Half of the twenty-six singled out by Cousteau would also enter the U.S., with the remaining half either not seeking to immigrate or not having necessary documentation. In all, over one hundred Cubans would arrive in the U.S. "You are a genuine hero," George Bush greeted long-time political prisoner Ricardo Montero-Duque in the vice president's West Wing office. "Your patience and triumph against totalitarianism is [sic] wonderful."[39]

While some Cubans were arriving in the United States, others were departing—but not without a fight. On November 20, 1987, the State Department announced that under another agreement with the Cuban government, the U.S. would be deporting about 2,500 *Marielitos* housed in American prisons. The next night, 1,000 Cuban inmates in an Oakdale, Georgia detention center and about 1,400 in an Atlanta maximum-security prison launched a riot. Attorney General Edwin Meese reacted immediately to the inmates' takeover of the facilities by offering them an indefinite moratorium on deportation and a "full, fair, and equitable review" of their immigration status. The inmates, who sought permanent resident status in the U.S., rejected the offer and prolonged the occupation.[40]

So Meese sent in Federal Bureau of Investigation agents while a SWAT team, armored personnel carriers, and helicopters surrounded the prisons. On November 24, Reagan signed an executive order authorizing the potential dispatch of federal troops if needed to quell the disturbance. Yet the prisoners only hardened their resolve, taking employees hostage and unfurling a banner, "Mr. Reagan, if you deny us freedom, you kill us."

The Oakdale rioters asked to see Georgia Democratic representative John Lewis, a veteran of the civil rights movement; Carla Dudeck, a leader of the Coalition for the Support of Cuban Detainees; Gary Leshaw, a civil rights lawyer; and Rev. Agustín Román, the Cuban-born auxiliary bishop of Miami, who a year earlier had joined the nation's other Cuban-American bishop, Rev. Enrique San Pedro of Galveston-Houston in appealing for mercy for those prisoners who were mentally ill and justice for those who had committed crimes in Cuba or the United States. On the tenth day of the standoff, the FBI played a videotape on four large televisions outside the Oakdale facility. "I want you to release the prisoners who are in your custody, and I want you to demonstrate to the world the good every Christian should have in his heart," Bishop Román said on the screens. He presented a document to the prisoners containing a seven-point agreement between the federal government and the bishops calling for a quick review of the detainees' causes and amnesty for their participation in the riot. "Sign the document," he said.

Then Bishop Román rode into the center of the detention center in a white pick-up truck. "My brothers, give me your weapons, give me your hostages," he implored. "No man can ask for freedom while denying it to others."

The detainees tossed their machetes, pipes, homemade spears, and sticks with protruding nails into a pile. Bishop Román said Mass for the detainees, and then witnessed their signing of the agreement. One of the hostages would recall that the Cubans treated the bishop "like the Pope."[41]

The Atlanta prisoners held out for a better deal, but they didn't get one. On the eleventh day of their ordeal, they too signed the agreement, and Bishop Román blessed it. Meese indicated that Bishop Román would be among those reviewing the inmates' cases, and the attorney general flew to Miami to meet with the bishop and begin the reviews.[42]

Vernon Walters, Reagan's Catholic ambassador to the United Nations, blamed the State Department's deportation directive for instigating the siege. "I would have perceived something like this would happen since I do keep track of Cuban matters," said the ambassador. "I would have said, 'You're going to have trouble the first night.'"[43]

The president, who played no public role in the crisis, had approved the agreement which Walters was criticizing. He had also endorsed the settlement negotiated by Bishop Román. And following the riots, he backed an amendment to the federal budget bill sponsored by Democratic senators Frank Lautenberg of New

Jersey and Lawton Chiles of Florida which repealed Reagan's ban on visas for Cubans in third countries and terminated a requirement that Cuban political prisoners had to have served at least a ten-year sentence before being eligible for immigration to the United States.[44]

Like his predecessors, Reagan nevertheless persisted in treating Haitian exiles as economic migrants rather than political refugees. So next to none were entering the United States legally. "In the wider sense, however, those Haitians are true refugees," *America's* editors insisted in January 1985, joining the bishops in urging Reagan to change course. He would not, beyond signing the Immigration Reform and Control Act the following year. The law narrowly permitted those Cuban and Haitian "special entrants" who had entered before 1982 to remain in the United States.[45]

Central American Refugees and the Sanctuary Movement

To the perennial problems of Cuban and Haitian refugees the Reagan era added a new source of anxious exiles—Central America. Civil wars in Guatemala, Nicaragua, and El Salvador—in which the United States played important roles—led to a large-scale exodus to the north. In Guatemala, the military had ruled the country since the Central Intelligence Agency helped it overthrow the democratically elected leftist government of Jacobo Árbenz in 1954. In 1960, a loose coalition of leftist guerillas, the Guatemalan National Revolutionary Unity (URNG), had launched its armed struggle against the military government and rightist militias. In El Salvador in 1980, the communist Marti National Liberation Front (FMLN) commenced an uprising against the military government and rightist militias. In Nicaragua in 1961, the leftist Sandinista National Liberation Front (FSLN) began its offensive against the government of rightist dictator Anastasio Somoza DeBayle. Shortly after overthrowing

Somoza in 1979, the Sandinistas accepted aid from communist Cuba and sent arms to the FMLN rebels in El Salvador.

By September 1980, two months before Reagan's election, the Immigration and Naturalization Service had apprehended almost twelve thousand Salvadorans, compared to almost four thousand four years earlier. Border Patrol agents estimated that for every irregular alien they captured, as many as five may have evaded them, so there may have been sixty thousand new Salvadorans in the United States in 1980 alone.[46]

In 1981, Reagan authorized the Central Intelligence Agency to begin training the contra rebels to try to overthrow the FSLN government. In June 1983 Reagan, who was sending billions of American dollars to the right-wing governments of Guatemala and El Salvador and the anti-communist guerillas in Nicaragua, would warn that communist victories in Central America would lead to "a tidal wave of refugees—and this time they'll be 'feet people' and not 'boat people'—swarming into our country seeking a safe haven from Communist repression to our south." The tidal wave had already begun, though most of the refugees were fleeing anti-communist governments, not communist ones.[47]

"There are dozens of wars, civil wars, and insurgencies in the world today, and almost all are in the Third World," Assistant Secretary of State for Human Rights and Humanitarian Affairs Elliot Abrams declared in defending administration policy. "Those who ask that all Salvadoran migrants be allowed to stay in the United States indefinitely must explain why the same treatment is not deserved by all another migrants from poor, violent societies to our south—now and in the coming years." In other words, most Salvadoran exiles were not political refugees, but economic migrants.[48]

Salvadoran labor activist Óscar Oliva told a different tale. "In 1983, I was arrested … by the National policemen with civilian clothes," Oliva would relate. "They gave me electric shocks on the ears and other parts of the body that, like the other methods of torture, did not work. Next thing they did was to tell me they were going to kidnap my family if I did not cooperate with them. They gave me two hours to make my 'choice.' When the time was up, I accepted to cooperate with them."[49]

Oliva's story, as well as those of thousands of other Salvadoran exiles, had inspired many religious Americans to come to their aid. The 1965 Immigration and Nationality Act had made it a crime punishable by fine or imprisonment for anyone who "knowingly or in reckless disregard of the fact that an alien has come to, entered, or remains in the United States in violation of law, . . . attempts to conceal, harbor, or shield from detection, such an alien in any place, including any building or any means of transportation." Yet many Catholics were choosing to evade this law. Following the example of Presbyterian Rev. John Fife and Quaker Jim Corbett in Tucson a year earlier, Catholic clergy and lay people across the country were participating in the "Sanctuary movement," an underground railroad of churches providing havens for Salvadoran refugees. Rev. Tony Clark transformed Sacred Heart Church in Nogales, Arizona into the first Catholic Sanctuary church. Since the Salvadorans were fleeing a U.S.-backed government which had failed to prevent death squads from murdering San Salvador's Archbishop Oscar Romero in March 1980, Catholics John and Joe Bangert of Brewster, Massachusetts spoke for many in the movement by asserting that "Sanctuary is a moral response to an immoral foreign policy."[50]

The Reagan administration viewed it differently. "One of the tactics in the political campaign for Central America has been to create a focus for concerted action by a temporary coalition of *ad hoc* supporters, e.g. the 'Sanctuary Movement,'" an administration internal memo asserted. "Since the focus is the nexus through which the members of the coalition are bound, if the focus be lost, then the possibility of concerted action would also be attenuated." The document added that "as the *ad hoc* coalitions become disorganized, it becomes possible to mobilize *ad hoc* groups against the guerilla's cause."[51]

Joseph Cardinal Bernardin of Chicago soon found himself in the middle of the dispute between the Reagan administration and the Sanctuary movement. In an April 1983 meeting with representatives of the Chicago Religious Task Force on Central America, a prominent link in the Sanctuary chain, the cardinal condemned the administration's Central American policies and urged an end to the deportation of all Salvadoran and Guatemalan refugees. Yet, echoing a confidential USCC legal memorandum, he also repudiated the Sanctuary movement, not only because it was against the law but because it further endangered the refugees it purported to help.

In a follow-up letter to Bernardin, the Chicago Religious Task Force on Central America defended itself against the cardinal's charges. To the objection that the Sanctuary tactics were illegal, the CRTFCA leaders replied, "In our April meeting you agreed that ... there have been and are circumstances that not only justify but necessitate that we disobey an unjust law in order to remain faithful to God." They considered "the slaughter of about 100,000 human beings and uprooting of more than one million others from their homes by U.S.-supported regimes in Central America in the past five years" as exactly such circumstances.

To the contention that Sanctuary workers were doing more harm than good to the refugees, the letter noted Bernardin's concerns that the movement jeopardized the "*de facto* sanctuary" being provided the refugees by Catholic and Protestant churches, that the archdiocese was already fulfilling the needs of the refugees, that the Sanctuary movement was publicly exposing refugees, that the movement was undercutting legislative lobbying by the bishops and others to change unjust refugee policies, and that the archdiocese was serving as a buffer between the INS and the refugees. The CRTFCA leaders responded that the Sanctuary movement was expanding upon, rather than undermining, the efforts of local parishes and the archdiocese. As for uncovering otherwise safely hidden refugees, the Sanctuary movement exposed the injustices that caused them to flee, thus accelerating rather than impeding the chances for legislative and administrative change. Rather than act as a neutral buffer between the federal government and the refugees, the church, as the recipient of federal largesse, was in some ways doing the government's bidding.[52]

But there was little danger of that. In their July 1983 "Statement on Central America," the American Catholic bishops espoused "a diplomatic course of action as a means of addressing the war in El Salvador and a method of reversing the presently dangerous course of U.S.-Nicaraguan relations."[53]

When Secretary of State George Shultz and Vice President George Bush blasted the bishops for allegedly siding with communists in the civil wars in El Salvador and Nicaragua, Archbishop Roach wrote a letter of protest to the White House. While acknowledging that "individual members may depart from and distort the authentic teaching of the Church's ministry," Roach said that "any hint that the fundamental vision and ministry of the Catholic Church are based on an alien ideology or serve its purpose must be rejected."[54]

The next day, Pope John Paul II arrived in Nicaragua, sounding like Shultz and Bush in attacking the "unacceptable ideological commitments" of Catholics sympathetic to the leftist Sandinista government. But the pontiff resembled Roach in calling upon wayward Catholics to show "obedience to the bishops" in Nicaragua who were toeing the anti-communist line.[55]

The American bishops continued to toe the anti-administration line. "Because the conflicts in Central America are fundamentally rooted in questions of social justice and the persistent denial of basic human rights for large sectors of the population," Washington's James Cardinal Hickey testified in October before former Secretary of State Henry Kissinger's National Commission on U.S. Policy in Central America, "the USCC has always opposed interpretations of the Salvadoran and Central American conflict which place primary emphasis on the superpower or East-West rivalry." Hickey criticized the administration's support for military remedies in El Salvador and Nicaragua, calling for a ceasefire in both countries that would allow for a regional cure to the indigenous political, social, and economic maladies which had long infected Central America.[56]

The "search for a military solution is futile and dangerous," Cardinal Bernardin declared, excoriating the administration's Central American approach at a December Mass commemorating the third anniversary of the murder of four American Catholic churchwomen by a right-wing paramilitary group in El Salvador. "It will not end the violence; it will not restore order and peace." Cardinal Bernardin's speech was so vitriolic that the president dispatched his Catholic Associate Director for Public Liaison Robert Reilly to lecture the cardinal on the administration's objectives in Central America and, in Reilly's words, "the facts on which they're based."[57]

Cardinal Bernardin was not a receptive student. In January 1984, at the conclusion of an all-day symposium on Bernardin's 1983 antinuclear war pastoral "The Challenge of Peace," the cardinal again lashed out at the president over Central America. Speaking just a few hours after Reagan had accepted the recommendations of the Kissinger Commission to pour over eight billion more dollars of U.S. aid into war-torn El Salvador, the cardinal urged a "basic redirection" in Central America. "The Catholic bishops have opposed the basic direction of U.S. policy in Central America since 1980," Bernardin noted, careful to include the Democratic Carter administration in his critique. "We have never been convinced of the wisdom of that policy, and I remain unconvinced of it today."[58]

Having reprimanded the bishops, Reilly tried reassuring them. "Whatever controversy may surround the situation in Central America, one agonizing aspect of it is all too clear and indisputable, and that is the terrible suffering of the hundreds of thousands of refugees in the region," Reilly wrote Detroit Archbishop Edward Szoka in January 1984. "Certainly the Catholic Church has had one of the largest hearts for those in need, helping through such agencies as

Catholic Relief Services. I know the President would warmly appreciate anything you could do to help bring the plight of these unfortunate refugees to the attention of Catholics in this country."[59]

At least the president and the bishops could agree on that. "The plight of the refugee is more than a story on the news," Bernardin remarked in February 1984. "It is the story of little children, women, men, the elderly. It is also the story of Jesus and the Holy Family as they fled to Egypt." He then appealed to the governments of El Salvador and neighboring Honduras to permit the over 20,000 people in refugee camps on the border of the two countries to remain there, rather than be moved for a third time.[60]

Unlike Cardinal Bernardin, some church leaders were expressing solidarity with the Sanctuary workers as well as the refugees. In February 1984, a week after the first arrest of Sanctuary personnel, a Catholic nun and lay worker accused of smuggling three Salvadorans into Texas, at least fifteen church groups called press conferences to protest the arrests. Among those meeting the press in nearby Albuquerque, New Mexico were Sister Rosemary Goins, coordinator for justice and peace for the Western Province of the Felician Franciscan Sisters, and Rev. Lorenzo Ruiz, a representative from the Catholic Archdiocese of Santa Fe. "Our country was founded as a sanctuary," said Sister Goins. "We are an immigrant people. We are a rich people. We need to show the world that America has a large heart." Father Ruiz flatly asserted that "our government and its policies are wrong."[61]

Other church leaders thought those policies were right. To combat the growing religious disenchantment with Reagan's Central American policies, Assistant to the President for Public Liaison Faith Ryan Whittlesey organized a White House Working Group on Central America, which listened to prominent voices on the administration side of the Central American schism. Among the speakers invited by the group were Monsignor John Foley, editor of the *Catholic Standard and Times* and a representative of the administration's team observing the 1984 presidential election in El Salvador, as well as Rev. Kenneth Baker, editor of *The Homiletic and Pastoral Review*, who served on the administration's unit observing the 1984 constituent assembly elections in Guatemala.[62]

While Monsignor Foley and Father Baker were preaching to the converted, their bishops were doing missionary work. Cardinal Bernardin, Cardinal Szoka, USCC president Bishop James Malone of Youngstown, USCC vice president Archbishop John May of St. Louis, USCC secretary Archbishop Thomas Kelly of Louisville, USCC general secretary Monsignor Daniel Hoye, John Cardinal Krol of Philadelphia, Archbishop John O'Connor of New York, and Archbishop Bernard Law of Boston lunched with the president for four hours at the White House in April 1984, the third time in four weeks that Reagan had met with Catholic officials in an election-year turnabout from the early days of his administration. "Although we admit that under the present situation some military aid is needed" in El Salvador, Bernardin feared that too many American weapons were on the way. "The only solution" to the war in El Salvador, Bishop Malone added, "is a political solution as contrasted with a military one."[63]

In January 1985, a federal grand jury indicted sixteen Sanctuary workers, including Rev. Fife, for transporting, harboring, smuggling, and conspiring to smuggle irregular aliens. After dropping charges against five of the defendants, the government tried the remaining eleven, five of whom were Catholic, including two priests and a nun. After three months of testimony by government witnesses, including informant Jesus Cruz, who secretly taped conversations in a Phoenix Lutheran church, the defense rested its case without calling a single witness. "When you're ahead twenty-seven to nothing," a member of the defense team confidently explained, referring to the prosecution's flawed arguments, "why bother playing the fourth quarter?"

In his closing statement, prosecutor Donald Reno said that

the government had based its case on "the law of the land, and there is no exception to it." But in their final remarks the defense team responded that their clients were following the dictates of their churches in helping refugees with a "well-founded fear of persecution."[64]

The jury largely sided with the prosecution, convicting eight of the eleven defendants, including Sister Darlene Nicgorski, who, while serving as a missionary in Guatemala, had once witnessed the government's execution of her parish priest. "If I am guilty of anything," Sister Nicgorski responded to the verdict, "I am guilty of the gospel."[65]

Nicgorski's five felonies for her role in the Sanctuary movement could have landed her in prison for twenty years. Instead, neither she nor her codefendants would serve time, and she would become one of Ms. magazine's "Women of the Year" for 1986. All obtained probation except one, who received a suspended sentence. Though several jurors expressed sympathy for the defendants and their views on immigration, they nonetheless felt obligated to uphold the law.[66]

The administration concurred. "If somebody breaks the law, guilt or innocence doesn't depend on the direction of the collar," Immigration and Naturalization Service district director William Johnston said, saluting the verdict. "You can't hide behind a clerical collar."[67]

Most of the bishops also agreed with the verdict. "The Sanctuary movement has confused the issue of ministry to immigrants by separating undocumented people into a special category," said Los Angeles Archbishop Roger Mahony, objecting to Father Luis Olivares designating Our Lady of Angels Church the city's first Sanctuary parish. "I am opposed to Sanctuary because it is illegal," Brooklyn Auxiliary Bishop Anthony Bevilacqua explained. "I do not feel at the present time that this [federal refugee] law is an unjust one." While he condemned the wanton violence plaguing El Salvador, Archbishop John Roach of Minneapolis-St. Paul, now president of the United States Catholic Conference, pronounced himself "absolutely convinced that we make progress by changing laws and not breaking them."[68]

The hierarchy's emphasis on the legal rather than the moral aspects of the refugee crisis unsettled the participants in the Sanctuary movement. "Unfortunately, the bishops as a group took the legal opinion of corporate lawyers instead of following the Holy Spirit," Sister Nicgorski would lament. Sacred Heart Church's Father Clark went further, undiplomatically branding the bishops "a bunch of cowards."[69]

Some prelates disagreed with the administration, however. Auxiliary Bishop Peter Rosazza of Hartford, Connecticut wished that his fellow prelates had more closely examined Sanctuary's moral as well as legal ramifications. San Francisco Archbishop John Quinn issued a pastoral backing the Sanctuary effort. "Is the inactivity of those who stand by and do nothing while they see the lives of human beings put into jeopardy morally justifiable?" asked Archbishop Rembert Weakland, whom Sister Nicgorski quoted in her sentencing statement. Weakland opened five Milwaukee churches to Salvadoran refugees. Bishop John Fitzpatrick of Brownsville founded the Casa Oscar Romero in San Benito, Texas for those fleeing Central America. After the arrest of the center's director, Jack Elder, and one of its volunteers, Stacy Lynn Merkt, for smuggling and transporting refugees, Bishop Fitzpatrick criticized the police, provided $27,000 of his own money for their bail, and testified on their behalf at the trial. The bishop's efforts were to no avail, as both defendants were convicted.[70]

Rather than demoralizing the Sanctuary movement, the Tucson trial galvanized it. Hugh Lacey, a professor of philosophy at Swarthmore College, testified at Elder's trial on the place of the Sanctuary movement in Catholic tradition. "The Church will be failing in its responsibility unless there are believers who hear the call to offer appropriate service to Central American refugees," said Lacey," and appropriate service requires that they be given refuge here." Mary Kay Meyer, a lay worker with the Sisters of St. Joseph in Concordia, Kansas, vowed to press the fight in the face of arrests and trials. "Our Savior's command was to take in strangers who are hurting," she pleaded. "That can't be illegal." Franciscan friars in seven states, comprising three-fourths of the members of the religious order, joined the Sanctuary movement. "They have told me of the oppression they have experienced, the torture they have endured, and the murder they have witnessed," Franciscan Rev. Floyd Lotito, the director of the San Francisco soup kitchen St. Anthony's Dining Room, recalled of the Salvadorans who had eaten there. "They have come to America for protection, for sanctuary, for survival."[71]

Before the indictments, only a few hundred people had registered for a national Sanctuary conference in Tucson at the end of January 1985. But following the indictments, twelve hundred people attended the conference. Among those groups embracing the movement at the gathering was the U.S. Catholic Mission Association, which coordinated societies sending Catholic missionaries in the United States and in other countries.[72]

Many of the faithful nevertheless continued to agree with the Reagan administration. Rev. Theodore Hesburgh invited Notre Dame alumnus José Napoleón Duarte, the newly elected civilian president of El Salvador, to speak at the university's 1985 commencement. Mark Rising of the University of Chicago's Calvert House attacked its decision to join the Sanctuary network as providing aid and comfort to the enemy in Central America. "No doubt, there have been many human rights violations by army personnel in El Salvador," Rising wrote. "But there have also been many human rights violations by the insurrectionists." Mike Rodriguez, president of the lay Catholic Concerned Citizens for Church and Country in Brownsville, protested his bishop's intervention in the Elder trial by appealing to Rome.[73]

Sanctuary had its critics within the network as well. "Sanctuary is independent of traditional political activism," Pat Corbett, the wife of the movement's cofounder, contended. "The movement is politically as well as religiously ecumenical." But to some Sanctuary leaders, including Renny Golden, the cofounder of the Chicago Religious Task Force on Central America, Sanctuary was inherently political. According to its newsletter *Basta* (Spanish for "Enough"), the CRTFCA originated as a means "to organize people of all religious persuasions to understand and challenge U.S. foreign policy toward Central America."[74]

In its newsletter and other documents, therefore, the CRTFCA advocated the end of American involvement in Central America. As a result, Sanctuary was merely a "humanitarian band aid" on a larger wound. "It's simply not true that Sanctuary transcends the political," Golden, a former Catholic nun, protested. "We have a responsibility not to take what could be the most beautiful position—what could be possible in other worlds—but to do what is historically possible." So Golden and her organization's cofounder, United Church of Christ minister Michael McConnell, believed that earmarking Sanctuary funds for refugees' family members "means pouring into resettlement work finances that could go toward further organizing of conscientization efforts toward stopping the war."[75]

Golden and other more radical members of the movement therefore grew frustrated with the disingenuous denials of political motives by more moderate Sanctuary members. When the conservative Institute on Religion and Democracy charged that Sanctuary's primary objective was "to undermine U.S. opposition to Marxist-Leninist movements in Central America," Rev. Robert Pfister, pastor of St. Boniface Catholic Church, a Sanctuary parish in San Francisco, dutifully scoffed. He assailed the Reagan administration's "myth that people run out of their country with guns made in the United States are not refugees." But Renny Golden admitted otherwise. "[In the] CRTF statement on goals of the Sanctuary movement," she asked plaintively in an internal memo, "can we ever say our intention is to stop U.S. intervention?"[76]

Such a motive should have been transparent given the composition of many of the network's clientele. To much of the Sanctuary movement, "Central America" was a political rather than a geographical and historical term, encompassing only those governments supported by the United States. To these activists, the Sandinistas were "revolutionaries" who had overthrown a U.S.-backed right-wing dictatorship. So while they welcomed Salvadorans and to a lesser extent Guatemalans, they largely shunned Nicaraguans who were fleeing the repressive leftist Sandinista regime. After the arrests in Texas, Bishop Fitzpatrick had appointed a new director of the Casa Oscar Romero, Sister Ninfa Garza, who admitted mostly Nicaraguans to the shelter. But Proyecto Libertad, a legal organization helping the San Benito Sanctuary movement, refused to represent Nicaraguans because, according to Jeff Larson, "We find that most Nicaraguans are here because of the economic situation."[77]

"Although I do not know that those fleeing persecution by the political Left were deliberately screened out, I never met any such person during my time in the East Bay," Susan Bibler Coutin of the East Bay Sanctuary Covenant in northern California would recall. "Certainly, East Bay Sanctuary workers tended to assume that Central Americans were fleeing persecution from the Right rather than the Left." She noted that a "questionnaire that asked potential asylum hearing witnesses to state their areas of expertise had no question regarding knowledge of persecution by the guerilla forces." When he discovered the blackballing of Nicaraguans by many Sanctuary groups, John O'Leary, who had previously assisted Vietnamese refugees, opened "New Exodus," an agency in the nation's capital ministering to Nicaraguan as well as Salvadoran and Guatemalan refugees.[78]

"Anger over U.S. policy in Central America makes the activist favor the Salvadoran over the Nicaraguan, the Afghan or the

Haitian," according to retired State Department officer David Simcox, analyzing the biases which were undermining the Sanctuary movement. "Among Salvadorans, the political activist is favored over the nonpolitical *campesino*, and the Salvadoran seeking to enter the country immediately is favored over the Salvadoran waiting his turn for legal immigration."[79]

The Catholic participants in the Sanctuary movement were not the only members of their church turning a blind eye to Sandinista repression. The National Catholic Rural Life Conference sent letters to the Senate Foreign Relations Committee calling for a freeze on U.S. military aid to El Salvador until true land reform had occurred. But while its executive director Gregory Cusack pronounced himself unsettled by the "violence embraced by some proponents of liberation theology," the NCRLC took no comparable action regarding Nicaragua, where a prominent priest serving in the government had proclaimed the compatibility of Christianity and Marxism.[80]

The Reagan administration was guilty of its own double standard, decrying human rights infractions by the anti-U.S. Nicaraguan government while downplaying abuses by the pro-U.S. Salvadoran and Guatemalan governments or the right-wing death squads those governments were unwilling or unable to control. So when Reagan claimed in April 1985 that Pope John Paul II "has been most supportive of all our activities in Central America," the Vatican distanced itself from the president's remarks.[81]

However political the Sanctuary movement was becoming, the Reagan administration appeared to be going to extremes to combat it. Though the administration and local police denied any connection to Washington, there occurred nearly three dozen burglaries of Sanctuary affiliates throughout the country in 1985. When Edward Haase, a member of a Central America "solidarity group" in Kansas City, returned after two months in Nicaragua, customs agents apprehended his diary and address book, as well as two articles he had written. The Federal Bureau of Investigation questioned members of the Committee on Solidarity with the People of El Salvador, and the group complained about the tapping of its phones, opening of its mail, and surveillance of its activities. A draft Defense Department memo branded the group's claims of providing food and medicine to refugees "disinformation."[82]

The Reagan administration was not administering all of the blows to the Sanctuary cause, however. In July 1986 the Outreach Committee of the Chicago Religious Task Force on Central America regretted that Cardinal Bernardin still "has not verbally supported Sanctuary and has made some terrible statements about Central America, such as his recent letter to [Nicaraguan President] Daniel Ortega denouncing the expulsion of . . . two priests." Thanks in large part to the cardinal, "there are no Catholic sanctuaries in Chicago."[83]

Other wounds to the Sanctuary movement continued to be self-inflicted. A January 1987 CRTFCA draft memo reviewed the "State of the Movement." On the plus side, Sanctuary had "injected a sense of morality into the debate on Central America," and arguably "has been a crucial factor in deterring Reagan from a more direct military intervention and use of U.S. troops in Central America." On the minus side, the movement had long since splintered between its Tucson branch, led by founders John Fife and James Corbett, who "recently proclaimed the death of Sanctuary [and] are now cooperating with the INS," and the Chicago branch, toward whom "distrust of CRTFCA and anything that smacks of organizing is rampant among certain people and groups." As a result, "the Sanctuary movement is comatose." The bottom line of Sanctuary's shortcomings was the bottom line: "An estimated $26 million/day in U.S. military and security aid goes to El Salvador, an incredible increase since 1982 when Sanctuary began."[84]

In September 1987, Pope John Paul II arrived in the United States and plunged headlong into the Sanctuary controversy. In San Antonio, the pope lauded the "great courage and generosity" of those "who have been doing much on behalf of suffering brothers and sisters arriving from the south." Though he did not explicitly identify the Sanctuary movement, an unnamed member of his entourage did, in an interview with the *Los Angeles Times*. When the *Times* headlined its story on the pontiff's remarks "Sanctuary Movement Endorsed by Pope," papal spokesman Joaquin Navarro-Valls rushed to issue a disclaimer. "While expressing compassion for undocumented aliens and admiration for those who seek to aid them," the pope, according to Navarro-Valls, "did not endorse any specific movement or group, nor did he encourage violation of the civil laws as a solution to this problem."[85]

In the face of the clear opposition of the president, the cloudy resistance of the bishops and the pope, and the gloomy prognostications of some of its members, the Sanctuary movement continued to grow. By August 1988, in the last year of the Reagan administration, there were 484 sanctuaries in the United States, and seventy-eight of them were Catholic—more than claimed by any other denomination. Since a majority of Salvadorans and Guatemalans and a plurality of Americans were Catholic, however, these numbers must have been deflating to some members of the Sanctuary network.[86]

Central American Refugees and Extended Voluntary Departure

While most bishops persisted in rejecting the means of the Sanctuary movement, they continued to share its ends. In 1981, the United States Catholic Conference pronounced itself in favor of Extended Voluntary Departure status (permission to remain in the country temporarily) for Salvadoran refugees. The State Department could legally ask the attorney general to grant such a classification if "there is widespread fighting, destruction, and breakdown of service and order" in the national home country. Since 1960, Cuba, Czechoslovakia, Cambodia, Vietnam, Laos, Lebanon,

Ethiopia, Hungary, Iran, Romania, Uganda, Afghanistan, Poland, and Nicaragua had received such a designation.[87]

The administration refused to add El Salvador to the list. "All EVD decisions require a balancing of judgments about their foreign policy, humanitarian, and immigration policy implications," Assistant Secretary of State Elliott Abrams testified on Capitol Hill in April 1984. With regard to foreign policy, the United States was dispensing over eight billion dollars in foreign aid to El Salvador while pursuing "various political and diplomatic efforts to resolve disputes and reduce violence." As for humanitarian concerns, "we asked the human rights office of the Archdiocese of El Salvador whether they believed that there was a pattern of persecution of deportees; they replied that they did not." Regarding immigration policy, "I do not believe that the appropriate response to the problems of poverty or violence in El Salvador is to allow any Salvadoran who wishes to simply live in America instead—any more than I think this is true for Guatemala, or Haiti, or Nicaragua, or Sri Lanka, or Afghanistan, or Iran, or Uganda, or Ethiopia, or Lebanon, or Vietnam, or Zimbabwe."[88]

Abrams's injection of the Archdiocese of El Salvador into his statement was an effort to undercut Catholic opposition to the Reagan Central American policy. Instead, it further antagonized some Catholics. Timothy Cardinal Manning of Los Angeles wrote Archbishop Arturo Rivera y Damas of San Salvador to verify the assistant secretary's assertion. He could not. "Salvadorans have returned to this country," the archbishop replied to the cardinal, "only to meet their deaths a few days later."[89]

Bishops Manuel Moreno of Tucson, Thomas O'Brien of Phoenix, and Jerome Hastrich of Gallup, New Mexico wrote President Reagan in January 1985 advocating the EVD designation for Salvadoran refugees. Two Catholic Democrats, Massachusetts Representative Joseph Moakley and Arizona Senator Dennis DeConcini, introduced their EVD bill two months later. "[T]he profoundization [sic] of the military conflict offers a future of greater pain, uncertainty, and suffering for the grand majority of Salvadorans," Archbishop Rivera wrote to the members of Congress, urging passage of the Moakley-DeConcini legislation. "During my visit to the United States, it was with profound concern that I was able to confirm, through numerous testimonies, that the authorities and members of the government of the United States have closed their doors and their hearts against the suffering of my people."[90]

"The religious community has played a very positive role in this legislation," DeConcini applauded, citing his own activities in his Arizona parish, the St. Vincent DePaul Society, the Newman Center, and the "Friendly House" halfway house for undocumented aliens. Yet he quickly acknowledged the rupture within and among the churches. "I'm at odds with some of my good friends in the religious community because of the Sanctuary movement. I just don't think that breaking the law is the way to operate," said the senator, separating himself from his cosponsor, an ardent supporter of Sanctuary's tactics and staunch opponent of Reagan's Central American strategy. But the churches' "long-standing credibility in dealing with aliens … has all brought a lot of credibility, that the church leaders that are involved in this are not just 'Johnnie-come-lately's' into this subject matter."[91]

The Reagan administration appreciated neither the role the churches were playing nor the legislation they were espousing. "Religious persons should not use the credibility they enjoy to market their personal, philosophical, and political beliefs," Assistant Secretary of State for Inter-American Affairs Langhorne Motley protested in July 1985. He added that it was "time to take politics out of the pulpit and the pulpit out of politics."

Noting that "in the last three years, Catholic officials have spoken before at least five congressional committees" to convey "their belief that military aid is useless and wrong," Catholic liberal Colman McCarthy took issue with Motley in the *Washington Post*. "With a new age of martyrdom now the reality in countries like El Salvador and Guatemala, the Church's appearances in political forums have been paid for in blood."[92]

They were not being paid for in votes. In 1986, after the House narrowly voted to include the Moakley Amendment granting Extended Voluntary Departure status to Salvadorans and Nicaraguans as part of the Mazzoli immigration reform bill, the conference committee removed it. The conference report of the Immigration Reform and Control Act then passed both houses, with the 1980 Refugee Act's prohibition on extending EVD to groups rather than individuals still intact. Moakley, DeConcini, and the bishops of their church swallowed their disappointment and endorsed the legislation. The president withdrew his veto threat and signed it.[93]

In June 1987, Acting Attorney General Arnold Burns announced that no deportations of Nicaraguans would occur before a final review of their cases by the Justice Department. The following month a group of House Democrats introduced a bill to ensure equal treatment of Nicaraguan and Salvadoran refugees. The measure would stop deportation of unauthorized immigrants from Nicaragua and El Salvador for two to three years. The bishops were among those supporting the legislation from the left. But the president was among those opposing it from the right. So it would die in the 100th Congress.[94]

Immigration Reform under Reagan

By the dawn of the Reagan era, immigration reform had become an economic as well as a moral imperative, a way of raising the country's international economic standing and its domestic alien underclass at the same time. "Rather than talking about putting up a fence," presidential candidate Ronald Reagan said during the 1980 primaries, "why don't we make it possible for them to come here legally with a work permit?" While he dismissed a "blurring of the borders" between the United States and Mexico, Reagan nonetheless insisted that "fences and armed guards are not the answer." Thus did Reagan frame the argument over immigration reform not in terms of reducing the flow of new arrivals, but legalizing it.[95]

Thus would the new president align himself with the U.S. Catholic bishops. Testifying before the House Subcommittee on Immigration, Citizenship, and International Law in March 1975, Monsignor George Higgins, Secretary for Research for the United States Catholic Conference, advocated "an across-the-board grant of amnesty with the necessary residency cut-off date for eligibility and adjustment of status, without chargeability against numerical ceilings." Higgins contended that without amnesty, irregular aliens "will be driven further underground," and "a permanent subculture will be created in the United States." Without amnesty, "it is doubtful that even massive expenditures of time, money, and effort on the part of the Immigration Service would ever lead to adequate controls."[96]

Yet the president and the bishops pitted themselves against most of the American people. According to a 1980 Roper poll, 80 percent of Americans wanted "to reduce the quotas of the number of legal immigrants who can enter the United States each year," while 91 percent supported "an all-out effort to stop the illegal entry into the United States of one and one-half million foreigners who don't have entry visas." A 1980 Gallup poll discovered that 72 percent of Americans would support "a law which would make it illegal to employ a person who has entered the United States without proper papers." 52 percent would oppose "a proposal to grant permanent resident status to all aliens who entered the United States illegally and who have been in the country seven years," as President Carter had espoused, while 62 percent believed that "everyone in the United States should be required to show an identification card such as a Social Security card." A member of Rep. Romano Mazzoli's staff informed the congressman three weeks after the election that "the public is clamoring for reform of our immigration policy since nothing has been done in over half a century."[97]

Michael Teitelbaum of the Ford Foundation, who served as staff director for the House Select Committee on Population from 1977 to 1979, attributed this public anxiety to six factors. First, the U.S. was receiving twice as many immigrants and refugees as the rest of the world combined. Second, immigration levels were approaching the highest ceiling in U.S. history, including the pre-1920s "open borders" era. Third, most estimates counted up to six million undocumented immigrants in the U.S. in the 1970s. Fourth, the 1965 Immigration and Nationality Act had inadvertently spawned a disproportionate number of Spanish-speaking regular and irregular immigrants. Fifth, the prospects for continued poverty and instability in the immigrants' home countries in the 1980s and the 1990s augured greater pressure on the American borders. Sixth, INS enforcement of U.S. immigration laws had become decidedly permissive.[98]

A City University of New York study calculated that the undocumented had filled as many as half of all the new jobs created in the stagnant economy of the late 1970s. "Concern over the number of illegal aliens in this country is growing," Commonweal editorialized in February 1981, "and unless economic development can be achieved in Mexico and throughout Latin America, the problem will not go away."[99]

During its two-and-one-half years of deliberations the Hesburgh Commission conducted hearings throughout the country. Many Catholic representatives shared their views on immigration reform with the panel, but none of them preached restrictionism.

Francisco Dominguez, director of the Catholic Charities Counseling Service of the Archdiocese of New York, advocated a "generous amnesty" for all unauthorized aliens. Rev. Francis Riley, director of the Centro de Asuntos Migratorios in National City, California, espoused "unconditional amnesty for all undocumenteds in the United States." Rev. Joseph Cogo, executive secretary of the American Committee on Italian Migration, favored a "three-tiered law whereby a separate preference system and percentages are given to each category of immigrants: family, workers, refugees." Rev. James Schulz of the Interfaith Coalition for Justice for Immigrants (composed of thirty-five Protestant, Jewish, and Catholic groups in the Chicago area) proposed "the elimination of the current quota system for all members of the immediate family to incorporate immigrants' concept of the extended family; the elimination of per-country ceilings and the distribution of quota numbers according to need, with recognition of special relationships the United States enjoys with particular countries; the institution of a preference category for minor U.S. citizens ... [and] a general amnesty program for undocumented persons." Zeferino Ochoa of the Chicago archdiocese's Latin American Committee posited that all parents of U.S. citizens should be citizens themselves. Sister Adela Arroyo lamented the "inhuman" working conditions at the INS.

Speaking for the bishops, Donald Hohl of the United States Catholic Conference Office of Migration and Refugee Services endorsed a "full grant of amnesty to all illegal/undocumented persons currently in the United States; permission for spouses and children to join those granted amnesty; increased [emigrant] ceilings for Canada and Mexico; and economic and technical assistance for the sending countries." Hohl opposed "sanctions against employers" for hiring the undocumented, and urged caution in adopting a national identification card "lest impatience prompts us to act impulsively, resulting in the erosion of human rights and the freedoms which we as a nation so jealously seek to protect." Alone among the representatives of his church who addressed the Hesburgh Commission, Hohl supported "tight control of our land and borders," though he didn't say how.[100]

In March, the commission issued its long-awaited recommendations, advocating amnesty for all irregular aliens, workplace verification to prevent more from coming, and an increase in the legal immigration quota from 270,000 to 400,000 (excluding refugees) for five years, then a reduction to 350,000. The commission also would continue to exempt the immediate relatives of immigrants from these limits. The report rejected, however, requiring a counterfeit-proof work permit for all Americans. It excluded a temporary worker program. And it offered no new prescription for border enforcement beyond a more "responsive" and "sensitive" Immigration and Naturalization Service. The USCC and the Jesuit Office of Social Ministries embraced the report in a letter to the White House, saluting its omission of a guest worker provision, which would have produced more unauthorized immigrants, lower wages for native-born workers, and an underclass ripe for social and economic exploitation. "It is past time for the American people to realize that the oft-referred-to 'tired, poor, and huddled masses yearning to breathe free' do very well for themselves," *Commonweal's* editors applauded the Hesburgh Commission report, "if they are given half a chance."[101]

President Reagan appeared to agree. Even as the Hesburgh Commission was advocating an increase in the number of immigrants, President Reagan's first budget was proposing a decrease in federal funding for border enforcement. "I'm very intrigued by a program that's been suggested by several border state governors and their counterparts in the Mexican States on the other side of the border," Reagan told CBS's Walter Cronkite in March in his first remarks on immigration since taking office. He alluded to "a proposal that we and the Mexican government get together and legalize this [illegal immigration] and grant visas, because it is to our interest that we might have a breaking of the stability south of the border."[102]

President Reagan nevertheless kept his distance from Father Hesburgh. Catholic White House aide Joe Ghoughassian counseled that "in his private statements to the Commission and news release statements," Reagan, while maintaining that his administration would prioritize immigration and refugee issues, should be careful to "speak in generalities." Heeding the advice of Donna Alvarado and Bill Gribbin of the Office of Policy Development, the vice president, not the president, received the report from Father Hesburgh in a White House ceremony. George Bush's remarks were deliberately vague, acknowledging the "complexity" of the issues addressed by the report, and only getting specific enough to stress the administration's "commitment to family reunification as [the] basis for immigration policy." Then, only five days after Hesburgh presented his findings, Reagan appointed his own Task Force on Immigration and Refugee Policy.[103]

By the end of April, Frank Hodsoll, the task force's White House representative, had declared the panel's mission "politically treacherous." On the one hand were "strong anti-alien feelings" and the fiscal and administrative costs of providing foreign workers with "equality of treatment and opportunity," and on the other hand was potential "all-out resistance" by "Hispanics, minority groups generally, the Catholic Church, and other religious groups, as well as civil rights groups" to "creating a legally sanctioned underclass of foreign workers or any attempt to increase enforcement without a generous amnesty program."[104]

Perhaps the thorniest issue that Reagan would have to resolve would be the question of a national identification card, which sparked a ferocious debate within his administration. Attorney General William French Smith had defended such an approach as little more than counterfeit-proofing Social Security cards. But White House aide Craig Fuller argued that devising a card would take too long and cost too much. Assistant Secretary of the Treasury Craig Roberts contended that it would address "the symptoms rather than the causes" of illegal immigration. William Niskanen of the Council of Economic Advisors believed that it would perpetuate rather than preclude document fraud. Secretary of Education Terrel Bell, Domestic Policy Advisor Martin Anderson, and Secretary of the Interior James Watt viewed it in much more sinister terms. Bell called it "Orwellian." Anderson saw it as "an indispensable tool of a totalitarian state." Watt likened it to the Book of Revelation's "Mark of the Beast."[105]

If these economic and ideological objections were not powerful enough, political considerations would persuade Reagan to rebuke his attorney general. Administration pollster Richard Wirthlin reported that adoption of a national identification system would be politically "disastrous." Counsel to the president Fred Fielding explained why. "The issue of government intrusion on individual liberty and privacy is one of those areas where liberal and conservative ideologies frequently converge," Fielding wrote. So at the last meeting of the task force, the president had characteristically rebuffed the attorney general not with hubris, but with humor. "Maybe we should just brand all the babies," Reagan suggested to Smith. "For about ten seconds everybody laughed and smiled," Anderson recounted, "and that was the end of the national identification card for 1981."[106]

"Illegal immigrants in considerable numbers have become productive members of our society and a basic part of our work force," Reagan said while formally accepting the recommendations of the task force in July. The report called for amnesty and a path to permanent residence for undocumented aliens who had been in the United States since before January 1, 1980, as well as the creation of a two-year, fifty-thousand-visa guest worker program for temporary employees.

"At the same time, in so doing," Reagan noted, "we must not encourage illegal immigration." He therefore also supported the task force's call for a 50 percent increase in spending on border enforcement (contrary to his proposed FY 1982 budget), fines for employers who knowingly hire irregular aliens, and a prohibition on the dependents of those given amnesty for entering the U.S. But he would not be requiring a national identification card for all Americans.[107]

For the National Catholic Rural Life Conference, the Reagan proposal would have been stronger without a guest worker provision. At their November 1981 board meeting, the directors of the NCRLC pronounced themselves "categorically opposed" to such a program. They charged that "importing foreign workers would have a serious adverse effect on domestic labor standards and would jeopardize the hard-won gains of our domestic work force in regard to wages and working conditions." Such a scheme would "enslave a vast number of Mexican laborers for exploitation and legalize the second-class status of Mexican laborers in the United States."[108]

The legislative process would have to wait, as Congress adjourned before taking action on the Reagan plan. Soon after the lawmakers returned to Washington in 1982, they devised an immigration scheme of their own. Senator Simpson and Representative Mazzoli introduced legislation which upped the ante on the Reagan proposal. Like the president's formula, the Simpson-Mazzoli design would grant amnesty to irregular aliens and would punish employers who deliberately added undocumented workers. But unlike the Reagan plan, it would push the date of entry for legalized aliens up from 1980 to 1982, would provide harsher fines for employers, would set an annual immigration quota (425,000), would omit a guest worker program, and would permit a national identification card.[109]

USCC General Secretary Msgr. Daniel Hoye assured the members of Congress, after the Simpson bill survived the Senate Judiciary Committee in June, of the bishops' support for the legislation because of its amnesty and legalization provisions. He nonetheless expressed "severe reservations" concerning the parts of the bill dealing with employer sanctions (for fear of employment discrimination) and family unity (because of the bill's elimination of the visas available to the adult, unmarried sons and daughters of adult U.S. citizens within the so-called "Second Preference" and of the visas accessible to brothers and sisters of adult U.S. citizens within the so-called "Fifth Preference"). He also challenged the addition of guest workers (out of concern that they become subject to the fluctuations of the economy).[110]

After amending the bill to restore the administration's January 1, 1980, cutoff date for amnesty, and refusing an amendment by Massachusetts Catholic Democratic senator Edward Kennedy to attach the "Fifth Preference" family reunification provisions for legal immigrants, the Senate voted 80–19 to send the measure to the House. From Washington, where the bishops were holding their annual fall meeting in November, Bishop Bevilacqua reiterated the USCC's reserved support for the bill, this time urging the House to do what the Senate had not—restore the Senate Judiciary Committee's January 1, 1982 cutoff date for amnesty, and the existing law's Second and Fifth Preference provisions, while extinguishing the guest worker program. "We tolerate employer sanctions," the bishop warned, but only as a "trade-off for fair and generous legalization."[111]

It would not matter. Under heavy lobbying by the bishops and Rev. Joseph Cogo, the Catholic priest who headed the American Committee on Italian Migration, the House Judiciary Committee deleted the changes to the Second and Fifth Preferences mandated by the Senate legislation. But the other parts of the Senate bill to which the bishops objected remained in the House version.[112]

Father Hesburgh prodded the House to finish the job. "As you know, I invested two years of my life in the formulation of the policy behind the bill," Hesburgh wrote to the Catholic Speaker of the House, Thomas "Tip" O'Neill of Massachusetts, in October. "Although it is not perfect and everyone can have some problems with it, it is far better than what we now have, and it does put forward a coherent U.S. policy on immigration and refugees that can be both workable and humane." Hesburgh thus implored O'Neill to take up the legislation in the lame-duck session between the November midterm elections and the January opening of the next Congress.[113]

The bishops joined Father Hesburgh in seeking a floor vote on the Mazzoli bill. "For ten years the [United States Catholic] Conference has urged Congress to adopt legislation to legalize the status of the many undocumented aliens who reside in this country," USCC General Secretary Msgr. Daniel Hoye wrote members of the House in December. "At the same time, we have opposed legislation to impose sanctions on employers who hire undocumented workers and which did not contain a generous legalization program."

Yet the Mazzoli bill still did not completely meet these standards. The bill's employer sanctions contained the potential for discrimination against Latino applicants, and the measure's distinction between temporary (those in the country since January 1, 1980) and permanent (those in the country since January 1, 1978) residents, with the denial of some federal benefits for both, was not generous enough. The bishops continued to support the bill, but they urged Mazzoli to amend it.[114]

The prelates also feared that the House might strip the bill entirely of its legalization provisions, leaving an enforcement-only approach. James Robinson, director of the USCC Office of Government Liaison, thus wrote the bishops and directors of state conferences encouraging an all-out telephone and telegram effort to ensure that legalization remained part of the legislation. "Many of the members of Congress report that they are under strong pressure from organized campaigns of opposition in their districts," Robinson wrote. "They are in need of expressions of support for legalization from the Catholic community."[115]

The bishops' effort fell short. They succeeded in retaining legalization and in helping bring the Mazzoli bill to the House floor. But after a passionate debate which lasted into the wee hours of two mornings, the House adjourned for the Christmas recess before coming to a vote. Mazzoli blamed the resistance from Hispanics and African-American organizations, labor unions, farm groups, business interests, and even the leadership of his party, for their shameless stalling. "Despite this opposition, the bill enjoyed widespread support, including that of the United States Catholic Conference," the congressman wrote his archbishop, Thomas Kelly of Louisville, in January 1983, "for which Senator Simpson and I are very grateful."[116]

Speaker O' Neill admitted that he was not "enamored" of the legislation, and only allowed the debate as a "courtesy" to Reagan. But the president didn't press hard for the Simpson and Mazzoli bills.[117]

And who could blame him? "Public opinion polls show that eighty percent of the American people want reductions in legal admissions [of immigrants]," Republican James Sensenbrenner of Wisconsin said, explaining why he was taking on the leader of his party in the White House. Then, in language which could not have pleased the leaders of the church, the congressman observed, "Compassion fatigue has, indeed, set in."[118]

So "was last year one big waste of time?" James Michael Hoffman, assistant director of the USCC'S Migration and Refugee Services, wondered as 1983 began. "Obviously not," he answered his own question, citing the Senate's overwhelming passage of the Simpson bill and the House's "116 pages of *Congressional Record* debate" on the Mazzoli bill. "Had this debate not occurred," Hoffman contended in his internal memo, "the chances for immigration reform during 1983 would be very slim indeed."

Hoffman noted that his office was considering a series of meetings around the country within the next few months "to allow Catholic leaders employed in local Catholic organizations to express their views and offer suggestions for immigration reform proposals for the Ninety-Eighth Congress." Hoffman thus remained amazingly upbeat following a disappointing year for his fellow Catholic immigration advocates.[119]

The Simpson-Mazzoli legislation would follow a familiar path in 1983. The administration again endorsed the Senate bill, which required worker verification for all businesses with four or more employees. It also maintained a "two-tier" approach to legalization, with those irregular aliens who were in the country before January 1, 1977 eligible to receive permanent legal status, but those who came between January 1, 1977 and January 1, 1980 having to wait at least three years to obtain permanent status.

The Senate again easily passed the Simpson bill, 76–18, in May. The bishops and other Catholic immigration advocates again mobilized to try to persuade the relevant committees in the House of Representatives to soften the Senate measure. Only this time, unlike 1982, they succeeded.

The House Judiciary Committee made worker verification optional, unless the employer had an earlier violation, and eliminated the "two-tier" approach to legalization, settling on the single cutoff date, January 1, 1982. The House Education and Labor Committee attached penalties for discrimination against Latino employees. While these changes pleased the bishops, they alienated the president. The Reagan administration could no longer support the Mazzoli bill, Attorney General Smith explained, "until modifications are made to tighten enforcement provisions and to significantly narrow the terms of legalization to address the Administration's budget concerns."[120]

Reagan's opposition to the amended Mazzoli legislation threatened to derail immigration reform. When asked if immigration reform was dead in the Ninety-Eighth Congress, Senator Simpson replied, "Nothing ever dies."[121]

"We're still alive," Representative Mazzoli, a Notre Dame alum, wrote Father Hesburgh in September, noting that the House Rules Committee would be considering sending his bill to the floor in the middle of October. With the prospect of more amendments in the rules committee and without the support of Speaker O'Neill and Democratic Majority Whip James Wright of Texas, Mazzoli nonetheless concluded that "our vital signs are weak."[122]

Administration intervention could not save the Mazzoli bill in 1983. But the measure finally would receive a floor vote and a victory, by a 216–211 margin, in June 1984. "Your name was cited during the debate more often—and always favorably—" Mazzoli wrote Father Hesburgh after passage of the bill, "than any other save those two 'crazies,' Simpson and Mazzoli." The Catholic congressman added warily, "I hope election year jitters do not scuttle the tremendous and worthy work done by all concerned—not the least of whom is Ted Hesburgh—over the last six years."[123]

There were ample reasons for "election-year jitters" in the Reagan camp. According to a July 1984 survey by administration pollster Richard Wirthlin, over half of Americans opposed amnesty for unauthorized aliens and almost three-quarters favored worker verification measures. "In the opinion of the American people," Wirthlin summarized his findings, "granting amnesty is a questionable solution that carries liabilities for the president." The best political outcome of Simpson-Mazzoli for Reagan, therefore, would be "deadlocking the bill in conference."[124]

Reagan would get his deadlock, not because of anything he did, but because of what his opponent did. After former vice president Walter Mondale, the Democratic nominee for president, assured the Hispanic Congressional Caucus of his opposition to Simpson-Mazzoli, Speaker O'Neill appointed several opponents of the legislation to the conference committee. A month before Mondale's presidential candidacy died in forty-nine states, the Simpson and Mazzoli bills perished in the conference committee.[125]

Things were going so badly for Reagan on the immigration front that even Mother Teresa was upset with him. "I am writing to ask your help in the matter of obtaining visas for our sisters in the U.S.A.," she wrote the president in October 1984. "Over the past year, it has become more and more difficult . . . ."[126]

Some members of his administration were agitated as well. At a June 1985 meeting of his Domestic Policy Council, many of the president's inner circle counseled caution toward immigration reform. Catholic White House aide Linda Chavez worried about the resistance of her fellow Latinos to the Simpson bill's enforcement provisions. "Your Administration has been accused of only being half-hearted in favor of the [immigration] legislation last year," White House aides Max Friedersdorf and M. B. Oglesby reminded Reagan in July.[127]

Reagan was fully engaged, however, at a Domestic Policy Council meeting that month. He cited cases of exploitation of undocumented employees by their bosses. He added that while affluence is a magnet for immigration, immigration is a magnet for affluence, in both the receiving and sending countries. New Attorney General Edwin Meese presented the president with three options: 1) support the legislation, 2) support the legislation but try to amend it, or 3) support the concept of the legislation, but not the bill itself. Reagan approved Meese's option two—an endorsement of the Simpson bill, with an amendment to provide for a guest worker program. Then the meeting adjourned, so President Reagan could meet with Senator Simpson.[128]

Within a month, Meese was testifying in favor of option two before the Senate Judiciary Committee. After hearing testimony by the bishops and Father Hesburgh, the Senate Judiciary Committee again cleared the Simpson bill, on a near party-line vote of 12–5, with only two Democrats in the majority. This latest version nodded to Meese by promising to defer legalization until a presidential commission had determined that the nation's borders were secure. An amendment from Massachusetts Catholic Democratic senator Edward Kennedy ensuring immediate implementation of the amnesty portion of the bill fell to a party-line vote.[129]

When the legislation reached the floor in September 1985, California Republican Pete Wilson, with the blessing of the president and over the opposition of the bishops and Hispanic groups, successfully inserted a guest-worker program. Then the bill passed by a wide margin, 69–30.

The immigration subcommittee of the House Judiciary Committee reported the Mazzoli bill in November. It contained broader protection for guest workers than the Senate bill, and included the antidiscrimination language the Senate had removed. But the House adjourned before the full committee could vote on the measure.[130]

In their "Resolution on Immigration Reform" passed at their November meeting, the bishops pronounced themselves opposed to what the Simpson and Mazzoli bills now included as offering too much on employer sanctions and too little on amnesty and the rights of temporary laborers. The National Catholic Rural Life Conference was part of a "rural coalition" which wrote Representative Rodino in November objecting to any guest worker program as exploitative.[131]

As the new session of Congress convened in 1986, key voices on Capitol Hill urged Reagan to inject himself into the immigration reform campaign. "Dear Ron," Senator Simpson wrote his friend in the White House in January, suggesting that Reagan include immigration reform in his upcoming State of the Union Address to help "get this damn thing done and off the national agenda."[132]

"If you agree with me that control of our borders is of critical importance to our nation," the Catholic House Democratic Majority Leader Representative Peter Rodino of New Jersey wrote Reagan in the same month, "I would request your personal involvement and leadership in the effort to enact legislation to accomplish that objective." To Simpson's dismay, Reagan would not mention immigration reform in the State of the Union. To Rodino's relief, Reagan would meet with Rodino, Simpson, Mazzoli, California Catholic Republican representative Dan Lundgren, and New York Republican representative Hamilton Fish IV, in an effort which Mazzoli said "should have laid to rest any lingering doubts my colleagues on the Hill have that President Reagan is very committed to the bill."[133]

In March 1986, President Reagan and Attorney General Smith met with Father Hesburgh and other supporters of the administration's immigration reform efforts on the fifth anniversary of the release of the Hesburgh Commission report. But some Catholics still had doubts. To arrest the influx of irregular immigrants, Rev. Frank Moan, national coordinator of the Jesuit Refugee Service, wrote in *America* in March, the Reagan administration "must cease supporting totalitarian regimes that deny the very human rights we consider essential" and cause the exodus of economic migrants to the U.S. "There are no illegal aliens in the Catholic Church," the nation's youngest archbishop, forty-nine-year-old Roger Mahony of Los Angeles, explained his resistance to a Reagan administration policy requiring all adult residents of federal housing to show proof of legal immigration status. In June, Mahony launched a five-year plan of outreach to the Latinos who comprised half the members of his archdiocese, 50,000 of whom turned out at Dodger Stadium to hear the archbishop kick off the campaign.[134]

After seven months of quarreling over the guest worker provisions, the House Judiciary Committee reported the Mazzoli bill, 25–10. The majority agreed to provide permanent residence status to farm laborers who had worked for at least sixty days in American agriculture between May 1985 and May 1986, set a formula for devising an annual cap on guest workers, and simplified requirements for growers to obtain temporary workers through the H-2 visa program.[135]

Six weeks later, when the full House again debated immigration reform, Mazzoli extolled the virtues of his legislation and paid tribute to its founding father. "This bill did not originally spring full blown from the fevered brows of Ron Mazzoli and Al Simpson," the Kentucky congressman reminded his colleagues. "It especially reflects the work of Rev. Theodore Hesburgh, CSC, president of my alma mater Notre Dame University, who headed the Select Commission on Immigration Reform, and whose magnum opus on the subject forms the outlines of the bill before this body today."

While one representative was citing Father Hesburgh in an effort to pass the bill, another was citing Father Hesburgh in an effort to defeat it. "Now, this is a far cry from the original Hesburgh Commission report that tied employer sanctions with a tightly drawn legalization program, a two-year program where people who have not been in the United States a long period of time received permanent residency status, and those who have been in for a much longer period of time received permanent status which led to citizenship," Wisconsin Republican James Sensenbrenner reflected. With the Rules Committee's adoption of an amendment sponsored by Texas Catholic Democrat Robert García to "sunset" the bill's employer sanctions after five years, Sensenbrenner added, "what we have, when this bill passes and plays out in five years, are no employer sanctions left, but millions of people who are on the road to citizenship and will be eligible for public assistance and free public education because they are here under color of law."

"What's wrong with sanctions? Shouldn't it be illegal to hire persons who are here without proper documents?" Garcia defended his amendment—and the position of his church. "In a word, no . . . . Because in our zeal to slap the hands of those who hire undocumented persons, we are also setting up a situation where employers would rather not hire a person of color because of the risk of a fine."[136]

After narrowly defeating the amnesty part of the legislation, the House voted 230–166 to send the rest of the bill to the conference committee. It had taken four years for the House and Senate to get this far. Yet it took only four days for the conference committee to report the final bill, which adopted the Senate language of a review of employer sanctions within three years, the House protections against employment discrimination and in favor of free legal representation for guest workers, and the House's legalization cutoff of January 1, 1982. The central tenets of the original Simpson and Mazzoli proposals—employer sanctions and amnesty—remained.

The final bill called for a 50 percent increase in the number of Border Patrol along the country's southwestern border. It authorized employer fines of $250 to $2,000 for a first offense, $2,000 to

$5,000 for a second offense, and $3,000 to $10,000 for a third offense for each unauthorized alien employee, for those with a "pattern or practice" of hiring the undocumented. It granted temporary status for those in the country unlawfully since January 1, 1982, with the promise of permanent status within eighteen months for those who were learning minimal English and knowledge of U.S. history and government. It also denied public nonemergency assistance to all able-bodied irregular aliens for at least five years.[137]

Although such workers probably comprised fewer than 15 percent of undocumented labor, western and southwestern growers overcame union opposition to create the Special Agricultural Worker (SAW) program as part of IRCA. This scheme would offer permanent residency to those with at least sixty days of seasonal farm labor experience with specified crops between May 1985 and May 1986. To assuage the concerns of growers who feared an exodus of legalized employees from their farms, the bill included a Replenishment Agricultural Worker (RAW) program. It permitted as many as 350,000 such temporary residents who worked at least ninety days in perishable agriculture for each of the next three years to qualify for permanent residency, and another two years to earn citizenship if the Departments of Agriculture and Labor certified a shortage of workers in perishable agriculture. The legislation also revised the Immigration and Nationality Act of 1952 to permit long-term undocumented immigrants present in the country before January 1, 1972 to revise their status to permanent residency.[138]

The House approved the conference report, 238–173, on October 15, while the Senate endorsed it, 63–24, two days later. Despite his reservations over the cost of the legislation and its antidiscrimination language, Reagan signed the Immigration Reform and Control Act on November 6, 1986. "Our objective is only to establish a reasonable, fair, orderly, and secure system of immigration into this country," said the president, "and not to discriminate in any way against particular nations and people."[139]

The bishops applauded Congress and the president for enacting a law that, in their view, was much better in its final incarnation that it had been when Senator Simpson and Representative Mazzoli introduced it. "It is against the common good and unacceptable to have a double society, one visible with rights and one invisible without rights," the bishops said in praise of the legislation. They then organized what Donald Kerwin would call "the country's largest network of 'qualified designated entities'—voluntary and community organizations that had permission from the Immigration and Naturalization Service to help unauthorized immigrants to fill out adjustment-of-status applications."[140]

By 1987, over one-third of all the Catholics in the United States were Hispanic. So when Pope John Paul II visited the United States in September of that year, he stopped in such heavily Latino cities as Miami, San Antonio, Phoenix, and Los Angeles.[141]

The pope's message in these Hispanic enclaves was one of diversity and inclusion, and he delivered parts of it in Spanish. Not only had it become clear almost a year after the passage of IRCA that many undocumented aliens were not learning English, but it was also apparent that they had not stopped coming to the United States. While the law's amnesty provisions were, to the delight of the church, easily enforceable, its employer sanctions, to the relief of the church, were not. Without the kind of transparent national identification card which the bishops and the president had always resisted, the American workplace remained rife with document fraud. "Opponents from the right and the left savaged it as 'a national ID,'" Simpson and Mazzoli would lament, "although it was not something that had to be carried on one's person [except] at the time of the 'new hire' employment or when applying for government benefits."[142]

Reagan aide Charles Smith also sounded several warning signals. "Estimates of persons eligible to become temporary residents, and eventually citizens, as a result of various provisions in the bill (e.g., amnesty, temporary agricultural workers, increase in H-2 workers) may be *low*," Smith wrote. He foresaw "a *shadow* effect that a) more persons, including dependents, may be here than estimated, b) many persons may *come* across the border illegally and claim eligibility as an individual or dependent, c) many persons legalized may seek to *bring in* family members, and d) the birth rate of those legalized may be relatively high." Successful implementation of IRCA would therefore require "that INS a) improves their border control procedures, and b) spends a much larger proportion of their effort on interior enforcement."

Smith added that "providing amnesty a) rewards lawbreakers, and b) reduces chances for entry into the United States for many persons waiting a long time for legal entry." He admitted that "since this bill does little to reduce the economic differences between the United States and Mexico, many Mexicans may still be attracted to the U.S. for work or public assistance as illegal aliens." Smith therefore advocated "border enforcement that includes deportation of illegal aliens deep into their home countries," while suggesting that "states should pass and enforce laws concerning illegal aliens, including employment and social services."[143]

Hugh Davis Graham identified the law's assets as "large numbers of hard-working, low-cost laborers and the economic benefits this brought to employers and consumers of immigrant services, including a strengthened worker-to-retiree ratio." But among its drawbacks were "low levels of migrant education and employment skills, increased lawlessness in the form of illegal entry and continued residence, ... migrant smuggling and its attendant corruption, asylum claims coached by immigration lawyers to disguise economic distress as political oppression, and depressed wages for all low-skilled workers."[144]

As explained by Betsy Cooper and Kevin O'Neill, legalization divided families between those who arrived before and after the amnesty cutoff date. Efforts to publicize, implement, and finance the law at the state and local levels were uneven. Affidavits to certify those eligible under the program were often fraudulent, and security checks were often haphazard.[145]

In the words of Reed Ueda, IRCA was "the most generous immigration law passed in U.S. history," featuring "novel and generous provisions for the legalization of illegal aliens" and augmenting "a host of allotments based on special needs and status." In sacrificing genuine border enforcement and worker verification for a magnanimous amnesty, Reagan caved in to what Otis Graham would call "a bizarre lobbying coalition including . . . Hispanic ethnic lobbyists . . . , big western growers, [and] religious leaders" like the American Catholic bishops.[146]

So almost as soon as the ink was dry on the Immigration Reform and Control Act, there were calls for tougher immigration reform. But those calls were not coming from the White House. In May 1988, the INS proposed that the administration shift its focus to legal immigration reform in order to reunite immigrant families more rapidly by eliminating all country preferences and most occupational distinctions, by reducing IRCA's five-year residency requirement to three, and by raising the quota of legal entrants to as many as 700,000 per year.[147]

The calls for tougher immigration reform were not coming from the U.S. Catholic hierarchy, either. In September 1988, two months before the election of George H. W. Bush, the bishops issued their newest "Statement of Principles on Immigration Reform." They "espoused family reunification, equality of treatment among the nation's valuable resources," and "every effort . . . to discourage illegal immigration by promoting just immigration law. " They concluded that the "right to migrate for work should never be displaced by the exercise of a nation's sovereign right to control its own borders."[148]

The bishops therefore largely remained on the side of the Reagan administration, which they had once opposed on employer sanctions, legalization cutoff, and family preference provisions of the Simpson and Mazzoli bills. But they still found themselves on the opposite side of many Catholics—and most Americans. "There was no political benefit," to immigration reform, Attorney General William French Smith would remember, "only travail for the sponsors"—and for the advocates from church and state.[149]

Conclusions

The failure of the Immigration Reform and Control Act to address the nation's overall refugee problem was a defeat for Catholic immigration interests and for the country. The law's failure to ensure enforceable immigration reform was a victory for the former, but a tragedy for the latter.

On refugee issues, the U.S. Catholic bishops and their supporters nonetheless could count some successes. They helped raise awareness of the Reagan administration's disparate treatment of Haitians, Cubans, Nicaraguans, Salvadorans, and Guatemalans. A group of American bishops helped procure Fidel Castro's release of Cuban political prisoners, and Bishop Román helped produce a fair outcome for the Oakdale rioters. The Sanctuary movement enlisted many Catholic congregants and a few Catholic prelates.

On the whole, however, the Reagan era was unkind to Catholic refugee advocates. They failed to persuade the administration to define most Haitians as refugees or to let them reach American soil. They demonstrated their own inconsistency, favoring Salvadorans and Guatemalans over Nicaraguans. They were unable to acquire Extended Voluntary Departure status for Central Americans. The Sanctuary movement alienated most Catholic congregants and prelates, while dividing over the scope of its mission.

On immigration reform, Catholic proponents suffered a few setbacks. In the Immigration Reform and Control Act they had to accept the promises of greater border safety and workplace verification. They had to swallow a guest worker program and less than ideal family preference provisions. There was no provision for assistance to the countries from which the immigrants came.

But these Catholics recovered far more than they relinquished. The law included the amnesty and the antidiscrimination language they sought. It excluded the national identification card they feared. And its enforcement provisions were so lax as to be laughable.

On both refugee issues and immigration reform, then, the country was the big loser. The inability of the president and the bishops to resolve both had led to the enactment of IRCA. The inability of IRCA to resolve both meant that a new president and some new bishops would have to wrestle with an old problem.

2. George H. W. Bush
1989–1993

FOR GEORGE H. W. BUSH, immigration was personal. Not only was the transplanted Texan a former border state congressman, but his second son Jeb had married a Mexican woman in a Catholic church. Although Jeb's conversion prompted a lot of soul-searching by his father, and while President Bush was otherwise inordinately attentive to Catholic concerns, immigration was not high on his list of priorities. So the Episcopalian president often found himself at odds with his erstwhile Catholic allies.[1]

Even as they were arriving at a rare rapprochement on legal immigration, the leaders of church and state were resuming their constant conflict over illegal immigration. But as that issue became more urgent, the president and the bishops became more reluctant. They did not want to deal with a dilemma which was growing more difficult by the day. So they settled for an easier issue.

Refugees

The Bush administration was not even a month old when Blair Dorminey of the National Security Council repudiated the refugee policies of Bush's former boss. Citing a February 1989 *Wall Street Journal* article by Douglas Bandow of the libertarian Cato Institute, Dorminey denounced the Reagan administration's roadblocks to the admission of refugees, especially those from Nicaragua, Indochina, and the Soviet bloc. He pointed to the combination of what Bandow called a "miserly" law which set an unreasonable standard for "well-founded" fear of persecution, and a "Kafkaesque bureaucracy" at the Immigration and Nationalization Service more intent on keeping refugees out than letting them in.[2]

As a result, according to Bandow, although there was an almost twenty-fold increase in the number of Soviet Jewish émigrés in the last two years of the Reagan administration (made possible by decreasing the total of Indochinese refugees), there was a backlog of 11,000 applicants in December 1988. The record for Haitians and Salvadorans was far worse. In 1988, the INS accepted only six of nineteen Haitian applicants, and in 1987 it admitted none of the sixty-nine who applied. In 1988, only twenty-nine of 805 Salvadoran applicants received asylum, compared to 110 of 3,932 applicants the year before. After admitting less than half of the Nicaraguan applicants in 1988, INS commissioner Alan Nelson promised to accept even fewer in 1989.[3]

"The INS considers [the] Meese memo [creating the Asylum Policy and Review Unit, which added an extra review step for Central American refugees] invalid," White House aide Robert Pastorino noted in March 1989. The INS seeks "to incarcerate and send back" the refugees.[4]

For Eastern Europeans, the record was mixed. In 1987 and 1988, the INS approved 461 of 627 Romanians, twenty-two of fifty-seven Czechs, 880 of 1,750 Poles, but only forty-eight of 1,963 Hungarians. "If President Bush is serious about promoting a 'kinder, gentler nation,'" as he famously posited at his party's national convention in 1988, Bandow asserted that "he needs to drastically overhaul" INS refugee policies.[5]

And, the *New Republic*'s Morton Kondracke suggested in April, he should replace Nelson with a more admissionist commissioner. Yet Kondracke argued that doing so would risk offending the president's close friend, Wyoming Republican senator Alan Simpson, cosponsor with Catholic Democratic senator Edward Kennedy of a bill to increase immigration levels below those championed by the Catholic Church and other more inclusionist interests.[6]

But Nelson survived into June, deporting thirty-nine Nicaraguans from the 150,000-member exile community in Miami. The commissioner also refused to forswear mass deportations of Nicaraguans. In the eighth year of the *contra* war, the INS found itself in unusual agreement with the Sandinista government about the plight of those fleeing the conflict. "We do a hell of a job sifting through those who have a real fear of persecution," INS spokesman Duke Austin boasted. He might have added that Nicaraguans were required to fulfill an extra step in the review process not accorded their Salvadoran, Guatemalan, and Honduran neighbors, of whom about 2,000 went home before the first Nicaraguan did.[7]

Nelson didn't last through June, however. Though he fought hard to save his job, denying it was in jeopardy and producing a film to explain why it should not be, Bush let Nelson go at the end of the month. His replacement would be Gene McNary, the highest-ranking official in St. Louis County, Missouri.[8]

Liberated from what a Justice Department official called the "embarrassment" of having to defend his INS commissioner, Bush continued to walk the tightrope of denouncing Sandinista repression in general while denying it in particular cases. "I am very concerned by a series of recent measures the Sandinistas have taken, including the ... electoral and media attacks on the National Endowment for Democracy, and attempts to prevent diplomats from observing political events," the president told the *Miami Herald* in late June. Yet "there have been no verified reports of retribution against the handful of people who have been returned to Nicaragua," a number which had now reached forty-two.[9]

The president's assurances had not prevented the introduction on Capitol Hill of a bill to postpone the deportation of Central Americans through a grant of Extended Voluntary Departure status. Nor had it prevented the administration, and Dorminey, from opposing such legislation. "I hope that the Congress will leave EVD, based as it is on foreign policy as well as domestic and humanitarian considerations," Dorminey wrote, "in the hands of the Executive." Testifying before the Subcommittee on Immigration and Refugee Affairs of the Senate Judiciary Committee in June, Acting Assistant Secretary of State for Inter-American Affairs Michael Kozak announced the administration's resistance to such action as an unnecessary and unjustified usurpation by the legislative branch of the rightful authority of the attorney general. "Conditions in El Salvador and Nicaragua," Kozak contended, "are not sufficiently serious to warrant extended voluntary departure status."[10]

The issue of Central American refugees just wouldn't go away. The announcement of a plan by the region's five presidents to disband the Nicaraguan *contras* by December, almost three months before the Bush administration's deadline, heightened the urgency of the refugee question. "Our primary concern must be for the personal welfare of some 60,000 brave people whom we have supported for the last seven years," Vice President Dan Quayle stated to the Veterans of Foreign Wars in August. "The bottom line is that they should not be forced to go back to Nicaragua until it is safe for them to do so and until conditions have been established for their normal reintegration into Nicaraguan society." Quayle added, "I can't tell you how long that process is likely to take, but it is indisputable that safe and democratic conditions do not exist in Nicaragua today; and until they do exist, it will remain a moral obligation of the United States to continue its humanitarian assistance to those people."[11]

Thus did the administration align its refugee policies with its foreign policy objectives in Central America. "The Deputy Attorney General's office is now holding up about forty deportations" of Nicaraguans, Dorminey wrote in an August memo. "Our hand should be strengthened by the Vice President's VFW speech."[12]

It wasn't. In October, the House passed the bill providing EVD status for Salvadorans and Nicaraguans as well as safe haven for Chinese students in the wake of the June 1989 Tiananmen Square massacre. When the legislation reached the Senate Judiciary Committee on Immigration and Refugees, Senator Simpson helped to stall it until the congressional session expired.[13]

"It will take a strong Administration effort, beginning immediately in January 1990," Alan Nelson, now advising the restrictionist Federation for American Immigration Reform, wrote Deputy National Security Advisor Robert Gates in December, "to let the Republican leadership and the entire Senate know that the Administration not only opposes EVD but will vigorously support the Republican leadership to defeat such [a] proposal." Nelson advised that the president issue a threat to veto any EVD bill.[14]

The president was in no hurry to transmit that signal. The next evening, at a dinner for the American cardinals, Bush promised to "do everything we can to bring to justice" the killers of six Jesuit priests in El Salvador in October. He pledged to continue to "oppose the export of revolution" to Nicaragua "until liberty's victory is won." But he made no mention of those fleeing the civil war conditions in both countries.[15]

And rather than responding to congressional concern about Central American refugees, the administration began the New Year replying to one of the cardinals, Boston's Bernard Law, about the status of Polish and Hungarian refugees. Cardinal Law, director of the United States Catholic Conference's Office of Migration and Refugee Services, as well as a close friend of the president who had delivered the invocation at the inauguration, wrote Bush protesting the "decision to make permanent the current suspension of adjudication of the approximately 20,000 existing Polish and Hungarian refugee applicants who do not have any previous ties to the United States," due to the shattering of the Iron Curtain in Central and Eastern Europe. "Although [the labor union] Solidarity has nominal control of the Polish government, the police and military are still in the hands of [communist] authorities," Cardinal Law explained. "Until the Polish penal code is revamped and the entire judicial and police system restructured" in both countries, he maintained, "we can expect human rights violations to continue."[16]

As with Central America, however, the administration did not share the Catholic bishops' viewpoint. Noting that "more than 40,000 Polish and Hungarian refugees have been admitted to the United States since 1981," James Budeit of the State Department's Bureau for Refugee Programs replied to the cardinal in February 1990, the administration "decided as of November 22, 1989 no longer to accept a new application for refugee status from Hungarians and Poles unless it can show that an individual is in immediate danger." And contrary to Cardinal Law's view, Budeit added that "institutionalization of political reform is well underway in Poland and Hungary, and we expect it to continue."[17]

So on this issue the president would again be rebuking his good friend, defying the American Catholic hierarchy, and disappointing many Eastern and Central European Catholics. By stiffening his stand toward Polish and Hungarian refugees, Bush risked alienating many natural political allies. "My work with the Catholic groups in the past campaigns brought me into frequent contact with Eastern European communities that are heavily Catholic," Thomas Melady, Bush's Ambassador to the Vatican, would warn the administration in December 1991. "The 'up' side of ethnic Catholic communities is that they voted heavily in favor of President Bush in the last campaign. On the negative side, they are sometimes difficult to deal with."[18]

The administration was difficult to deal with for too many Central American refugees. In January 1990, citing budget constraints, INS commissioner Gene McNary had ordered the release of over 1,200 undocumented political asylum applicants from the detention center in Bayview, Texas. At the beginning of February, however, McNary abruptly ended this permissive policy, announcing the infusion of eleven million dollars to expedite the adjudication process and expand the detention facilities to house up to ten thousand detainees in tents as well as dormitories. "The message for Central America is: don't just drop in on our doors unannounced," McNary warned at an on-site press conference. "We're going to defend our borders, and if someone comes across the border illegally, they are going to be detained." McNary vowed that Central Americans would not be able to "duplicate what happened last year," when thousands of them slept on the streets while they awaited asylum hearings.

At the nearby asylum hearing for Raul Lopez Martinez, the self-described eight-year veteran of El Salvador's National Police pleaded his case to stay in the United States. If he returned to his country, Lopez contended, he would be a target of the communist guerillas. "It seems to me that you are threatened for your work, not your political opinion," immigration judge Glenn P. McPhaul responded. "There is no evidence on record that the respondent would be persecuted throughout El Salvador." At the end of the two-and-one-half-hour hearing, the judge ordered his deportation. "I'm going to have to go die in my country," Lopez wept. "This is a place," court interpreter Modesto Canales reacted, "where a lot of tears are shed."

McNary defended the INS's three percent approval rate for Salvadoran asylum seekers. "A better way of life, a better job, better conditions don't qualify, and if they came here for those reasons, our job ... is to deport them." And, before that, his agency's job was to detain them, in what McNary called "conditions not like the Ritz Carlton."[19]

Others had a different view. Three Catholic nuns joined ten Catholic, Protestant, and Jewish laypersons on a tour of the INS border detention centers in February. "A Guatemalan mother told us of fleeing with five children after witnessing the assassination of her fourteen-year-old son; a Salvadoran man related his difficult eighteen-day journey—much of it on foot—undertaken after the murder of his brother," the trip's organizer, Mary McCann of the Chicago Religious Task Force on Central America, related. "In Mexico he was robbed, separated from his sister-in-law, and his papers were destroyed by Mexican immigration officials." McCann noted that "many refugees imprisoned in the detention facilities told us that excessively high bail ($1,500–$3,000) keeps them detained for months and years, unable to join relatives in the United States." Linking the massive influx of Salvadorans into the United States to the "heightened religious persecution manifested in the brutal assassination of two church workers and six Jesuit priests by the Salvadoran military," McCann urged that children be spared detention, that asylum seekers be provided competent legal assistance, that "safe haven mechanisms" replace detention centers, and that the Bush administration stop encouraging human rights violations by funneling aid to the Salvadoran and Guatemalan militaries.[20]

"Recent events concerning the adjudication of asylum claims in South Texas have been commented on extensively in the press," an Asylum Policy and Review Unit memorandum acknowledged. And like many journalists, the unit took issue with the INS's restrictive interpretation of asylum status. Citing the report of the United Nations High Commission for Refugees on the South Texas entry point, the memo lamented that the "INS is more interested in why the applicant is coming to the U.S., rather than seeking to ascertain why the applicant left his own country. This completely contradicts the policy of asylum."[21]

A federal court agreed. As a result of a settlement known as ABC, about 190,000 Salvadoran and 50,000 Guatemalan asylum seekers who had entered the United States in the 1980s could remain until special adjudication procedures had decided their fate. And as part of the Immigration Act of 1990, the attorney general for the first time obtained the authority to declare "Temporary Protected Status" for undocumented immigrants, suspending but not preventing a return to their homelands due to dangerous political or social conditions there. In what Aaron Bekemeyer would call a "victory for the Sanctuary movement," the agreement with the Bush administration authorized new hearings of all asylum cases since 1980 and training sessions on international human rights for asylum officers and immigration judges, to be conducted by secular and religious (including Catholic) organizations.[22]

A free election ousted the Sandinistas in Nicaragua in 1990, and a United Nations-brokered peace agreement would halt the civil war in El Salvador in 1992. The easing of the Central American refugee crisis was welcome news not only to President Bush but to American Catholics, whose church had badly divided over their nation's policies in the region. Catholic liberals had applauded *America*, *Commonweal*, *Our Sunday Visitor*, the *National Catholic Reporter*, and the *Catholic Worker* for their denunciations of U.S. aid to the Salvadoran and Guatemalan governments and the Nicaraguan *contras* (legally before 1984 and after 1986, illegally in between). Catholic conservatives had opened the pages of *Catholicism in Crisis*, *National Catholic Register*, *The Wanderer*, and Catholic publisher William F. Buckley's *National Review* to find affirmations of those policies. And the American Catholic bishops, by adopting liberal positions on Central America alongside conservative postures on contraception and abortion, had struggled for the allegiance of both groups.[23]

In 1991, the tide of revolution overwhelmed the shores of Yugoslavia, where strongman Slobodan Milosevic met Croatian revanchism with Serb repression. Following a September meeting with Cardinal Law and Jozef Cardinal Glemp of Poland, Newark Archbishop Theodore McCarrick urged President Bush to condemn the slaughter. "I know you are in New Jersey tonight, where thousands of people from Croatia in my Archdiocese grow daily more concerned over the destruction of their ancient land and its people," the archbishop pleaded with the president in a heartfelt, handwritten letter, "at the hands of one of the few remaining Communist dictatorships in Europe." But Bush would say little and do less about the conflagration in the Balkans.[24]

Haitian Refugees

Before Bush could address somebody else's refugee crisis, he had to confront his own. Six days after Archbishop McCarrick's letter, the Haitian military exiled the country's first democratically elected president, former Catholic priest Jean-Bertrand Aristide. The administration responded by removing aid and embargoing trade to the newly installed military junta.

The administration did not respond by welcoming Haitian exiles to the United States. In accordance with its 1981 agreement with the hemisphere's most impoverished country, the U.S. instead was sending them home. "As of November 19, we had picked up nearly 2,200 Haitians," Deputy Assistant Secretary of State for Inter-American Affairs Robert Gebhard informed the House Judiciary Committee the next day. "Seven of these boats had over 100 Haitians on board; none of these craft was over forty feet in length. For example, on November 14 the cutter *Confide* interdicted a forty-foot sailing vessel with 238 Haitians aboard [and] . . . no life jackets, no flares, no radio, no beacons, no charts, no navigational equipment."

So the administration turned the boats around. "In response to a difficult situation," Gebhard asserted, "our overriding concern has been to save lives."[25]

Some American Catholics wanted the administration to do more than that. "Persons willing to risk their lives in the dangerous passage from Haiti to this country are not coming for frivolous reasons," USCC president Archbishop Daniel Pilarczyk of Cincinnati wrote President Bush in November 1991. "They are coming to escape violence and oppression that has once again become intolerable." On behalf of his fellow bishops, Pilarczyk implored the president to grant Temporary Protected Status to the boat people so as to provide a "welcome to the stranger in need that is so deeply a part of national tradition"—and that of his church.[26]

And, for now anyway, part of the Constitution. . . . Miami

District Court Judge C. Clyde Atkins answered in 1992 by halting the return of two-thirds of the 15,000 Haitian refugees so they could obtain a fair hearing of their pleas for political asylum in the United States. "We are under a court order not to repatriate voluntarily any of the Haitian boat people," Princeton Lyman, director of the Bureau for Refugee Programs, replied to Archbishop Pilarczyk. Yet the administration continued to argue that "the belief that they can get to the United States is one of the major factors prompting the extraordinary outflow of Haitians onto the high seas"—and the death of hundreds who would never reach their destination.[27]

The Supreme Court appeared to agree. Without giving a reason, the high court reversed Judge Atkins's ruling, mandating the removal of 10,000 refugees being held at the Guantánamo Bay Naval Base in Cuba. So in May Bush issued an executive order allowing the Coast Guard to return Haitian refugees to their home country. To Cardinal Law this policy was "morally questionable." To New York's John Cardinal O' Connor, it was "morally reprehensible."[28]

And to some Catholics, it was audaciously inconsistent. After all, the U.S. government seemed to place such a priority on the lives of Cubans fleeing the oppressive dictatorship there. "We should not grant preferential treatment for persons of certain countries for political reasons," Catholic Democratic congressman Joseph Moakley of Massachusetts said, criticizing the double standard produced by the Cuban Adjustment Act of 1966, which permitted Cubans who had been in the United States for only a year to become permanent residents. Quoting Miami Archbishop Edward McCarthy's testimony before the Hesburgh Commission in December 1979, America's editors noted that "only fifty-five of 9,000 black Haitians" received political asylum then, "while there is no publicly recorded case of any one of some 10,000 predominantly white Cuban boat people being denied admission." Archbishop McCarthy had charged the Carter administration with "institutional racism" then. And America's editors were not ruling it out now.[29]

But the Bush administration was. As *America's* editors conceded, the administration was willing to provide about one-third of Haitian exiles with an asylum hearing. And as for comparisons with Cuba, Secretary Gebhard saw none. "Cubans are fleeing one of the world's remaining Communist dictatorships," said Gebhard. "They fear returning to it for no other reason than that it is a crime in Cuba to leave without an exit permit." He concluded, "Those conditions do not apply to Haiti."[30]

"Frankly, if Castro fell, you would see the exodus going the other way," President Bush had said when he weighed in on the alleged double standard in a November 1991 television interview in Miami. "I just think that he's swimming totally against the tide," said the president, in an unfortunate choice of metaphors, "whereas in Haiti they're at least trying to go the democratic route."[31]

Cardinal Law attempted to heal the rift between the bishop and the president by inviting Bush to speak at his committee's National Migration Conference in Washington in June 1992. But Bush's Associate Director for Public Liaison Jane Leonard counseled against it. "My concern would be the Haitian refugee issue," Leonard wrote, "and our position versus theirs on it."[32]

The president would decline the invitation. Two weeks after receiving Law's letter, however, at the urging of the bishops and the American Jewish Committee, Bush appointed the cardinal to chair his Commission on Legal Immigration Reform.[33]

But Bush would not change his position toward Haitian refugees. "Yes, the Statue of Liberty still stands, and we still open our arms to people that are politically oppressed," said Bush at a campaign stop in Marietta, Ohio, in May. "I will not, [however], because I have been sworn to uphold the Constitution, open the doors to economic refugees [from] all over the world."[34]

In October, when a USCC campaign questionnaire asked the presidential candidates, "Do you support legislation that would give due process rights to 'excluded aliens' (e.g., Haitian boat people and Mariel Cuban detainees)?" Bush's Domestic Policy Advisor Roger Porter reminded the president, "We oppose." So Bush responded, "The immigration policy of the United States is fair and color-blind. Of the more than 35,000 Haitians served, almost one-third were judged eligible to pursue their claims. To date, more than 10,000 Haitians have entered the United States based upon a preliminary claim for asylum."[35]

And when a Miami reporter informed Bush in October that "there are 11,000 people that your own asylum offices in Guantánamo, for six months before June, said had credible fears of persecution in Haiti," the president promised to "take a look at it."[36]

He wouldn't get the chance. Two weeks later Bush failed in his reelection effort, and the refugee problem would soon become someone else's. But it still belonged to many Catholics, three-fourths of whom ended the Bush era in support of Haitian repatriation, even as their bishops continued to oppose it.[37]

Immigration Reform

George Bush had not spent a lot of time in Texas recently. Since his two terms in Congress representing that state from 1967 to 1971, Bush had served as Ambassador to the United Nations, special envoy to China, and Director of the Central Intelligence Agency. In 1980, he ran for his party's nomination, only to lose to former California Governor Ronald Reagan. So Bush needed a reminder of just how vexing his home state's illegal immigration problem had become.

The reminder came in the form of the 1989 Texas Immigration and Border Study. The survey found that 87 percent of Texas voters, who saw the problem firsthand, viewed illegal immigration as a problem, and 67 percent considered it a "very serious" problem. Sixty-two percent of Texas voters advocated strict enforcement of the laws against employing unauthorized aliens. Seventy-eight percent backed a border toll to pay additional border personnel,

77 percent espoused greater federal spending on border security, and 65 percent favored a border fence. A "strong majority" approved of annual quotas on legal immigration.

Hispanic Texan voters even more vigorously opposed illegal immigration, with 91 percent in favor of more border security, 80 percent behind more federal spending on the border, and 79 percent supporting a border toll. Seventy-eight percent endorsed limits on legal immigration, and 73 percent sought a border fence.[38]

In other words, most Hispanic Texans, many of whom were Catholics, rejected the teachings of the church on immigration as alien to their circumstances. In their September 1989 pastoral, "Relieving Third World Debt," the United States Catholic bishops asserted that "interdependence is a fact of economic—indeed of all—life," and that "co-responsibility, justice, and solidarity" should govern relations between the people of the developed and developing worlds. "To be truly Catholic—to be universal," Sister Teresa Kane, past president of the Leadership Conference of Women Religious, wrote in *Commonweal* in November 1989, "is to have a profound religious conviction that we are obliged by our catholicity to have a hunger and thirst for justice—not only for the citizens of the U.S.A. but for people of other nations and religions."[39]

The president would side with neither his fellow Texans nor the Catholic Church. Rather than revisit illegal immigration, Bush would choose to confront the more manageable and less menacing matter of legal immigration. After a year of study, Bush's Departments of State, Justice, and Labor as well as the Office of Policy Development, the National Security Council, the Domestic Policy Council, the National Science Foundation, the Council of Economic Advisors, and the Office of White House Counsel had, by February 1990, devised a proposal for legal immigration reform. Such a plan, these agencies agreed, should rest on three pillars: the continued admission of citizens' immediate relatives, the continued reliance on family reunification of immigrants, and an increased emphasis on skill-based immigration. The Bush design would raise the annual limit on all legal immigration from 440,000 to 630,000; would increase the annual level of skilled immigrants from 54,000 to 150,000; and would admit 25,000 more close relatives at the expense of fewer distant relatives of immigrants.[40]

The Bush proposal placed the administration largely in line with S.358, an immigration reform bill cosponsored by Massachusetts Catholic Democrat Edward Kennedy and Wyoming Republican Alan Simpson, which had passed the Senate in 1988. But it put the administration in opposition to S. 448, sponsored by Illinois Democratic senator Paul Simon, which would double the number of Second Preference visas for the spouses and children of permanent residents, and H.R. 4300, sponsored by Connecticut Democrat Bruce Morrison, which would lift the legal immigration quota to 800,000 instead of the 630,000 in the Bush and Kennedy-Simpson scheme.[41]

In a September letter to the Catholic Democratic Speaker of the House Thomas Foley of Washington, Bush's Department of Justice objected not only to the House legislation's higher immigration ceiling, but to its expansion of the "immediate relatives" designation to include immediate relatives of permanent resident aliens, among other provisions. The DOJ explained that "treating immediate relatives of legal permanent residents as equivalent to immediate relatives of United States citizens would create a disincentive for 'green card' holders [legal permanent residents] to naturalize."[42]

The American Catholic hierarchy raised objections to the administration. Citing the bishops' 1988 "Principles for Legal Immigration," Bernard Cardinal Law, chairman of the USCC Committee on Migration, urged that "family reunification must be affirmed as the basic precept driving a just immigration policy." According to the cardinal, the expansion of the term "immediate relatives" in the Morrison bill, by removing limits on spouses and minor children of permanent legal residents, was more sympathetic to family reunification than the Kennedy-Simpson and administration approaches.[43]

The House bill also contained an amendment, sponsored by Catholic Democrat Joseph Moakley of Massachusetts, which would bestow Extended Voluntary Departure status on exiles from war-torn El Salvador, Kuwait, Liberia, and Lebanon. The Bush administration disapproved of this addendum, which would remove the attorney general's administrative discretion over EVD cases, and could add as many as half a million aliens to the U.S.[44]

The Bush-backed Kennedy-Simpson legislation sailed through the Senate, 81–17, in July, while the Morrison bill passed the House with the Moakley Amendment, 231–92, in November. Negotiations between the Bush administration and House and Senate conferees begat a compromise resulting in a ceiling of 700,000 immigrants for the first three years of the legislation, and 675,000 thereafter. Skill-based immigration would more than double from 54,000 to 140,000 per year, and family-based immigration would increase from 216,000 to 226,000 annually in all categories, including the contested group of immediate relatives of legal permanent residents. The statute created a new category, the H-1B visa, to attract college graduates with special skills, especially in the rapidly growing information technology field. To the chagrin of Congressman Moakley, the talks pared his EVD extension to cover only those fleeing El Salvador, and for only eighteen months. To the consternation of Kennedy, Simpson, and Bush, however, the revised Moakley Amendment remained in the final bill.[45]

Under pressure from the Hispanic Congressional Caucus, Simpson agreed to remove his proposal in the conference committee of a pilot program in which three states would devise drivers' licenses which identified legal residents. The only enforcement mechanisms remaining in the bill were the streamlining of deportation procedures for criminal aliens, the addition of 1,000 Border Patrol agents, and the creation of a nine-member commission which would report to Congress on the nation's immigration situation by 1994. The resulting Immigration Act of 1990 breezed through the Senate 89–8, on October 26, and navigated the House, 264–118, the next day. On November 29, Bush signed the law, the first major legal immigration reform measure in twenty-five years.[46]

"This bill is pro-growth and pro-family, and has received strong endorsement from the business and the ethnic communities," Bush's Domestic Policy Advisor Roger Porter, who had helped negotiate the compromise, wrote the president after the conference committee had reached agreement on an immigration reform bill "that the Administration can enthusiastically support." It had not only produced unusual agreement between the Republican president and the Democratic Congress on a major piece of domestic policy, but, thanks to its inclusion of spouses and minor children of permanent legal residents, it had elicited even more extraordinary concord between the White House and Catholic immigration advocates.[47]

But raising the limit for legal immigration would do little to deter illegal immigration, even as the nation's unemployment rate soared above 7 percent. In less than two years, Porter would be visiting the U.S.-Mexican boundary in California and reporting to Bush the Border Patrol's gloomy projection that "more than a million will illegally immigrate through the San Diego sector during this fiscal year." Most ominously, Porter added, "border patrol officers uniformly reported that those apprehended are more aggressive, difficult, and rougher-looking than in the past."[48]

"This is a frightening situation," the president said in a handwritten note dispatched to Porter and Chief of Staff Sam Skinner. "We must do something."[49]

The American Catholic bishops wanted to do something, but their goal was to make it easier for unauthorized immigrants to enter the country, not harder. So, following their truce over the Immigration Act of 1990, the bishops would return to the front lines in their battle with the president. "Do you support legislation which would repeal sanctions against employers who hire undocumented people?" the bishops queried the presidential candidates in their October 1992 campaign questionnaire.

Bush's answer was a firm no. "To help ensure that all Americans are gainfully employed, I have called for bolstering the enforcement of laws against hiring illegal workers," the president responded. "In particular, I have hired fifty new investigators to crack down on those employers who hire illegal immigrants."[50]

That was not what the bishops wanted to hear. To the bishops and other Catholic admissionists, President Bush was shutting the doors of the White House to their pleas for an even more liberal immigration policy. Within three months, however, a new president would reopen them, and the dialogue would begin again.

Conclusions

The Bush era continued the pattern of the Reagan years in pitting the president against Catholic leaders on refugee issues and immigration reform, only to have them converge in the interest of passing legislation. As before, however, the law was a stopgap measure which merely postponed an answer to the country's divisive dilemma of illegal immigration.

On refugee issues, Catholic advocates nevertheless could declare victory on several fronts. They won in court, where Salvadoran and Guatemalan asylum seekers received permission to remain in the country. They won in Congress, where the Immigration Act of 1990 authorized Extended Voluntary Departure status to Salvadoran exiles, and Temporary Protected Status to undocumented aliens who feared returning to their homelands. They won at the peace table, where an end to most of the fighting in Central America alleviated (though it did not end) the refugee crisis in the United States.

But Catholic refugee advocates also fought several losing battles.

They failed to secure greater numbers of refugees from Hungary, Poland, El Salvador, and Guatemala. They failed to prevent the administration from adopting a more restrictive interpretation of asylum and a more expansive policy of detention. They failed to keep the administration from continuing to turn back Haitians, even as it continued to welcome Cubans.

On immigration reform, these Catholics won when the Immigration Act of 1990 increased the quota for legal immigrants, maintained the Second Preference for the spouses and minor children of citizens, and extended the Second Preference to the spouses and minor children of permanent residents. But they lost when it did not raise the ceiling even higher.

The country was both the better and the worse for all of these efforts. Americans could cheer the willingness of Catholics, Congress, and the president to bargain over legal immigration and Central American peace. But they could bemoan the unwillingness of Catholics, Congress, and the president to confront illegal immigration, even as many congregants and constituents demanded that they do so.

3. Bill Clinton

1993–2001

FOR BILL CLINTON, immigration was political. In 1980, President Jimmy Carter permitted Cuban dictator Fidel Castro to empty his jails and mental health facilities—and send many of the inmates to Fort Chafee in Arkansas, where Clinton was the governor. Clinton, the third Democratic president since the Immigration and Nationality Act of 1965, would never forgive the second for the action that sent prisoners to his state. And many Catholics would never forgive Clinton, the consummate politician, for his countless zigs and zags on refugee issues and immigration reform.

Though politics colors every president's policies, Clinton's malleable ideology defined his refugee and immigration policies even more than the incongruities of his predecessors defined theirs. He therefore alternately fulfilled and frustrated the hopes of Catholic admissionists, who sought a chief executive with whom they could work, instead of one with whom they would fight. Yet because he was so attuned to public opinion, Clinton often listened more intently to the Catholics in the pews than to the Catholics in the pulpits.

Haitian Refugees

During the 1992 presidential campaign, Bill Clinton fiercely criticized President George H. W. Bush for his policy of forcibly repatriating those escaping the desperately poor island nation of Haiti. Candidate Clinton vowed to be more compassionate in his response to the Haitian boat people, and more expansive in his interpretation of their status as political refugees. Some Catholics, a plurality of whom gave him their votes, looked forward to the fulfillment of his promise.[1]

Shortly after his inauguration, however, President Clinton adopted a policy remarkably similar to that of his predecessor. Like Bush, Clinton ordered the Coast Guard to intercept Haitian vessels and return the passengers to their home country. He also imposed a naval blockade to prevent most Haitians from even contemplating such a voyage. Only three weeks after taking office, Clinton found himself defending a policy he had only recently stopped deriding.

"My policy is not the same as President Bush's policy," Clinton insisted at a town meeting in Detroit in February 1993, "because I am committed to putting more resources there to process people who want to be political refugees and can meet the standard, and bring them to the United States." Thus did Clinton double the Immigration and Naturalization Service's capacity to interview refugee applicants in Haiti, and he sent a technical team to Haiti to facilitate the application process.[2]

If Clinton's approach was different, however, his rationale was not. "I did what I did because of the evidence that people in Haiti were taking the wood off the roofs of their houses to make boats of questionable safety, to pour in thousands of numbers to come to this country," said the new president, sounding a lot like the previous one, "when we know for sure hundreds of them would die on the high seas coming here, in a human tragedy of monumental proportions."[3]

And like his predecessor, Clinton was going to court to validate his repatriation policies. In March, the Supreme Court heard arguments over the Clinton administration's constitutional authority to return the exiles to Haiti. "Are you having second thoughts about your criticism of George Bush's Haiti policy during the campaign," a reporter wanted to know, "given that today you went to court to essentially support his position?"

Clinton conceded that "maybe I was too harsh" in his attack on Bush, but he was still not willing to admit that he was pursuing a similar track. "There's a big difference between what we're doing in Haiti and what they were doing in Haiti," he protested. "Something that was never brought up before but is now painfully apparent," Clinton contended, "is that if we did what the plaintiffs in the court case want, we would be consigning a very large number of Haitians, in all probability, to some sort of death warrant."[4]

Not only had Clinton offered the same argument ten days earlier, but Bush had repeatedly used it in justifying his repatriation decision. And like the argument of the Bush administration, this argument carried the day in the Supreme Court and in the court of public opinion. In June, the high court, by an 8–1 margin, upheld the Clinton policy on the grounds that the Refugee Act of 1980 had granted asylum only to those exiles who reached U.S. soil. So the Clinton method of intercepting Haitian boat people at sea was constitutional.[5]

Chairman of the Joint Chiefs of Staff General Colin Powell, who served both presidents, would recall that candidate Clinton "had criticized the Bush policy of sending Haitian refugees back home." But President Clinton soon "recanted on that one."[6]

And most of the American people applauded. An August 1993 *Newsweek* poll asked, "Should it be easier or more difficult for people from the following places to immigrate to the United States?" Only 20 percent thought it should be easier for Haitians to enter the country, while 55 percent sought to make their task more difficult, a percentage exceeded only by the 61 percent who desired a higher bar for Middle Eastern immigrants.[7]

The American Catholic bishops begged to differ. At their November meeting, they pleaded for recognition of the causes of the flight of refugees from countries such as Haiti, and empathy toward those who were fleeing. "While it is true that no one country can respond totally or take in all those seeking freedom and a new life," the bishops said in their policy statement, "the world of nations cannot simply shut its eyes or doors."[8]

President Clinton opened the doors slightly in April 1994, announcing that a group of exiles picked up by the Coast Guard just off American shores would not be returning to Haiti. The president explained that since the Haitians were within four miles of the American border and had suffered abuse by some on their boat, they had received permission to stay in the United States. But Clinton maintained that he was not changing administration policy.[9]

Not yet, anyway. Two weeks later, with Trans Africa leader Randall Robinson on the twenty-seventh day of a hunger strike and the Congressional Black Caucus escalating its criticism, the policy changed, and the president owned up to it. "We will continue to interdict all Haitian migrants at sea, " Clinton announced in May, "but we will determine aboard ship or in other countries which ones are bona fide political refugees [instead of interviewing them only in Haiti]."

Yet if Clinton was now willing to concede change where he had been unwilling to confess continuity, he would not fully accept the potential consequences of his decision. "Are you in danger, sir, of sending signals that could open up the floodgates to Haitian refugees?" a reporter would wonder. "I hope that we will not have a flood of refugees," the president replied, "but we are increasing our naval resources to deal with them."[10]

Then came the flood. Instead of the expected 2,000 exiles per week, the Coast Guard was rescuing as many as 3,000 per day. "I continue to urge all Haitians to avoid risking their lives in treacherous boat voyages," Clinton pleaded. On July 4 alone, 140 Haitians drowned. By July 7, 16,000 had boarded Coast Guard vessels. So Clinton again reversed course. He announced that his government would send Haitians who met the definition of political refugees to safe havens in the Caribbean such as Panama and Cuba. Clinton's refugee policy, the Congressional Black Caucus lamented, "changes by the moment."[11]

It would change dramatically in September 1994. "This year, in less than two months, more than 21,000 Haitians were recovered at sea by our Coast Guard and Navy," Clinton stated in an address to the nation on television the night of September 15. "Today, more than 14,000 refugees are living at our naval base in Guantánamo." To stanch this unremitting flow and to relieve the suffering of those Haitians left behind, Clinton announced a United Nations–backed American invasion of the island. "We never should have stopped the refugees," Clinton admitted to Catholic Democratic senator George Mitchell of Maine.[12]

But military force would prove unnecessary. Hours before the invasion was to begin, the diplomatic troika of former president Jimmy Carter, former chairman of the Joint Chiefs of Staff General Colin Powell, and former Georgia senator Sam Nunn convinced Haitian strongman Raoul Cédras to step down and restore Jean-Bertrand Aristide to power. Rather than reversing Haitian boats, Clinton was now turning around American planes.[13]

The flow of Haitian refugees diminished greatly, though many already in the United States would never return to Haiti. In 1998, Clinton would sign legislation permitting Haitians who had remained in the U.S. to become permanent residents. The American Catholic bishops welcomed this rare piece of "good news" about Haiti. Two years later, however, in 2000, the Clinton administration received only forty-nine Haitian refugees.[14]

In his memoir, Clinton would finally acknowledge the continuity between his Haitian refugee policy and that of President Bush. But he argued that the increased processing of refugees had saved more Haitian lives. He made no mention of Randall Robinson, the Congressional Black Caucus, or the Catholic opponents of his shifting strategies.[15]

Cuban Refugees

In addition to inheriting the Haitian refugee crisis from President George Bush, Clinton would grapple with a Cuban refugee problem which had developed its roots under President Dwight Eisenhower. The Cuban Revolution of 1959 continued and showed no signs of ending anytime soon, and neither did the exodus of Cubans from that communist enclave.

In September 1994, three years after the dissolution of its benefactor the Soviet Union, Cuba agreed to allow an increase in legal Cuban immigration to the United States to as many as 20,000 per year. When Fidel Castro reenacted his Mariel stunt by unloading Cuban misfits on American shores, Clinton abruptly reversed himself, turning in the opposite direction from his pivot on Haiti. Cuban exiles would not receive automatic entrance into the United States. They would first join Haitians at Guantánamo for immigration hearings. While he had taken over a year to reverse course on Haiti, Clinton mused, he had needed only three days, thanks to Castro, to change his mind on Cuba.[16]

In May 1995, however, Attorney General Janet Reno declared that, like the Haitian migrants before the U.S. invasion, the Cuban exiles would have to apply for admission to the U.S. in Havana. A revision of the 1966 Cuban Adjustment Act forbade Cubans from entering the country by boat or via Guantánamo Bay Naval Base, where the torrent of Haitian and Cuban refugees had strained the base's resources and threatened American servicemen. Under this new "wet foot, dry foot" policy, however, Cubans who reached American soil could remain in the U.S. and apply for expedited permanent resident status.[17]

In January 1999, with the president impeached and his political survival now in the hands of the United States Senate, Clinton welcomed Pope John Paul II to St. Louis. "Remember, he's seventy-nine," Clinton confided to biographer Taylor Branch. "He's got Parkinson's.

He's been shot. And he had bad knees to start with. But his mind is very sharp." The ailing pontiff then proceeded to give Clinton a piece of that mind, vainly urging the president to lift the four-decades-old U.S. embargo of Cuba.[18]

The following year, Clinton's Cuban refugee policy would take center stage when six-year-old Elián González floated ashore in an inner tube supplied by his mother before she drowned trying to transport him to freedom in the United States. In the ensuing custody battle between Elián's great-uncle in Florida and his father in Cuba, the administration sided with the latter. Following a predawn raid by federal agents, Elián returned to Cuba.[19]

The raid antagonized some Americans, and, coming in an election year, solidified Republican George W. Bush's presidential campaign among Florida's large, mostly Catholic, Cuban-American population. "The fact that Elián's father loved him and had been a good parent," Clinton would defend his decision to return Elián, "should count more than the poverty or the closed and repressive policies of Cuba." In the same year that Elián González returned to Cuba, 3,184 Cubans acquired refugee status in the United States.[20]

Asylum Reform

The considerable attention paid to the Haitian and Cuban refugee situations distracted from the larger question of overall American refugee policy. By 1993, the Immigration and Naturalization Service had accumulated a backlog of over 300,000 applications for asylum from foreigners in the United States. Unable to handle such a caseload, the INS was simply releasing most of the applications, many of them with work authorizations, pending hearings for which many applicants failed to show up.[21]

The discovery of a Chinese alien smuggling ring and the bombing of New York's World Trade Center by followers of Sheik Omar Abdel-Rahman heightened the urgency of asylum reform in 1993.

As a result, legislation to address the INS backlog began circulating through both houses of Congress. "The key legislative issue seems to be preventing the abuse of political asylum," Clinton aide Diana Yin explained in June, "targeting the lenience of officials and procedures which allow asylum seekers into the country."

Yet the Clinton administration, while appearing to endorse a legislative solution, preferred an executive decision. "Both [Massachusetts Catholic Democratic senator Edward] Kennedy and [Wyoming Republican senator Alan] Simpson have draft bills to . . . revise the political asylum process," Yin wrote. "However, Simpson and Kennedy are supposedly working together with the Administration on a draft bill."[22]

In July, President Clinton, Vice President Al Gore, and Attorney General Janet Reno introduced legislation hatched by a twelve-member administration task force (headed by Gore) in consultation with key Democrats in Congress. The proposal included a provision for "expedited exclusion" hearings to occur at entry points into the United States, and only those with a "credible fear" of persecution in their home countries would advance to a full hearing. "Of course, some deserve asylum [but] most do not, under our laws," Gore asserted. "Many never even show up for a hearing, and immediately become part of the large and growing illegal alien population."[23]

But the legislation would apply only to those 15,000 annual potential asylees who got caught unlawfully entering the country, not the 100,000 who didn't get caught yet who applied for asylum anyway, or the 30,000 who neither got caught nor sought asylum. And for the vast majority of those creating the backlog in the asylum system, the administration was not offering to overhaul the system, but simply to streamline it. "These changes will be costly," Office of Management and Budget director Leon Panetta, a Catholic, warned in July, "but will deter frivolous applications and reduce our direct spending in the future."[24]

The administration hoped that its proposal would preempt

more aggressive plans such as one sponsored by Kentucky Catholic Democratic representative Romano Mazzoli, which would mandate an increase in the number of INS asylum offices and toughen the requirements for asylum applicants to receive work permits, or a measure approved by the Senate Judiciary Committee which would have facilitated INS exclusion of asylum applicants missing proper documentation. The administration's strategy also could rescue many members of Congress from a vote they really didn't want to make.[25]

The Clinton administration's executive end run also possessed the political virtue of appeasing refugee advocacy groups, including Catholic ones. While conceding that the " present procedures are too protracted because they [INS facilities] are hopelessly under-staffed," Rev. Richard Ryscavage of the bishops' Office of Migration and Refugee Services nevertheless worried that by "conducting quick interviews in circumstances in which legitimate asylum-seekers are generally tired, confused, and frightened, we will be risking their return to imprisonment, torture, and even death." So the year would end not with an asylum reform bill, but with a nonbinding statement in an omnibus crime bill conveying the Senate's desire to hasten the processing of INS applications and deportations.[26]

But in the midst of the nation's rising restrictionism, catalyzed by the historic Republican takeover of both houses of Congress and the triumph of California's anti-undocumented immigrant Proposition 187 in November 1994, Congress would pass the Illegal Immigration Reform and Immigrant Responsibility Act of 1996. Although Catholic refugee advocates had succeeded during the committee process in helping to soften its major tenets, the new law was decidedly more restrictive than before. The act would permit summary exclusion of immigrants, broaden the basis for deportation, and mandate "the detention of all immigrants, including permanent residents, facing deportation for most criminal violations until the resolution of the case." It would severely tighten requirements for suspension of deportation for aliens who had resided in the U.S. for a long time, set an annual cap of 4,000 for such suspensions, and require migrants to be in the United States for ten, rather than seven, years to be eligible for a suspension. It also would establish a pilot program in Anaheim and Ventura County, California authorizing law enforcement officials to screen suspects in local jails prior to arraignment. The program would spread to other communities beginning in 1997.[27]

The legislation also would institute, as of October 1997, a one-week deadline for INS adjudication of "expedited exclusion" at the nation's entry points. Yale law school professor Peter Schuck determined that prior to the law, when virtually all immigration court decisions were subject to appeal before judges who were independent of the Justice Department and were serving life terms, immigrants won up to 40 percent of their appeals. But "expedited exclusion" afforded applicants (most of whom were not applying for asylum but were fighting charges of document fraud) no such appeals. This policy would disproportionately affect Nicaraguans and Salvadorans as well as Guatemalans, whose thirty-six year civil war finally ended in 1996. So Clinton attacked this requirement, promising to "seek to correct provisions in the bill that were inconsistent with international principles of refugee assistance, including the imposition of rigid deadlines for asylum." But he signed it anyway.[28]

Clinton repeated this pledge in a trip to Costa Rica in May 1997. Then he went a step further. If Congress didn't repeal "expedited exclusion," the president vowed that he would.[29]

"Huh?" Domestic Policy Advisor Bruce Reed wrote in the margin of the *Washington Times* story on Clinton's latest promise, wondering how the president planned to pull it off.[30]

"You tell me," Clinton appeared to instruct Reed and National Security Advisor Samuel Berger. So they arrived at a plan for Clinton to revise the policy unilaterally by invoking his foreign policy authority as commander in chief.[31]

He wouldn't have to. Clinton was able to persuade Congress to delete what George Anderson of *America* called "one of the pernicious aspects of the 1996 legislation." Revised versions of the law gave Nicaraguan refugees preferential treatment and, in the aftermath of Hurricane Mitch, the hemisphere's worst storm in two centuries, which ravaged Central America in November 1998, granted a temporary reprieve to Salvadorans, Guatemalans, and Hondurans.[32]

That was still not good enough for many Catholics. In February 1999, Bishop Nicholas DiMarzio of Camden, New Jersey, chairman of the USCC Committee on Migration, testified in Congress that the 1996 law separated families, vitiated human rights, and undermined conventional norms of fairness. In November 1999 in Baltimore, the Catholic Legal Immigration Network (CLINIC) joined the Lutheran Immigration and Refugee Service and the Florence Immigration and Refugee Project in sponsoring a conference they called "Open Wide the Doors." At the convocation, CLINIC attorney James Haggerty lashed out at the 1996 law's provisions for mandatory detention of unauthorized migrants (including those fleeing persecution in their home countries) rather than paroling them into the community, where they might have friends and relatives. When added to the administration's increased use of expedited exclusion in place of hearings before an immigration judge, as well as its move to privatize some detention centers, the Clinton policies had nearly doubled the number of detainees in the United States.

Three former detainees shared their harrowing stories with the conference attendees. During their sixteen months of detention in San Pedro, California, Yudaya Nanyonga of Uganda and a married couple, José and Amalia Molina of El Salvador, each stayed in separate units, without any means of communication between them.[33]

In the last full year of the Clinton administration, the country would admit 72,143 refugees. At their June 2000 meeting, the American Catholic bishops nonetheless lamented that despite a substantial rise in the number of the world's refugees, the United

States was accepting 42 percent fewer refugees than in 1992. In their November 2000 statement, "Welcoming the Stranger Among Us: Unity in Diversity," the bishops regretted that the 1996 law still "included provisions that allow summary exclusions of asylum seekers from this country without the benefit of review of their asylum claims by an immigration judge."[34]

Immigration Reform

During the 1992 presidential campaign, Bill Clinton excoriated President Bush for being overly restrictive toward irregular immigrants. As president, however, Clinton would assail Bush for being overly lenient.[35]

"Economic restructuring, the end of the Cold War, and the growing predominance of neoliberal policies," according to Kathleen Arnold, had joined with longstanding anti-Mexican racism to harden American attitudes toward unauthorized entrants. So in July 1993, the new president unveiled a four-pronged strategy for addressing illegal immigration. He would strengthen border enforcement, improve workplace verification, assist the states in their immigration efforts, and deprive irregular immigrants of all public benefits except emergency medical care and public education for their children. Clinton also appointed former Texas Democratic congresswoman Barbara Jordan to chair the congressionally-mandated Commission on Immigration Reform, which would include administration officials among its membership.[36]

With 60 percent of Americans viewing current immigration levels as "bad," and with only 20 percent considering their nation a "melting pot," Clinton was preaching to an increasingly more vocal choir. "We must not—will not—surrender our borders to those who wish to exploit our history of compassion and justice," the newly restrictionist Clinton vowed.[37]

The new president's new tone alarmed some Catholics. "Quite

apart from the fact that no one recommends surrender of the borders," America's editors wrote in reaction to Clinton's remarks, "this characterization of our national history conveniently overlooks the U.S. annexation of California in 1848, an imperialist move that today's Mexican migrants are peacefully reversing." New York's Catholic Democratic governor Mario Cuomo maintained that undocumented immigrants' "fresh, new infusions of energy, enterprise, and hope should be welcomed, not shunned. Earlier immigrants built a nation; the new immigrants can help us save it."[38]

Such discord would not deter the president. "Without a more evolved policy argument," White House aide Stephen Warnath wrote in August, "we simply cannot effectively counter the enticing logic of the opposing view: the Federal government is responsible for controlling the borders."[39]

A "more evolved policy argument" was not forthcoming. So the Clinton administration adhered to its position. "In both the short-term and the long-term," White House aides Rahm Emanuel and Ron Klain argued in September, "the Administration's objective with regard to immigration should be to strike an aggressive posture."[40]

The next month the Jordan Commission issued its preliminary findings, which called for worker verification through a registration database and a national identification card, aid to the states to fight illegal immigration, denial of welfare and nonemergency benefits to the undocumented, stronger border control, and the imprisonment and deportation of irregular aliens. "The Administration and the Commission," Emanuel and Klain calculated, "agree on ninety percent of the issues."[41]

Some Catholics did not. "As pastors, we are deeply concerned about the growing hostility toward immigrants evident now in some parts of our society and even, sad to say, supported by some public officials," the American Catholic bishops lamented in their policy statement at their November meeting. "In the context of

Catholic social teaching and, indeed, in the light of the Judeo-Christian heritage, such an attitude is not acceptable."

But it was becoming widespread. The bishops' statement came in the wake of the passage of Proposition 187, a California ballot initiative to deny public health, education, and welfare services to the undocumented, which passed over the objections of the bishops as well as the president. "The lie of Proposition 187 was, if you vote for denying services to illegal immigrants, you will be better off somehow," stated Los Angeles's Roger Cardinal Mahony, reacting to the success of the measure. "Emotionally based responses are not overcome by rational argument, discussion, or appeal to Scripture." Fifty-one percent of California Catholic voters agreed with the cardinal.[42]

"I thought it was unfair to the children and counterproductive and self-defeating," Clinton would say to explain his opposition to Proposition 187. To the delight of Mahony and Clinton, Proposition 187 would never become law, as a federal court would preclude its enactment.[43]

But the November 1994 elections had also ushered in the first Republican Congress in four decades, and the new majority was even more intent on restricting immigration than the old. United States Catholic Conference representatives met in January 1995 with new Senate Majority Leader Robert Dole of Kansas to convey their uneasiness with the new political climate. "We oppose making national policy out of anti-immigrant sentiment such as that expressed in California's Proposition 187," they told the Republican senator, "and we do not consider depriving people of basic human rights as a suitable discussion of the failures of federal immigration policy."[44]

Just as the bishops were stepping up their immigration efforts, so too was the president. In his State of the Union Address in January, Clinton pledged to "do more to speed the deportation of illegal aliens who are arrested for crimes, to better identify illegal aliens in the workplace as recommended by the Commission headed by former Congresswoman Barbara Jordan." In February, Clinton issued an executive directive to the heads of all departments aimed at "first, protecting our borders; second, protecting the interests of our workers in the workplace; third, removing more criminal aliens; and fourth, providing more assistance to the States which are burdened with the problem of illegal immigration." But rather than write a bill of his own, Clinton would let Congress do it for him.[45]

Congress wanted to wait for the Jordan Commission, which issued its final findings in June. The report recommended a reduction in legal immigration from 800,000 to 550,000 per year, including 50,000 refugees and 100,000 workers with special skills. Siblings and adult children of U.S. residents would no longer receive preferential treatment. The commission also required businesses to pay immigrants with work-related visas 5 percent above the prevailing wage to eliminate the incentive for foreign labor, and it reiterated its previous call for a national worker verification system.[46]

Clinton called the report "an excellent framework to achieve gradual reductions in the level of legal immigration. This is a goal and objective I share."[47]

So did many members of Congress. Republican Lamar Smith of Texas produced a House bill which merged provisions on legal and illegal immigration, while Republican Alan Simpson of Wyoming authored Senate measures which confronted each issue separately. All three bills adopted many of the Jordan Commission's proposals.

The most controversial provision in any of the three measures was an amendment to the House legislation sponsored by California Republican Elton Gallegly which would have barred the children of irregular immigrants from attending public schools. Clinton deemed this provision unduly punitive toward children, and threatened to veto any legislation which retained it.[48]

Many Catholics rejected all three of the congressional measures, with or without the Gallegly Amendment. In July in "One Family under God," the bishops' Committee on Immigration blasted the Gallegly Amendment as "mean-spirited and essentially short-sighted, since the well-being of the whole community is affected by the well-being of all its children." *America* similarly denounced the Gallegly Amendment as an invitation to return to "the nineteenth-century nativist movement that sought to blame national problems on those of foreign birth."[49]

"Due to the considerable proportions reached by the illegal migrants phenomenon," Pope John Paul II observed in July, "legislation in all the countries should be brought into harmony, also for the more equitable distribution of the burdens of a balanced solution." The pontiff warned against the "use of administrative regulations, meant to restrict the criteria of family membership, which result in unjustifiably forcing into an illegal situation people whose right to live with their families cannot be denied by any law."[50]

Neither the bishops' direct opposition nor the pope's indirect influence could slow the inexorable march toward immigration reform. After passing both houses of Congress in June and July of 1996, a hybrid of the House bill and both Senate measures went to the president's desk. Clinton signed it on the last day of September, in the last full year of his first term.[51]

The Illegal Immigration Reform and Immigrant Responsibility Act of 1996 did not contain the Gallegly Amendment. Nor did it include Senator Simpson's provision for a toll-free telephone number to verify worker identification through Social Security and INS records, which, thanks in part to resistance by the bishops, had shrunk to a voluntary pilot program in three states. Nor did it reduce legal immigration levels or cap refugee ceilings at fifty thousand, as the Jordan Commission proposed and Clinton had embraced, only to change his mind in an improving economy during an election year, when business, Latino, and Catholic votes were precious. Nor did it repeal the "Fifth Preference" admission of siblings of U.S. citizens, as Clinton had endorsed until, as White House aide

Lanny Davis would admit, Asian campaign contributions, Microsoft, and the Catholic Church helped steer him in the opposite direction.[52]

But it did call for a doubling of Border Patrol agents from 5,000 to 10,000 by 2001, construction of the second and third tiers of a fourteen-mile border fence south of San Diego, and the development of biometric alien identification cards. It toughened penalties for smuggling aliens and using false documents while eliminating judicial review of deportation appeals. It outlawed the payment of Social Security benefits to unauthorized entrants. In an effort to curb abuse of food stamps and disability payments by legal immigrants, it stiffened the criteria for sponsorship of immigrants. Clinton lauded the new law as "landmark immigration reform legislation that builds on our progress of the last three years. It strengthens the rule of law by cracking down on illegal immigration at the border, in the workplace, and in the criminal justice system—without punishing those who live in the country legally."[53]

No sooner had Clinton signed the restrictionist measure than he and the country began to retreat from it. The National Association for the Advancement of Colored People (NAACP) altered its historic restrictionist stance and joined hands with the Congressional Hispanic Caucus in favor of liberal immigration policies and affirmative action considerations. In 1998, Attorney General Janet Reno called off worksite inspections for undocumented aliens. The number of HI-B visas for skilled workers (to be hired only if there were no available qualified native-born workers) would grow from 65,000 in 1990, when the program began, to 195,000 in 2000. In 2000, INS Associate Commissioner Robert Bach conceded that, unless they committed a crime, if undocumented aliens evaded capture by the Border Patrol, they were pretty much left alone.[54]

In the same year, the Catholic president of the American Federation of Labor-Congress of Industrial Organizations, John Sweeney, announced that, in an effort to organize the heavily undocumented low-skilled service industry of restaurant, hotel, janitorial, and do-mestic workers, the union was reversing its traditional opposition to illegal immigration. The addition of organized labor to African Americans and Latinos on the admissionist bandwagon meant that Democratic presidential candidates, like Vice President Al Gore in 2000, had to join the cause as well.[55]

They would have plenty of company. In 1993, when Clinton took office on the heels of a recession, 63 percent of Gallup's respondents found immigration harmful, and only 26 percent saw it as helpful. Numbers like that had helped effect Clinton's original about-face, from the admissionist candidate of the 1992 campaign to the restric-tionist president who signed the 1996 law. But in 2000, in the midst of a booming economy, Gallup now discovered that only 40 percent of Americans considered immigration to be hurting the country, while 44 percent believed that it was helping. These new numbers contributed to Clinton's second reversal, which was less significant only because he could not run a third time.[56]

The 1996 law nonetheless remained on the books, and it was still symptomatic of a nativist climate to some Catholics. "The word 'reform' in the title suggests that it was meant to bring about a change for the better," George Anderson wrote in *America* in May 1998. "But from the perspective of many immigrants, its provisions have made their struggle to remain in the United States more des-perate." The National Catholic Rural Life Conference denounced the meager wages, horrible working conditions, and INS raids at fruit and meatpacking plants. A letter to Congress signed by Spo-kane Bishop William Skylstad, representing the NCRLC, helped save a federal legal services program for migrant workers. James Haggerty, regional counselor for the bishops' Catholic Legal Im-migration Network (CLINIC) in New York, castigated the "abusive" interpretation of the 1996 law by the INS. With the number of im-migrants imprisoned while facing deportation proceedings expect-ed to reach 15,000 in 1999, CLINIC joined Lutheran immigration agencies in producing a video, "Know Your Rights," to help educate detainees.[57]

At the National Legislative Conference on Immigration and Refugee Policy in Washington in the spring of 1999, INS commissioner Doris Meissner vigorously defended her agency's mandate under the new law. Mark Franken, executive director of Migration and Refugee Services for the USCC, just as strongly denounced it. The country's sentiment had dramatically deteriorated, Franken regretted, from the generosity with which it had received the dregs of Fidel Castro's society in 1980 to the mean-spiritedness behind the INS's enforcement of the 1996 law, which was tripling the daily numbers of detainees.[58]

So the bishops sought its repeal. In March 2000, Roger Cardinal Mahony of Los Angeles and Bishop Nicholas DiMarzio of Camden, New Jersey joined the AFL-CIO's John Sweeney in introducing "Fix 96," a joint effort to help change the 1996 immigration law. They urged the federal government to grant amnesty to irregular immigrants, respect the civil and employee rights of undocumented laborers, repeal employer sanctions against hiring unauthorized entrants, and enact economic and foreign policies which addressed the causes of illegal immigration.[59]

The bishops unanimously endorsed this endeavor at their November meeting. In their statement "Welcoming the Stranger Among Us: Unity in Diversity," the prelates observed that "while the changes in the law have enabled many to adjust their status to that of permanent resident, the 1996 immigration legislation has made this option more difficult for the vast majority." In the spirit of "solidarity," they pledged to "continue to work at the national level to promote recognition of the human rights of all, regardless of their immigration status, and to advance fair and equitable legislation for refugees and prospective immigrants."[60]

In December, with the country still digesting the contentious presidential election, Congress included in section 245(i) of a budget bill a provision granting a four-month opportunity for as many as 500,000 unauthorized entrants to apply for permanent resident status. A month before leaving office, in the wake of a 36 percent increase in illegal immigration over the last six years of his presidency, Clinton signed the legislation.[61]

Welfare Reform

Immigration was such a dominant concern in the 1990s that it invaded numerous realms of federal policy. Welfare reform was one of them. As a presidential candidate, Bill Clinton had famously promised to "end welfare as we know it," and the status quo had included benefits for legal immigrants. The Republican Congress which arrived in Washington in January 1995 sought to end this practice and, if he was to keep his promise, President Clinton would have to go along.

Even before the seismic midterm jolt delivered by the GOP, some Catholics were worried that Clinton's architecture for welfare reform would not spare legal immigrants. "The sad turn of events appears to be that those charged with developing plans for reform now find themselves turning to programs for other poor families to find necessary funding," Catholic Charities president Rev. Fred Kammer wrote to his childhood friend in the White House in February 1994. "Refugees are singled out, but they are not the only ones who seem to be falling outside a Reaganesque 'truly needy' category."[62]

"As you know, there is no easy answer" to the welfare quandary, Clinton replied to Father Kammer. He promised to share Father Kammer's letter with his White House Working Group on Welfare Reform.[63]

"We applaud your leadership in seeking reform of the welfare system," United States Catholic Conference president Archbishop William Keeler of Baltimore wrote Clinton in March. But "we believe that such efforts would be severely undermined if financing reform jeopardizes the well-being of thousands of legal immigrants and their families who have sacrificed to sponsor them."[64]

"I appreciate your insight on this important issue," the president assured the archbishop. "I welcome your continued participation in the process."[65]

The bishops' participation would only increase as the Republicans seized the reins on Capitol Hill. "We are not defenders of the welfare status quo, which too often relies on bureaucratic approaches, discourages work, and breaks up families," Auxiliary Bishop John Ricard, chairman of the USCC Domestic Policy Committee, wrote to the Republican House Ways and Means Committee chairman, Representative Willis Archer of Tennessee, as his panel embarked on a welfare reform hearing in January 1995. Yet "we cannot support punitive approaches that target immigrants and propose to take away the minimal benefits that they now receive, especially those targeted to pregnant women and children."[66]

The president agreed with the bishops. According to his biographer Taylor Branch, Clinton considered the proposed ban on benefits to legal immigrants a product of "*ad hominem* politics, milked from anti-foreign sentiment, and therefore unconscionable." In a March letter, Health and Human Services Secretary Donna Shalala informed Archer of the administration's resistance to denying all welfare benefits to legal immigrants.[67]

The president and the bishops joined forces to try to stop the Ways and Means Committee from reporting a bill with such a prohibition. In an April meeting at the White House, Clinton conveyed to Washington's James Cardinal Hickey his "shared concerns on welfare reform."[68]

Under the existing immigration law, immigrants needed a sponsor to sign an affidavit attesting that they would not go on welfare. If they tried to receive Aid to Families with Dependent Children (AFDC), Supplemental Security Income (SSI) assistance, or food stamps, their sponsor's income would disqualify them in most cases. The sponsor's affidavit was not legally binding, however, so legal immigrants had access to the welfare system at about the same rate as nonimmigrants.

The Jordan Commission recommended in June that such affidavits be legally enforceable. But it advised that the "safety net provided by means-tested programs" remain available to legal immigrants.[69]

The Republicans didn't agree. The House passed a welfare reform bill which made sponsors' affidavits legally enforceable, but which, with limited exceptions, barred immigrants from obtaining AFDC, SSI, food stamps, and emergency and nonemergency Medicaid.[70]

So the Catholics and Clinton shifted their attention to the Senate, where the finance committee had reported legislation similar to that of the House. Like the House bill, the Senate version would eliminate aid to legal immigrants by counting their sponsors' income as available to them even after naturalization. And it would deny emergency and nonemergency Medicaid coverage to legal immigrants, including pregnant women and children.[71]

"The consequences of this bill, especially in regard to the children of this country," Joan McGuinness Wagner, president of the National Association of Catholic Life Ministers, wrote the president in June, "are very frightening." Catholic Charities issued an "Action Alert" urging its members to write their senators requesting a vote against the bill's anti-immigration provisions. The group targeted fourteen senators, including six Catholics, for special lobbying.[72]

Father Kammer suggested that Clinton threaten a veto to compel the senators to modify the measure. "We will be with you," he pledged to the president in June, "and so will the bishops and many others."[73]

The bishops were with the president later in the month, sending a letter espousing their "principles and priorities on welfare reform," including support for immigrant aid, to every member of the

Senate. Among the "many others" in the Catholic community who shared Clinton's opposition to the GOP bills was Sister Catherine McNamee, president of the National Catholic Educational Association. "I urge you to veto welfare reform that destroys the nation's social safety net," she wrote the president of the nation.[74]

But the Senate majority was not with these Catholics or with Clinton. The anti-immigrant tenets remained, as the Senate passed the welfare reform bill by a resounding 87–12. With the notable exceptions of emergency Medicaid, short-term emergency disaster relief, school lunches, food stamps for children, public health assistance for immunizations, Head Start, and foster care and adoption services, the legislation outlawed needs-based aid to legal immigrants for five years.[75]

The administration's posture toward the House and Senate bills was to "continue to push legally binding affidavits of support; support reform to slow the growth of SSI use by elderly immigrants with a legally-binding affidavit to ensure family financial support." But it would " oppose any requirement that would kick current elderly and disabled off the program; [and] support the more reasonable restrictions on [welfare] eligibility over broader, harsher restrictions in each case. . . ."[76]

If a teen cutoff, a mandatory food stamp block grant or block grants for child welfare, and school lunch were parts of the conference bill, Domestic Policy Advisor Bruce Reed and White House aide Rahm Emanuel advised that Clinton veto the legislation. As for the "difficult-to-improve areas" like "immigrant cuts," the president "should make a lot of noise without signaling a veto, so even if you sign this bill you reserve the right to soften these cuts as part of the reconciliation."

Reed and Emanuel prescribed an "aggressive campaign" by the administration to sway the conference committee. Such an effort should enlist the "Catholic Church, Religious Groups, and the Pro-Life/Pro-Choice Coalition[s]."[77]

The bishops were an easy sell. In November, USCC president Bishop Anthony Pilla of Cleveland reminded Clinton to resist "provisions which unfairly deny essential help to immigrants, even legal immigrants."[78]

The Catholic-Clinton alliance helped trigger two vetoes, one in December 1995 and the next in January 1996. When a third welfare reform bill reached Clinton's desk at the end of July, Bishop Pilla again pressed the president to "veto this legislation and continue to work for genuine welfare reform which will strengthen families and protect children."[79]

And then the coalition crumbled. Though "I am deeply disappointed that the congressional leadership insisted on attaching to this extraordinary important bill a provision that will hurt legal immigrants in America," Clinton explained that the other parts made the bill "significantly better than the bills I vetoed." Since "I am convinced this never would have passed alone," Clinton would, as Reed and Emanuel had suggested, "send legislation to Congress to correct" the anti-immigrant stipulations.[80]

This assurance did not mollify Clinton's erstwhile Catholic allies. "We are very disappointed with your decision to sign such a reckless and dangerous welfare reform bill," Father Kammer and Bishop Joseph Sullivan of Catholic Charities wrote Clinton in August. "We urge you to establish an effective mechanism to track the effects of this legislation on the women, children, and immigrants who will no longer be eligible to receive assistance." Bishop Pilla, speaking for the USCC, wrote Clinton lamenting the president's signing of the "deeply flawed" legislation.[81]

"As you know, this was a very difficult decision," Clinton responded to Bishop Pilla. "I am . . . deeply disappointed that the Republican leadership insisted on using welfare reform to cut off assistance to legal immigrants."[82]

The Catholic Health Association blamed the Republicans too. "CHA strongly agrees with the President's judgment that this particular provision has nothing to do with welfare reform ... and it [is] not right," the organization asserted in an August press release. "The new welfare legislation will undoubtedly increase the financial burden of many hospitals, including Catholic ones, which serve a disproportionate share of legal immigrants."[83]

Within a week of the CHA statement Clinton directed the secretary of agriculture to grant waivers letting states extend the certification of eligibility periods for legal immigrants seeking food stamps. Under the new law, benefits to lawful immigrants and their children ended when certification began. Clinton also instructed the attorney general to expedite naturalization of legal immigrants so they could receive welfare benefits as U.S. citizens.[84]

Catholic leaders prodded Clinton to do more. "In response to the very harsh provisions affecting legal immigrants and refugees in the welfare statute, you stated on several occasions that you intended to ease the provisions regarding legal immigrants and Food Stamps," Catholic Charities Deputy Director for Policy Sharon Daley reminded Clinton in December.[85]

Clinton refused to apologize for his decision to sign welfare reform into law. "Some of you think I made a mistake when I signed the welfare reform bill, and I don't," the triumphant president told a group of religious leaders, including Archbishop Theodore McCarrick of Newark, at the White House in January 1997. "My objective here is, once and for all, to take the politics out of poverty and to treat all able-bodied people the same at the community level."[86]

To his critics, though, Clinton's signature had more to do with politics than poverty. Catholic Democratic senator Daniel Patrick Moynihan of New York, who had led the charge against the legislation, said of Clinton's about-face, "If it were fourteen weeks *after* the election, he'd say no."[87]

About fourteen weeks after the election, in March 1997, the president proclaimed that the next fiscal year's budget "would return SSI and Medicaid benefits to more than 350,000 immigrants who become disabled entering the United States, and it would also continue to provide essential cash and medical assistance for low-income immigrant children." Clinton added, "Now our goal must be to mobilize support" for this budget.[88]

The mobilization effort commenced two weeks later at a White House briefing for immigration advocates attended by Jack Bresch of the CHA, John Kromkowski of the Catholic University of America, Kara Morrow of the Jesuit Social Ministries, Jennifer Consilvio of the Jesuit Conference, and Cynthia Phillips of the USCC. Lamenting that without administration action "charity groups may become these immigrants' only source of income support" under Republican proposals to block-grant immigration funds to the states, White House representatives assured the visitors that "restoring benefits to legal immigrants is an absolutely critical part of the Administration's agenda for the year." They added that "the president is talking about this issue as he travels the country."[89]

Indeed he was, and by August Clinton had succeeded in persuading Congress to remove some anti-immigrant portions of the welfare reform law. But that hardly satisfied his Catholic critics. "There is a serious problem among immigrants and their families as they attempt to access Food Stamps, Women with Infant Children, Medicaid, the [State] Children's Health Insurance Program, and other programs," Kathy Thornton and Mary Elizabeth Clark of the Catholic social justice lobby Network complained to the president in March 1999.[90]

"The important goals of the Medicaid and SCHIP programs are undermined when states are not permitted to use federal funds to provide preventative and other basic health services to lawfully present immigrants," Father Kammer wrote Clinton in November 2000. The Kammer letter arrived two months after the president had sent congratulations to his "dear friend" Father Kammer on the ninetieth anniversary of Catholic Charities. "Each day you show us the power of faith in action," Clinton wrote, "and your commitment to serving others reinforces our nation's fundamental values of community, responsibility, and compassion."[91]

Church and state indeed had much in common as the Bill Clinton era came to an end. But on immigration, despite Clinton's meaningful overtures, the Catholic activists and the American president were nearly as far apart as ever.

Conclusions

President Bill Clinton treated many of the refugee and immigration maladies which his predecessors had failed to cure. His varying remedies, however, alternately attracted and repelled Catholics, and helped and harmed the country.

Catholic refugee advocates welcomed the president's heightened processing of Haitian and Cuban migrants, temporary reprieve for Central Americans fleeing Hurricane Mitch, and resistance to lower refugee quotas and expedited exclusion. But they lamented the dramatically different numbers of Haitian and Cuban refugees, his interdiction of Haitian vessels, his signing of legislation which included expedited and summary exclusion, and his failure to achieve significant asylum reform.

Catholic proponents of immigration reform applauded Clinton's opposition to Proposition 187, the Gallegly Amendment, and lower caps for legal immigration; his restoration of some welfare benefits to authorized immigrants, and easing of the path to permanent residency for unauthorized immigrants; and the Illegal Immigration Reform and Immigrant Responsibility Act's retention of the Fifth Preference for siblings of citizens as well as its omission of legal immigration quotas. But they condemned his signing of one law which deprived legal immigrants of welfare benefits, and another which called for a longer border fence, increased Border Patrol, and biometric identification cards.

President Clinton deserved credit from the country for his

measured, moderate approach (on immigration reform, if not on refugees) to implementing the recommendations of the Jordan Commission. But he deserved blame for largely deciding not to enforce them. And in their polarizing pleas for amnesty for the undocumented and the repeal of sanctions for employers, Catholic immigration advocates offered a fearful foreshadowing of what was still to come.

4. George W. Bush

2001–2009

FOR GEORGE W. BUSH, immigration was ideological. Like his father, Bush knew firsthand the ramifications of the nation's porous southern border. Before his Texas governorship had concluded, the younger Bush was speaking of "compassionate conservatism," paying homage to the American people's reverence for self-reliance and reputation for generosity. "Family values," Bush insisted, "don't stop at the Rio Grande."[1]

Bush's sentiments would align him with many American Catholics, who would award him the lion's share of their votes in his 2004 reelection campaign. But his record would fall short of his rhetoric, as his words and actions would follow the path of most of his party and much of the populace after September 11, 2001, away from comprehensive immigration reform and toward punitive border enforcement. When the president and most of the country returned to their embrace of comprehensive immigration reform, however, Catholics on the far ends of the issue helped prevent its enactment.

Immigration Reform before September 11

George W. Bush's interest in immigration was in part a product of his own experience, growing up in a household with a "second mother," a Mexican housekeeper named Paula Rendón. "Bush genuinely believed that immigration was part of America's great story," Andrew Wroe and Jon Herbert write, "but this was not the reason he pursued it." Wroe and Herbert contend that Bush viewed immigration reform as a key to unlocking Hispanic inclusion in the "permanent Republican majority" envisioned by his political guru, Karl Rove.[2]

While personal predilections and political calculations undoubtedly helped steer Bush's course, immigration reform was above all a centerpiece of the new president's dedication to "compassionate conservatism." The brainchild of Christian evangelical University of Texas professor Marvin Olasky, "compassionate conservatism" attacked government responses to poverty while extolling church antipoverty efforts. It was in harmony with St. Thomas Aquinas's quest for "the common good" through "distributive justice," which dictated the "subsidiary" of society, and "commutative justice," which required the "solidarity" of society. Thus was Bush's domestic agenda, in the words of his chief speechwriter Michael Gerson, "inspired, at least in part, by Catholic social teaching."[3]

The George W. Bush administration was not even a month old when the new president began to practice his newfound principles. In February 2001 he traveled to Mexico to meet with that country's president, Vicente Fox. Both leaders brought to the meeting the report of a commission sponsored by the Carnegie Endowment for International Peace in the United States and the Instituto Tecnológico Autónomo in Mexico and cochaired by former Clinton envoy to Latin America Mack McLarty, former Mexican Undersecretary for Foreign Affairs Andrés Rozental, and Bishop Nicholas DiMarzio of Camden, New Jersey. The two leaders agreed to devise an immigration plan based on the commission's blueprint by the time of Fox's scheduled visit to the White House in September.[4]

Bush and Fox would meet three more times during the first eight months of the administration, seeking to forge what the American president expected to be his "signature foreign policy legacy," the improvement of U.S.-Mexican relations. But in the early months of his presidency, Bush spent more time clarifying what he was against than explicating what he was for on immigration reform. "There will be no blanket amnesty for illegals," he insisted in August at his home in Crawford, Texas.[5]

Not all the omens were bad for immigration advocates, however. In August, while a Democratic immigration task force prepared to support the Republican president, representatives of the United States Conference of Catholic Bishops (formerly the United States Catholic Conference) discussed immigration reform with State and Justice Department officials in Washington.[6]

President Fox arrived in Washington on September 5 for the Bush administration's first official state dinner. The Mexican head of state surprised his host by pressing for what he called "regularization," a program of uncontrolled amnesty for all irregular immigrants residing in the United States. "I made clear that would not happen," Bush would recall. "I believed amnesty—making illegal immigrants automatic citizens—would undercut the rule of the law and ensure further illegal immigration."[7]

While the American president was discouraging his Mexican counterpart, the Catholic Church was encouraging him. In a revised edition of the document "The Church and Racism," originally authored in 1968, the Pontifical Council for Justice and Peace was denouncing "zero immigration" laws and warning of racial prejudice against immigrant populations. The statement, prepared for the United Nations Conference on Racism which concluded in Durban, South Africa on September 7, urged governments to avoid creating a "subcategory of human beings" by subjecting the unborn, the poor, and the migrants to a "new and terrible form of slavery."[8]

Refugees after September 11

Four days later, nineteen Al Qaeda suicide bombers crashed planes onto American soil, killing almost 3,000, damaging the American economy, and rattling the American psyche. Among the casualties of the 9/11 invasion, it would turn out, were many of the world's refugees seeking shelter in the United States. Before the attacks, over 20,000 refugees had received approval for entry into the United States. Yet within three months after the attacks, and seven weeks later than required by law, President Bush had reduced the quota of prospective refugees from 80,000 in FY 2001 to 70,000 in FY 2002.

The State Department then reported that due to the dramatic reduction in the processing of applications, it was unlikely that more than 45,000 refugees would enter the United States in FY 2002, which began on October 1. "In the absence of that [asylum] document from October 1 to the third week in November," Mark Franken, executive director of the United States Conference of Catholic Bishops' Office of Migration and Refugee Services, lamented, "no refugees were coming in."[9]

Bill Frelick, director of the nonprofit United States Committee on Refugees, noted the tragic irony that refugees—already the most scrutinized newcomers to the United States—were suffering due to the heinous acts of men who were in the country on lawfully obtained visas. And the Bush decision meant not only fewer opportunities for refugees to escape persecution in their home countries, but fewer federal funds to feed and house them upon arrival in the U.S.[10]

The smaller federal role in refugee assistance imposed greater pressure on Catholic relief organizations. Of the five million refugees accepted by the United States in the previous fifty years, Catholic agencies had settled 1 million. By 2001, 106 dioceses had refugee resettlement coordinators.[11]

But they could not bear the burden alone. "The United States must not shrink from its global leadership role," the U.S. Catholic bishops asserted in their November pastoral "Living with Faith and Hope After September 11." They urged the Bush administration not to abandon its responsibility of "offering protection to refugees who flee terror in their homelands." They sought a meeting with Attorney

General John Ashcroft to discuss, in the words of the USCCB's Mark Franken, "the refugee protection issue and the protection of due process and civil liberties for non-citizens." And they pleaded with President Bush to raise the refugee ceiling to 95,000 for FY 2002.[12]

"Obviously, the environment has changed drastically," observed Kevin Appleby, director of the USCCB Office of Migration and Refugee Services. "The brunt of Homeland Security has been focused against those of non-citizen status: immigrants, refugees, the undocumented, and non-immigrants who are here on visitors' visas." He predicted that the lowered quota and reduced funding by the U.S. would have a ripple effect throughout the world. *America*'s editors prodded Congress to "summon the political will to help bring an end to the crisis in refugee admissions."[13]

But Congress had little inclination to let more people into the United States at a time when most Americans wanted to keep them out. In Gallup's 2002 Minority Rights and Relations poll, its first post-9/11 survey, only 51 percent of whites and 46 percent of African Americans would consider immigration to be good for the country.[14]

If September 11 had ushered in a frightening new era, however, there remained disturbing echoes of a troubled past. A boat containing 167 Haitians reached shore in Florida in December 2001. As of March 2002, these Haitians were still in detention centers in the southern part of the state. Auxiliary Bishop Thomas Wenski of Miami implored Attorney General John Ashcroft to press the Immigration and Naturalization Service to release the Haitians from detention. "Since asylum seekers do not present a danger to the community or a rule of flight," Bishop Wenski wrote, "these individuals should be released to family or supportive community members, such as Catholic Charities, during the pendency of the immigration proceedings."[15]

And accompanying yet another saga of Haitian exiles reminiscent of the dramas of the previous three presidencies was the familiar accusation of a double standard in U.S. refugee policy. "Cubans ... are not treated this way," *America* editorialized in August 2002. "If they are interdicted at sea, they are sent back, but if they reach our shores seeking asylum, they can remain and not be detained while their asylum claims are being processed." The USCCB's Appleby concurred that when it came to the victims of this depressing double standard, "It's always the Haitians."[16]

Like his predecessors, Bush recognized yet defended the double standard. "The immigration law ought to be the same for Haitians and everybody else," said the president in November. Bush explained that "the difference, of course, is that we don't send people back to Cuba, because they're going to be persecuted. And that's why we've got a special law on the books regarding Cubans."[17]

The Bush administration would not heed Bishop Wenski's request, so he would try again in May 2003. The bishop called the detention of Haitians "a dangerous precedent for detaining asylum seekers for the purpose of deterring future migrations of those fleeing persecution."[18]

Yet it appeared to be working. In 2002, according to the United States Committee for Refugees, the United States had admitted only 27,000 refugees overall, down from 70,000 the year before, and the lowest number in thirty years. By September 2003 the administration had forcibly repatriated 1,500 Haitians.[19]

To Reed Lubbers, United Nations High Commissioner for Refugees, forcible repatriation was a violation of human rights, the kind that countries like the United States were claiming were under assault by terrorism. "Here and in other countries that have raised fortress-like barriers against those fleeing persecution," *America* editor Rev. Thomas Reese charged, "these rights ... are now in danger."[20]

On the eve of another presidential election year, the American bishops in October 2003 issued "Faithful Citizenship: A Catholic Call to Responsibility." Among their prescriptions for cures to the nation's social ills was a "more generous immigration and refugee policy."[21]

None would be forthcoming. "I have made it abundantly clear to the Coast Guard," Bush observed in February 2004, "that we will turn back any refugee [from Haiti] that attempts to reach our shore."[22]

If Bush had any intention of downplaying the refugee issue in his second term, the Catholic Church was determined not to let him. Only three weeks after Bush defeated Massachusetts Democratic senator John Kerry, Pope John Paul II commemorated the World Day of Migrants and Refugees with a ringing reaffirmation of the rights of refugees. "Christians must above all listen to the cry for help that comes from a multitude of migrants and refugees," the Holy Father intoned, "but they must then foster, with active commitment, prospects of hope that will herald the dawn of a more open and supportive society."[23]

But first the Congress would have to listen. In April, Bishop Gerald Barnes of San Bernardino, California, chairman of the USCCB Committee on Migration, wrote the House and Senate conferees on the Emergency Supplemental Appropriations Act of 2005, expressing the bishops' opposition to the bill's Real ID Act. This provision would permit judges to deny asylum to those who could not provide documentation proving their persecution, would prevent applicants who could not prove they were in the U.S. legally from obtaining driver's licenses, and would extend construction of the border fence between San Diego and New Mexico. Bishop Barnes deplored the act's "extraordinarily harmful impacts on asylum seekers."[24]

It survived the conference committee, however, and the president signed the bill into law. In November, Bush called for expansion of the "expedited removal" process, enabling Border Patrol agents to order deportations. *America*'s editors decried this proposal as "especially harmful to asylum seekers who are fleeing persecution." Orlando Bishop Thomas Wenski, speaking for the USCCB, condemned it for putting "*bona fide* refugees and other vulnerable migrants at risk of wrongful deportation."[25]

Just when it seemed that matters could not get worse for Catholic refugee advocates, another makeshift Haitian boat washed ashore in Florida, where the Coast Guard was detaining its 101-member crew in March 2007. If the administration would only release the detainees, Miami Archbishop John Favalora promised, "the Church stands ready to make sure that these people have a place to go and people to take care of them while they make their claim" for asylum. But the president would not free the Haitians.[26]

In August and September 2008, four hurricanes ravaged Haiti, killing 800 and leaving 1 million homeless. The names of the storms, wrote Marc Lacey of the *New York Times*, "Haitians spit out like curses: Fay, Gustav, Hannah, and Ike."[27]

Many Haitians resorted to eating "mud cookies," concoctions of salt, vegetables, shortening, and dirt. With Haiti suffering from the hemisphere's highest mortality rate for infants, children under five, and mothers, President René Préval appealed to Bush for Temporary Protected Status for Haitians in the United States, and an eighteen-month reprieve such as that granted to Nicaraguans, Salvadorans, and Hondurans by the prior Bush and Clinton administrations. On behalf of the bishops, Chicago's Francis Cardinal George wrote Bush in October that "Haiti meets the standards of TPS because it has experienced political turmoil, four natural disasters, and severe food shortages in the previous eight months alone." But Homeland Security Secretary Michael Chertoff denied the request of the Haitian president and the American bishops, a fitting climax to eight years of futility for the people who lived on an island, and the bishops who felt like they did.[28]

In one of his last acts in office at the end of December 2008, the president signed the William Wilberforce Trafficking Victim Protection Reauthorization Act, which Congress had passed unanimously in an effort to combat sex trafficking. The statute mandated that the Department of Health and Human Services place with family members or others those unaccompanied children who entered the United States from countries other than Mexico or Canada, until they could obtain a hearing before an immigration judge. By the end of the Bush administration, the country was accepting 60,108 refugees. This number was up from the anxious aftermath of 9/11, but down from the final year of the Clinton administration.[29]

Immigration Reform after September 11

The ease with which the September 11 hijackers had gained entry into the United States pushed border security to the forefront of the immigration debate. And, according to Robert Draper, it robbed Bush of much of the creativity and improvisation that immigration reform would demand.[30]

In May 2002, Bush joylessly signed the Enhanced Border Security and Visa Entry Reform Act, which added Immigration and Naturalization Service personnel, required biometric identification cards for foreign visitors to the U.S., and mandated that all incoming ships and airplanes provide a list of their passengers and crews. Having brandished the stick of border security, Bush lamented that there would be no carrot of leniency toward undocumented migrants in the law. "The bill doesn't have everything I wanted," the president admitted in his signing statement, regretting that temporary extension of the 245(i) program for long-time residents to achieve legal status was not part of the legislation.[31]

It didn't have everything the U.S. Catholic bishops wanted, either. At their November meeting, the American hierarchy approved the first-ever joint statement with their Mexican counterparts, "Strangers No Longer: Together on the Journey of Hope." The document called for a program of "earned legalization" for all undocumented aliens in the U.S., a guest worker plan to provide employment, a living wage, and workplace protection for foreign-born laborers; reform of the immigration system to promote family re-unification; and endorsement of policies which addressed the global inequities that prompted illegal immigration to the U.S.[32]

The bishops' declaration was a resounding rejection of the restrictionist fervor which was sweeping the United States and approaching the White House. Auxiliary Bishop John Manz of Chicago, who represented the U.S. bishops in Mexico City while Bishop Talavera Ramírez of Coatzacoalcos attended the meeting in Washington, would recall the atmosphere of "fear and xenophobia" which engulfed his country in the wake of the terrorist attacks.[33]

The bishops futilely resisted Bush's transfer of the Immigration and Naturalization Service from the Justice Department to the new Department of Homeland Security as potentially "detrimental to the civil rights of people who look or sound 'foreign.'" They effectively lobbied to strip twelve anti-immigrant provisions from a House intelligence bill. Yet Bush began to approach the Catholic position in January 2004. He unveiled a guest worker plan under which unauthorized immigrants would receive a work permit for three to six years, after which they would return to their home countries and apply for U.S. citizenship.[34]

The Bush proposal was conservative. "An opportunity society," the president told the League of United Latin American Citizens in July, promotes "a policy of justice and fairness toward those who come to America to live and work." It was also compassionate. Immigration reform was "an important part of a compassionate America," said Bush in Hudson, Wisconsin in August. "I mean, why would you want to have a system where the employer is illegal, the worker is illegal, and if the worker gets harmed, he or she is fearful of bringing a complaint for fear of not being able to fulfill their function?"[35]

But Bush's position did not go far enough for many Catholics. Donald Kerwin, executive director of the bishops' Catholic Legal Immigration Network (CLINIC), complained that the Bush plan did not offer a path to permanent residency. The immigrants "would be here with their families, building up equities," Kerwin explained, "and yet after the six years they would be facing deportation." Rather than waiting in a fifteen-to-twenty-year line for lawful reentry into the United States, Verghese Chirayath wrote in *America* in May, "It is most likely that after their six years are up, the workers will not return to their home countries, but will go into hiding in the U.S." Echoing "Strangers No Longer," Coadjutor Bishop Thomas Wenski of Orlando advocated "truly comprehensive immigration reform that will provide opportunities for legalization for the undocumented currently living in the United States, [and] temporary worker provisions with full protections and a path to permanency."[36]

"The immigration officer is in back; they're getting everybody," a coworker warned Olga Santana, an undocumented Mexican restaurant worker in Green Bay, Wisconsin in June. But it was too late, as immigration officers arrested her along with eleven others. When the day of Olga's deportation hearing arrived, however, Sister Melanie Maczka, who operated a resource center for Green Bay's Hispanic immigrants, drove to Chicago to testify for her. Not only was Santana the only one of the twelve to avoid deportation, but nine years later the single mother of three would become a United States citizen. "If there literally was no hope for you to provide for your family," Sister Maczka would recount her testimony, "wouldn't you go somewhere else?"[37]

George W. Bush thought so, and in the midst of the 2004 presidential campaign, the president inched closer to the church's stance. In his October 13 debate with Kerry, Bush espoused earned legalization alongside more aggressive border control and workplace enforcement. The Catholic challenger agreed, matching the incumbent president point by point.[38]

Most Americans disagreed. In the October aftermath of the 2001 invasion, 58 percent of Americans polled by Gallup wanted to reduce immigration, and as of January 2004, 55 percent opposed Bush's guest worker proposal. So the president would have every reason to steer clear of the immigration minefield in his second term.[39]

But he wouldn't. "Mr. President, the Senate Republicans recently listed their priorities, and immigration reform wasn't on it," a reporter observed at Bush's press conference in January 2005. "It will be one of my priorities," the president replied.[40]

Immigration also remained a priority for the U.S. Catholic bishops. The bishops "have grown increasingly disturbed by the current political discourse surrounding immigration," Washington, D.C.'s Theodore Cardinal McCarrick, a consultant to the USCCB's Committee on Migration, lamented at a press conference in May, "in which newcomers are characterized as a threat to our nation and not a benefit." McCarrick praised the president for swimming against the political tide in pursuing immigration reform. "If he hadn't begun the conversation," the cardinal said of the president, "this issue wouldn't be on the table."[41]

McCarrick nonetheless took aim at Bush's guest worker proposal, complaining that it would do little to reunite the families whom illegal immigration had torn apart. The cardinal therefore announced that the bishops were joining with over a dozen other Catholic groups to launch Justice for Immigrants, a campaign "to try to change the laws so that immigrants can support their families in dignity, families can remain united, and the human rights of all are respected." The effort would seek to educate the public, create legal networks to assist immigrants, and shape public opinion in favor of immigration reform. McCarrick cited the twenty-year shift in Catholic opinion from support to opposition to the death penalty as an example of the effectiveness of such a campaign.[42]

Justice for Immigrants would utilize the USCCB's Migration and Refugee Services, Catholic Campaign for Human Development, Office of Domestic Social Development, Office of International Justice and Peace, Secretariat for Hispanic Affairs, and Catholic Legal Immigration Network. It would also enlist the Catholic

Health Association, Catholic Charities, Catholic Relief Services, National Catholic Association of Diocesan Directors of Hispanic Ministry, National Council of Catholic Women, National Catholic Education Association, United States Jesuit Conference, Leadership Conference of Women Religious, Conference of Major Superiors of Men, National Association of State Catholic Conference Directors, Catholic Migrant Farmworker Network, Irish Apostolate USA, and Roundtable, an association of diocesan social action directors.[43]

The campaign was off to a rocky start on Capitol Hill, where the House of Representatives was debating a measure sponsored by Republican congressman James Sensenbrenner of Wisconsin, chairman of the Judiciary Committee, which would build a 700-mile fence along the U.S.-Mexico border, would tighten worker verification, and would not only transform first-time illegal immigration from a civil offense to a felony, but would make assisting irregular immigrants a felony as well. An amendment by California Democrat Howard Berman, which would have created a guest worker program similar to the Bush proposal, failed in committee.[44]

"It is an extremely punitive bill which is far broader than illegal immigration, and if enacted, would unduly harm immigrants and their families," San Bernardino Bishop Gerald Barnes, chairman of the USCCB Committee on Migration, wrote House members on December 14. "Moreover, the bishops are deeply disappointed by the bill's enforcement–only focus and absence of reforms in the U.S. legal system that would address our current immigration problems more comprehensively."[45]

Two days later, the House passed the bill anyway. The Border Protection, Antiterrorism, and Illegal Immigration Control Act of 2005 sailed through by a 239–182 vote. If the bill ever became law, Roger Cardinal Mahony of Los Angeles declared in March 2006, he would instruct the priests of his archdiocese to defy it. But there was little chance the Sensenbrenner bill would survive the Senate, where Catholic Democrat Edward Kennedy of Massachusetts and Republican John McCain of Arizona had introduced legislation which would afford undocumented aliens a way to citizenship.[46]

Kennedy and McCain's Secure America and Orderly Immigration Act won the endorsement of the president. "I know people are saying, 'well, the House bill didn't have a temporary-worker program in there,'" Bush told a group of foreign journalists in March, "and I think any bill should be a comprehensive bill, including a temporary worker program."[47]

The Kennedy-McCain approach also won the qualified endorsement of the bishops, for whom Bishop Barnes had testified before the Senate Judiciary Committee in favor of an expanded guest-worker program, earned legalization, and easier family reunification. "It is this proposed legislation," *America's* editors approved, "that most closely reflects the thinking of the U.S. and Mexican bishops in their 2003 pastoral."[48]

Finding themselves on the same side for a change, the bishops and the president joined forces to press for passage of the Kennedy-McCain legislation. In March, eleven days before the Senate Judiciary Committee's verdict on the Kennedy-McCain bill, over 160 state Catholic Conference and diocesan social action workers participated in a conference call with USCCB lobbyists. "Put as much pressure on her as possible," Kevin Appleby, director of public policy at the bishops' Migration and Refugee Services, implored, urging the California representatives to prod that state's Democratic senator Diane Feinstein, viewed as a swing vote on the legislation. As for Catholic Republican Sam Brownback of Kansas, a co-sponsor of the bill whom Majority Leader Bill Frist of Tennessee was trying to dissuade, Appleby advised the Kansas bishops' conference, "He needs as much love as we can give him."[49]

By the end of the month, the Senate Judiciary Committee had approved Kennedy-McCain. Feinstein joined all the other Democrats, while Brownback was one of only two Republicans who voted to send the bill to the floor. The committee action heartened the bishops. In an April letter to all senators, Bishop Barnes lauded the legislation for permitting agricultural workers already in the United States to legalize their status and seek permanent residency, and for allowing all the children of irregular immigrants to regularize their status and attend college as state residents.[50]

The committee's decision also encouraged the president, who invited fifteen religious, business, agricultural, and political leaders to the White House in April. Bush praised the gathering's "constructive and important dialogue" on immigration reform. "If Congress handled things the way that meeting was handled," said Denver Archbishop Charles Chaput, one of three church representatives at the conclave, "we'd be in good shape."[51]

The bishops and the president would have been in better shape if more Catholics had agreed with them on the Senate bill, but there was much disagreement, especially from the right. *First Things* editor Rev. Richard Neuhaus would decry Cardinal Mahony's "conceptually confused but unmistakable attack on the nation-state . . . which has no warrant in Catholic social doctrine." New York Republican representative Peter King regretted that "it's become politically correct within the Catholic Church to take these very liberal positions." Fox News host Bill O'Reilly deplored the Catholic "sanctuary churches" which helped undocumented migrants "evade authorities," including the Long Island parish where "I was an altar boy." Colorado Republican congressman Thomas Tancredo, a former Catholic and current defender of the punitive Sensenbrenner bill, reminded Archbishop Chaput that "a majority of churchgoers" disapproved of comprehensive immigration reform. The archbishop did not argue with the congressman, adding that "we need to educate, educate, educate."[52]

There were also numerous Catholic opponents of the House bill, who attacked it from the left. Cardinal Mahony called for prayer and fasting to undo the House's damage. Tulsa Bishop Edward Slattery and Milwaukee Auxiliary Bishop Richard Sklba embraced

Mahony's earlier pledge of noncooperation should the House bill become law. "When it becomes a crime to love the poor and serve their needs, then I will be the first to go to jail for this crime," Bishop Slattery vowed, "and I pray that every priest and every deacon in this diocese will have the courage to walk with me into the prison."[53]

Over 100 cities held rallies to denounce Sensenbrenner's enforcement-only prescription, which Bush now said he could support. "I look across this historic gathering and I see the future of America," Senator Kennedy addressed 500,000 protesters on the National Mall. "I want to pray for all the Representatives and Senators and the president of the United States, because they have become atheists," Rev. José Hoyos, head of the Spanish apostolate for the diocese of Arlington, Virginia, said when he spoke at the rally sponsored by the Washington Archdiocese's Office of Justice and Service, Catholic Charities of the Arlington Diocese, and the Catholic social justice lobby Network. "If they were Christians they would not pass this kind of law." Recalling that fifty years earlier his predecessor Patrick Cardinal O' Boyle had repudiated racial discrimination at a similar event, Cardinal McCarrick told the throng that "we gather in prayerful protest against another [kind of] discrimination, that of the immigrant who comes to our country seeking a better life for himself and his family."

Some of those immigrants were among those listening to Cardinal McCarrick. "We are the ones who make people's houses," said Verónica Artuga, a student at Freedom High School in nearby Woodbridge, Virginia. "We're people who just want to work," added Romel Palomino, who had arrived in Washington from El Salvador twenty-eight years earlier. "We're not criminals."[54]

And down the street other Catholics were listening to the immigrants. In a letter to the bishops a week after the Washington rally, Representative Sensenbrenner, along with Catholics Henry Hyde of Illinois and Peter King of New York, all fervent advocates of the House bill, promised to work to remove its prohibition of "Good

Samaritans" aiding the undocumented, and to reduce its penalties for being in the country unlawfully.[55]

A week later, sensing a shift in the political landscape, Cardinals Mahony, McCarrick, and William Keeler of Baltimore met at the White House with Bush's political maven, Deputy Chief of Staff Karl Rove, and other close aides to the president. While they supported most of the Senate bill, the cardinals informed Rove that they opposed its expedited removal of irregular aliens along the border and denial of protection to asylum seekers. Then, joined by Sean Cardinal O'Malley of Boston, they conveyed the same message on Capitol Hill to Catholic Democratic Senators Edward Kennedy of Massachusetts and Richard Durbin of Illinois as well as Democratic Senate Minority Leader Harry Reid of Nevada and Republican Senate Majority Leader Bill Frist of Tennessee.[56]

In May, in the first-ever nationally televised, prime-time presidential address on immigration, Bush returned to his support for a temporary worker program, earned legalization, and worker verification. But he also advocated requiring all immigrants to learn English, promised to double the Border Patrol, and, for the first time, proposed to deploy the National Guard on the border. Most of the public applauded, with 69 percent of the respondents in a Fox News poll backing a guest worker scheme, 74 percent embracing earned legalization, and 81 percent endorsing greater border protection. But Bishop Barnes transmitted the prelates' apprehension over "the introduction of military personnel, because there has not been an adequate public discussion about its implications, especially for the treatment of migrants." *Commonweal's* editors, while saluting Bush's attempt to "steer a middle course" between mass deportation and blanket amnesty, nevertheless called his dispatch of the National Guard "problematic."[57]

Some Catholics thought it was overdue. "Contrary to his faux-pious rhetoric," George Neumann wrote in *National Review Online*, Cardinal Mahony was "speaking not for the Catholic Church but for himself, using, in a textbook example of clericalism, the prestige and trappings of his Episcopal office to advance nothing more than his personal opinion in favor of open borders." Congressman King was even more blunt, suggesting that the bishops devote less attention to immigration and "spend more time protecting little boys from pedophile priests"—a pointed reminder of the American church's sexual abuse scandal.[58]

Within two weeks of the Bush speech, the Senate passed a version of the Kennedy-McCain legislation (now cosponsored by Pennsylvania Republican Arlen Specter) by a 62–36 tally, with twenty-three Republicans and one independent joining thirty-eight Democrats in the majority. The measure would permit those unauthorized entrants who had been in the United States for at least five years to apply for citizenship after undergoing background checks, paying fines and back taxes, and enrolling in English classes. It would allow those who had been in the country for between two and five years to apply for citizenship at border checkpoints. The bill would provide for 370 miles of border fencing, funding for more Border Patrol agents, and $20,000 fines for employers who hired unauthorized aliens. It also would create an H-2C guest worker visa. By including a path to citizenship and excluding a "Good Samaritan" clause penalizing those who aided undocumented immigrants, the Senate legislation differed greatly from the measure which had passed the House the previous year.[59]

Bishop Barnes, speaking for the United States Conference of Catholic Bishops, called the bill's passage "a historic moment for our nation." He nonetheless noted that the bishops did "not agree with each and every provision" in the legislation. While praising the bill's "comprehensive approach," he encouraged both houses of Congress to "make changes to our family-based immigration system to reduce the waiting time for families to be reunited," and to "either eliminate or ameliorate the harsh enforcement provisions found in both the House- and Senate-passed versions of the legislation."[60]

The president applauded the Senate vote. Yet the House and Senate could not bridge their vast differences. Bush would sign an immigration bill in 2006, but not the one he and the bishops wanted. Instead, he enacted the Secure Fence Act, which authorized seven hundred more miles of fencing along parts of the U.S.-Mexican boundary, and a "virtual fence" along most of it. By the end of 2006 his administration would double the number of arrests of irregular immigrants and the number of Border Patrol agents over the previous year.[61]

By then midterm election-year politics had intervened, with members of both parties running against the president on immigration reform—Republicans from the right and Democrats from the left. Immigration again took a back seat to Iraq and the economy in November 2006, as Democrats recovered control of both houses of Congress for the first time in a dozen years. The existence of more Democratic advocates of comprehensive immigration reform and fewer Republican opponents on Capitol Hill seemed to bode well for the president and the bishops. At the Democratic House of Representatives retreat in February 2007, Catholic Luis Gutiérrez of Illinois urged Bush to reignite the immigration campaign.[62]

He would. Bush traveled the country touting the Kennedy-McCain bill, now co-sponsored by Arizona Republican Senator Jon Kyl. "Now is the time," Bush told the National Catholic Prayer Breakfast in April 2007, "for the United States Congress to get a bill to my desk that I can sign."[63]

But, in an effort to overcome the chasm with the House of Representatives, this bill was quite different from the previous one. Although the 2007 version contained more lenient legalization guidelines than the 2006 Senate bill, it was less clear in ensuring a path to citizenship. It replaced some family-based visas with work-based visas. Rather than providing provisional visas to temporary workers as the 2006 measure had, the new bill mandated that the guest laborers return home after two years and work in the United

States for a total of no more than six years. And the new legislation included stricter worker verification and fewer due process provisions for detainees than the old one.[64]

The United States Conference of Catholic Bishops again enlisted in the lobbying effort, sending Orlando Bishop Thomas Wenski to Capitol Hill to testify before the House Subcommittee on Citizenship, Refugees, Border Security, and International Law in favor of the Senate bill. "As providers of pastoral and social services to immigrants throughout the nation," the bishop began," we in the Catholic Church witness the human consequences of a broken immigration system every day in our parishes, social service programs, hospitals, and schools. Families are divided, migrant workers are exploited and abused, and human beings unnecessarily die in the American desert."

Bishop Wenski then devoted nearly all of his statement to bemoaning what the Senate legislation had excluded. He implored the committee to add a path to permanent residency for temporary workers, to restore the parents of native-born citizens to the family preference system, to delete the requirement that aliens return to their home countries before applying for permanent citizenship, to strengthen due process protections for detainees, and to curtail the indefinite detention of aliens awaiting deportation decisions. Unlike the president, the bishop demonstrated little concern for border enforcement, devoting only five sentences of his over thirteen pages to the topic. Alongside a nebulous nod to "security," Wenski conveyed the bishops' gratitude for the Border Patrol's valiant efforts to "identify and rescue migrants who are in distress." And he said nothing about worker verification.[65]

Some Catholics were tired of waiting for the Senate bill. In May, inspired by the example of Chicago minister Rev. Walter Coleman's providing refuge for Elvira Arellano in his Methodist church, the ecumenical New Sanctuary Movement was born in Chicago, New York, Los Angeles, San Diego, and Seattle. This reincarnation of the

Sanctuary effort of the 1980s, which had shielded Central American refugees, promised food, clothing, shelter, and legal and physical protection for the undocumented. "We want to put a human face to the very complex immigration laws and awaken the consciousness of the human spirit," Rev. Richard Estrada, associate pastor of Our Lady Queen of Angels Catholic parish in Los Angeles, said to explain why his church would be harboring a Guatemalan gardener.[66]

The advent of the New Sanctuary Movement would make the legislative task of McCain, Kennedy, and Bush even more difficult. "I think that they need to consider the fact that they might place themselves in jeopardy, in terms of violation of federal law," former immigration officer Brian Perryman said in reacting to this latest exercise of civil disobedience, "and I'm not talking about misdemeanors. I'm talking about felonies." Immigration and Customs Enforcement spokeswoman Virginia Kice reminded the NSM's founders of her agency's "authority to arrest those who are in violation of our immigration laws anywhere in the United States." She did not indicate, however, whether that authority ended at the doors of a church.[67]

"We believe that what we are doing is really calling forth a higher law," Kim Bobo of the immigrant advocacy group Interfaith Worker Justice said in defense of the new movement, "which is really God's law, of caring for the immigrant." But not all Catholics agreed. Some churches feared the legal consequences about which Perryman and Kice warned. Still others did not share Bobo's conception of God's law. "Christ expected his followers to treat criminals in prison the way they would treat him," wrote Brooke Levitske of the Acton Institute for the Study of Religion and Liberty, "but he said nothing about busting them out of prison." She added that "American churches ought to venerate and cherish the law because it is the guarantor of religious freedom." The rule of law, after all, was the "sustainer of the free and prosperous society that draws immigrants to the States."[68]

And the law could always change. In June, Illinois Democrat Barack Obama unsuccessfully sponsored an amendment, backed by the bishops, to replace the Senate bill's provision for rewarding permanent resident status according to the nation's economic climate with the existing system's reliance on family preference. But another amendment to curtail the measure's temporary worker plan after five years, proposed by North Dakota Democrat Byron Dorgan and endorsed by Obama and organized labor, passed by only a single vote, seriously jeopardizing the legislation.[69]

"He was awful," Republican Senator Lindsay Graham of South Carolina, a staunch partisan of the Kennedy-McCain-Kyl bill, would unjustly single out Obama. "I hated his guts. I thought he was so disingenuous."[70]

By July, "we were within a vote or two of getting the comprehensive reform bill passed," Bush would recall. So he asked the new Senate Majority Leader Harry Reid of Nevada to hold the Senate in session over the weekend before the Fourth of July recess. Instead, Reid called a cloture vote to cut off debate on a comprehensive reform measure authored by Republicans Chuck Hagel of Nebraska and Mel Martínez of Florida. When the cloture vote failed, Reid simply adjourned the Senate. Then, Bush would remember, "Senators went home and listened to angry constituents stirred up by loud voices on radio and TV." If immigration reform had passed the Senate, however, "we didn't have 218 votes" to win in the House, Congressman Gutierrez would recall.[71]

Even the children of the undocumented found themselves in the middle of the increasingly turgid national debate. The Development, Relief, and Education for Alien Minds (DREAM) Act offered those offspring of unauthorized entrants who were not themselves born in the United States temporary and potentially permanent legal status as a reward for two years of college or military service. But the legislation could not muster the sixty votes necessary to surmount a Senate filibuster. "Instead of investing in young persons who will return three-fold what we put into their education," the USCBB's Appleby lamented, Congress had succumbed to the "politics of immigration."[72]

And many Catholics continued to immerse themselves in it. From 2005 to 2007 workplace arrests of undocumented immigrants had increased tenfold. In December 2006 alone, Immigration and Customs Enforcement (ICE) agents apprehended almost 1,300 immigrants in six cities. "They told us not to run, but to sit down," Salvadoran worker María Ayala said, describing the March 2007 raid at the Michael Bianco clothing factory in New Bedford, Massachusetts. The ICE agents handcuffed Ayala and her fellow laborers, then deprived them of food and water for most of the day. "A worker doesn't deserve that kind of treatment," Rev. Richard Wilson, pastor of New Bedford's Our Lady of Guadalupe Church, asserted, opening his doors to the Bianco workers.[73]

Resistance by the churches of the New Sanctuary Movement to this more aggressive law enforcement spread to about fifty cities. In February 2008, Bishop John Wester of Salt Lake City, chairman of the USCCB Committee on Migration, and Coadjutor Bishop Jaime Soto of Sacramento, chairman of the Catholic Legal Immigration Network (CLINIC), wrote Homeland Security Secretary Michael Chertoff, appealing for an end to raids by ICE agents "near churches, schools, hospitals, and social service agencies."[74]

In April, the Democratic House of Representatives earned accolades from Catholic immigration activists for its passage of a bill extending a visa program for religious workers. Yet the introduction of another House measure indefinitely detaining immigrants until they learned of their status provoked a stern letter of protest from Network, the Xaverian Brothers, Catholic Charities of Houston and Syracuse, and sisters from the Maryknoll, Dominican, and Immaculate Heart of Mary orders.[75]

Even the pope seemingly could not rise above the country's toxic tone. In April, Pope Benedict XVI, while meeting with President

Bush in Washington, delicately promoted immigrant rights and family reunification, while adroitly evading the details of the American dilemma. While meeting with the U.S. bishops, the pontiff spoke of immigrants as "people of faith," adding that "we are here to welcome them."[76]

The pope's generous generalities were nonetheless specific enough to incite predictable reactions from both sides of the country's—and the church's—political divide. Representative Tancredo snarled that the Holy Father's "job description" did not entitle him to "engage in American politics." Cardinal Mahony viewed Pope Benedict's statements as not-so-veiled references to the ICE raids at five chicken plants that had resulted in the arrests of over 200 alleged undocumented immigrants. Though federal officials insisted that the timing was coincidental, Cardinal Mahony saw things differently. "I thought it was very inappropriate" to conduct the raids "in such a blatant way when the Pope was coming," the cardinal maintained, "when he has been so outspoken in defending the rights of immigrants."[77]

The pope was not just speaking, however. While the Holy Father was touring the United States, his Pontifical Commission for Latin America was funding one-sixth of the cost of construction of a Brothers on the Path shelter for Central American emigrants in southern Mexico. From the shelter in the city of Ixpetec along the Isthmus of Tehuantepec, the refugees would ride freight trains to the northern border of Mexico before unlawfully entering the United States. "The Church's mission is to provide assistance to people in need," Kevin Appleby of the United States Conference of Catholic Bishops Migration and Refugee Services said in defense of the pope's donation, which would help safeguard the Central Americans from Mexican violence. "There's no broader intention to promote illegal immigration."[78]

There would be more immigration raids—and more indignation from the Catholic power structure. In May, ICE agents stormed a Postville, Iowa meatpacking plant, arresting over 200 employees for aggravated identity theft, fraudulent use of Social Security numbers, and violation of U.S. immigration laws. Over 400 undocumented parishioners found refuge in Postville's St. Bridget Catholic Church, where they stayed for six days and consumed over a thousand meals. Most of the workers accepted a plea deal that dropped the identity theft charges in return for a five-month detention and the elimination of any possibility of legal permanent residency or citizenship. "Some of the weakest members among us are bearing the brunt of the suffering," Archbishop Jerome Hanus of Dubuque said in reaction to the raid of the factory in his diocese, "while legislators and other leaders, as well as many of us in the general public, have failed to give the issue the priority it deserves."[79]

In September, while the bishops' administrative board was meeting in Washington, ICE was executing raids in New Mexico and Rhode Island. "We have witnessed firsthand the suffering of immigrant families," Bishop Wester spoke for his fellow prelates, "and are gravely concerned about the collateral human consequences of immigration enforcement raids on the family unit." Bishop Thomas Tobin of Providence, Rhode Island joined fifteen Catholic pastors in that state in calling for a moratorium on such actions.[80]

There would be no moratorium. In October, Bush began to implement the Secure Communities program, which expanded President Clinton's 1996 pilot programs to fourteen jurisdictions, authorizing local law enforcement officials to fingerprint, detain, and deport criminal aliens. "We will continue to enforce the law and, I would stress, we do that in a professional way," ICE spokeswoman Kelly Nantel responded to the bishops' outrage, "with an acute awareness of the impact that enforcement has on the individuals we encounter."[81]

The bishops remained unpersuaded. "In truth, intermittent work-site raids, increased local law enforcement, and the creation of a wall along parts of our southern border, among other efforts, have done little to address the challenges presented by illegal immigration," Bishop Thomas Wenski of Orlando, chairman of the USCCB Committee on International Justice and Peace, concluded in the *Washington Post* in October, two weeks before the 2008 presidential election. "Seventy percent of the undocumented have lived in this country five years or more," Wenksi wrote, "and have no homes to return to." The bishop abhorred the "policy vacuum" which had emanated from the failure of comprehensive immigration reform. So did many of the Catholic rank and file. An October Zogby poll commissioned by the bishops discovered 69 percent of Catholics in favor of earned legalization, up from 49 percent just two years before.[82]

And so did George W. Bush. "If I had it to do over again, I would have pushed for immigration reform, rather than Social Security [reform], as the first major initiative of my second term," the president would relate. "The wildfire of opposition that erupted in 2006 and 2007 might not have raged as hot in 2005," before the Iraq War and the American economy took turns for the worse and the midterm election campaign energized the outer edges of both parties.

Bush hoped that "at the minimum, I was able to take some of the shock out of the third rail." He wished that "our work on Social Security and immigration reform will provide a foundation for a future president to reform both."[83]

John McCain would not be that future president. The Republican heir apparent, shell-shocked by his party's rejection of comprehensive immigration reform, won the GOP nomination by stressing enforcement and renouncing amnesty. Then the forlorn champion of comprehensive immigration reform lost the election anyway, to Illinois Democratic senator Barack Obama, who had once supported the Kennedy-McCain bill. But, in an unfortunate omen for Catholic immigration advocates, Obama didn't want to talk about it either.

Conclusions

The horror of September 11, 2001, regrettably produced a radically restrictionist climate which victimized refugees and undocumented workers alike. By the end of the George W. Bush administration, however, the populace and the president had largely returned to the center of the immigration debate. But unfortunately for the nation, too many House Republicans, Senate Democrats, and Catholic immigration activists clung tenaciously to the extremes, and an increasingly unpopular president could not move them to the middle.

Catholic refugee activists had little reason to cheer the Bush years. The president signed the Real ID law, dramatically reduced the refugee ceiling, returned almost all Haitian exiles, perpetuated the alleged double standard between Haitians and Cubans, and denied Temporary Protected Status to Haitian hurricane victims. Even the rise of refugee admissions from their post-9/11 nadir could not assuage Bush's Catholic critics.

On immigration reform the record was somewhat better. Catholic admissionists were elated when the House of Representatives pared a dozen anti-immigration portions from its post-9/11 intelligence legislation in 2002, when the Senate passed comprehensive immigration reform in 2006, and when Bush lobbied for the 2006 and 2007 Senate bills. They helped persuade House Republicans to reconsider the "Good Samaritan" provisions of their 2005 legislation, they helped convince each other to join forces in Justice for Immigrants in 2005, and they helped coax the public toward comprehensive reform by the end of the Bush years.

But Catholic immigration advocates were despondent when Bush transferred the Immigration and Naturalization Service to the new Department of Homeland Security; signed the 2002 Enhanced Border Security and Visa Entry Reform Act without temporary extension of permanent resident status for long-time residents;

and pursued greater immigration enforcement through the Secure Communities initiative, workplace raids, belated support for the 2005 House bill, and calls for more fencing, Border Patrol, and even the National Guard to police the country's southern border. The failure of the DREAM Act discouraged them; the founding of the New Sanctuary Movement divided them.

Yet the disappointments of the Bush years emboldened them. Rather than revisit their immigration positions, the bishops and other Catholic admissionists reinforced them. Their calls for legalization became cries for citizenship. Their attitude toward border enforcement went from begrudging acknowledgment to unabashed antipathy. They practiced cooperation in the Senate, but, to the detriment of their cause and of the country, they incited conflict almost everywhere else.

5. Barack Obama

2009–2013

FOR BARACK OBAMA, immigration was ethnic. Himself the son of a Kenyan immigrant, the president "with the funny name" understood that, although over 40 percent of the country's unauthorized population were those with expired visas, the issue had largely attached itself to Latinos, until 2011 the country's fastest-growing minority and, despite inroads by Ronald Reagan and George W. Bush, a reliable Democratic voting bloc.[1]

Just when many Hispanics, most of whom were Catholic, were growing as disillusioned with this president's performance on immigration issues as they had with his predecessors, he abruptly changed course to a more inclusionist view. But he postponed comprehensive immigration reform until after his reelection, so Catholic leaders still found themselves in a familiar position for much of his tenure—opposite the president. Then, when the Senate controlled by the president's party passed a bill supported by Catholic leaders, the Republican House of Representatives refused to vote and the Catholic leaders refused to budge. Democrats had never seemed so distant from Republicans, and the Catholic hierarchy had never seemed so far from the Catholic rank and file.

Refugees

No American president, it seemed, could avoid dealing with a crisis in Haiti. In February 2009, Department of Homeland Security Director of Policy Susan Cullen announced that the Obama administration would continue its predecessor's policy of deporting undocumented Haitians. So in March, Francis Cardinal George of Chicago again wrote to the White House, urging Obama, as he had George W. Bush, to grant Temporary Protected Status as a "mantle of protection" aimed at "alleviating the suffering of the Haitian people." But again, the president refused the entreaties of the cardinal.[2]

And again, accusations of a double standard emerged from Catholic quarters. "Over the past decades," *America*'s editors reminded the new administration, "people of Haiti's neighbor island, Cuba, received far more generous treatment from the United States" under the Special Cuban Migration Program of 1994, which granted 20,000 annual visas to Cubans and allowed those without visas to seek asylum upon reaching American shores. "By contrast, the policy toward Haiti has been harsh, marked by mandatory detention and lack of access to counsel."[3]

And that was *before* a monstrous earthquake rocked Haiti in January 2010. About 250,000 Haitians lost their lives, and the Inter-American Development Bank estimated that the disaster robbed Haiti of between 8 and 14 billion dollars. By the end of the year Haiti was in the throes of a cholera epidemic which infected over 500,000 people, or 5 percent of the country's population. Within two years, a ruthless tropical storm had pelted the makeshift tents housing the 400,000 displaced survivors of the 2010 earthquake.[4]

This unholy trinity of environmental calamities inflicted even more despair upon a long-suffering populace, whose economy was already so feeble that remittances from Haitians abroad were accounting for one-fifth of it. But these tragedies awakened the innate generosity of the American government and its people. Public and private pledges of relief assistance exceeded 4 billion dollars, thanks to an international campaign spearheaded by former presidents Bill Clinton and George W. Bush. Yet by August 2012, the United Nations could account for less than half of those funds. "People are feeling very angry, very frustrated, very let down," said Ken Hackett, president of Catholic Charities, which was overseeing the recovery effort. "In terms of challenge, this rivals anything I have seen in forty years and probably supersedes it," Hackett reflected on his way to a Mass concelebrated by Robert Cardinal Sarah of the Pontifical Council for Unum (the Vatican's humanitarian relief agency), New Orleans Archbishop Gregory Aymond, and Portland, Maine Archbishop Richard Malone on the first anniversary of the earthquake.[5]

Donald Kerwin, vice president for programs at the Migration Policy Institute, was among those Catholic voices assailing the Obama administration's refugee policies in the aftermath of the latest Haitian tragedies. "After the 2010 Haitian earthquake, the Obama administration announced that it would continue to intercept and repatriate Haitians by boat, and would detain those who reached the United States," Kerwin wrote. "On January 20, 2011, DHS [the Department of Homeland Security] resumed deportations to Haiti. One [individual in] the first groups of deportees reportedly died of cholera within a week of his return."[6]

Beyond Haiti, in September 2009 the administration had undertaken a review of its refugee assistance programs. It pledged "robust refugee assistance" by fiscal year 2013.[7]

Three months later the administration had revised the Bush policy of incarcerating asylum seekers while they awaited the adjudication of their claims. According to Edward Alden of the Council on Foreign Relations, the White House "wants to demonstrate that it's possible to be tough without being unfair and inhumane."[8]

The Obama administration admitted 56,424, or 70 percent, of all refugees referred by the United Nations High Commission on Refugees to be resettled in the United States in FY 2011. In FY 2013, 27, 546 immigrants filed "credible fear" asylum claims, up from 10,730 the year before and 3,273 in FY 2008. But noting that "asylum filings and grants have decreased since 2001," Kerwin decried the 9/11 mentality which continued to undergird U.S. refugee policy under Barack Obama, as it had under George W. Bush. Mark Hetfield, president of the Hebrew Immigrant Aid Society, added that "removals at the border soared from 113,462 in FY 2008 to 240,363 in FY 2012." The bishops also expressed concern about a pilot program launched by the State Department to institute DNA testing to combat fraudulent claims by alleged family members seeking to join asylees in the United States. Seyou Berhe, a Somali-born official with the refugee service of the Archdiocese of Arlington, Virginia, observed that in many developing countries, "family" was not simply a biological term. "If my brother were killed in Somalia, and I saved his child," Berhe explained, "according to my culture, that child is mine."[9]

Immigration Reform Before 2012

"As soon as this election is over and a new government is sworn in," Archbishop José Gómez of San Antonio told the Missouri Catholic Conference in his keynote address in October 2008, "we need to insist that our leaders roll up their sleeves and get to work on comprehensive immigration reform." A month later, Barack Obama, who backed earned citizenship, border control, and workplace enforcement, handily won the election over John McCain, whose comprehensive immigration reform bill had failed the previous year.[10]

Even before he took the oath of office, President-elect Obama met in January 2009 with Mexican President Felipe Calderón, who had instituted a policy of amnesty for undocumented migrants making their way through his country to the United States. Obama assured Calderón that they shared a desire to repair "the broken U.S. immigration system" by "fostering safe, legal, and orderly migration."[11]

Yet the American president seemed in no hurry to do so. Having been elected largely due to the financial meltdown which had discredited the Bush administration's economic stewardship, Obama set out to fix the American economy sooner, and deal with immigration reform later. "To some degree the collapse of housing construction in the country slowed down the flow of illegal immigrants to the country," the new president explained to reporters in March. And, he added, "Obviously, we've got a lot on our plate right now."[12]

Even some American Catholic bishops were counseling patience. Bishops Elden Curtis of Omaha, Fabian Bruskewitz of Lincoln, and William Dendinger of Grand Island conducted listening sessions throughout Nebraska, after a federal immigration raid at a Swift plant in Grand Island had drawn national attention. "As believers in the message of Jesus Christ," the prelates observed, "we Catholics need to realize the positive effect that respect, understanding, charity, patience, and hospitality can have for these, our brothers and sisters in the body of Christ."[13]

In June, Obama assembled legislative leaders at the White House to discuss comprehensive immigration reform. "We had a big 'Rah, rah, let's do immigration reform meeting,'" Senator McCain would remember. But there was no follow-up. There was still too much acrimony between the 2008 presidential candidates, both of whom had retreated from their once solid support for comprehensive immigration reform. "My hands aren't totally clean in this, either," McCain admitted, adding that "I was never called again."[14]

In August, to preempt further judicial activity, Immigration and Customs Enforcement director John Morton announced the closing of the Don Hutto Family Residential Facility in Taylor, Texas, an immigration detention center whose abysmal conditions had prompted a lawsuit by the American Civil Liberties Union. Morton also promised to assess the rest of the detention system, which was housing over three times as many immigrants as it had only a decade earlier.[15]

Morton's announcement heartened those in the vanguard of the immigration reform movement, such as Pat Murphy and JoAnn Pesch, two elderly Sisters of Mercy who were devoting their twilight years to ministering to immigrant detainees in the Chicago area. Twice a week for almost three years, they had been visiting McHenry County Jail in Woodstock, Illinois, where about 250 of the 650 inmates were unauthorized migrants awaiting deportation. And every Friday, they were traveling to the federal detention center in Broadview, the final step in the deportation process, where they prayed the rosary and boarded buses with those who had received deportation sentences, along with a couple dozen other clergy and lay immigration activists who had enlisted in the Sisters' army. "The immigrant detainees are different than the criminal detainees," Sister Persch asserted. "They most likely are never going to see their families (in the States) again. And they're going back to places that they don't know." The unassuming nun then downplayed her selfless efforts. "It's like in an emergency room when they bring the chaplain in," she stated matter-of-factly. "There's nothing you can do, but your presence, your compassion, your prayer . . . brings comfort to them."[16]

There was much an American president could do about immigration reform, but this chief executive decided not to try. By this time Obama's major priority had shifted from the still struggling economy to the country's ailing health care system, which he had pledged to reform. In his September health care message to Congress, Obama promised universal coverage—except for irregular immigrants. "You lie!" South Carolina Republican representative Joe Wilson bellowed, interrupting the president.[17]

As Obama tried to evade the contentious conflict over immigration, the bishops were determined to return him to it. Six Hispanic bishops met with members of Congress in September to urge them to include the undocumented in any health care legislation. "The reason this comes up," Coadjutor Bishop Jamie Soto of Sacramento reminded the president and the nation, "is Congress has previously failed to deal with comprehensive immigration reform."[18]

But that was about to change, the administration and the

bishops agreed. "I've been dealing hands-on with immigration issues since 1993," Obama's Catholic Secretary of Homeland Security (and former Democratic governor of Arizona) Janet Napolitano recalled, "and what I have seen makes reform far more attainable this time around." The passage of Obama's health care proposal would "mean there's a momentum in the country" for comprehensive immigration reform, Bishop John Wester, chairman of the USCCB Migration Committee, forecast from the bishops' meeting in Baltimore in November.

To make these dreams come true, the bishops authorized a massive postcard campaign coupled with a social media blitz on Facebook and Twitter, to help entice Congress to take up comprehensive immigration reform. "We want to increase Catholic grassroots support for immigration reform," Antonio Cube, national manager for the bishops' Justice for Immigrants campaign, said as he introduced this latest effort, "but we also want to show members of Congress a strong Catholic voice and strong Catholic numbers in support of immigration reform."[19]

Then Congress passed Obama's health care plan, the Affordable Care Act, on a party-line vote. So many Catholics hoped for the momentum which Bishop Wester had expected. Speaking to a crowd of 250,000 on the National Mall in March 2010, Los Angeles's Roger Cardinal Mahony promised that the church would not relent in its commitment to comprehensive immigration reform.[20]

But the administration would. The president invited a group of immigration advocates to the White House in March, only to tell them they should be up the street on Capitol Hill instead. He could do nothing, Obama insisted, without the support of Congress. "I am not a king," said the president.[21]

That evening, at a meeting with a group of congressmen led by Illinois Catholic Democrat Luis Gutiérrez, Obama was more conciliatory. "Look who I am," said the country's first minority chief executive. He reassured his guests that he "knew what it feels like for people not to be treated fairly." Then he recalled his promise "to be your partner as we work to fix our broken system," and added that "that's a commitment that I reaffirm today."[22]

Yet only a month later, Obama told reporters aboard Air Force One that he would not be seeking comprehensive immigration reform in 2010. After not securing a single Republican vote for his health care initiative, the president would not bother to try to persuade the legislature on immigration reform. "I've been working Congress pretty hard," said Obama, "so I know there may not be an appetite immediately to dive into another controversial issue."[23]

Stymied in Washington, the bishops set their sights on Arizona, where the legislature was debating a bill which would require state and local police to verify the immigration status of those for whom they had a "reasonable suspicion" that the person might be in the country illegally. The impetus for the measure, S.B. 1070, was the unsolved murder of rancher Rob Krentz, whose wife Sue hoped that the legislation could do what her four a.m. rosaries had so far failed to do—"get me through this."[24]

Mrs. Krentz's bishop was praying for S.B. 1070's defeat. Bishops Thomas Olmstead of Phoenix, Gerald Kicanas of Tucson, and James Wall of Gallup, New Mexico (whose diocese includes part of Arizona) rejected the bill's "punitive" and "costly" procedures. "We know that past waves of immigrants to this country—many of whom were our grandparents and great-grandparents—were not barred from entering our nation, did not require documentation, [and] were not treated as criminals once they were here," Bishop Joseph Galante of Camden, New Jersey said in reacting to the legislation. "And we know from experience how they greatly enriched our nation."[25]

The church could not deter the state. After the bill passed and Republican governor Jan Brewer signed it at the end of April, Cardinal Mahony pilloried it as "the country's most retrogressive, mean-spirited, and useless anti-immigrant legislation." The cardinal nevertheless thanked the governor for rejuvenating the somnolent immigration reform movement. Mahony cited the haste with which the measure passed in the face of "a torrent of opposition generated across the country" as ballast for his counterintuitive conclusion.[26]

The torrent of opposition reached the White House. "Our failure to act responsibly at the federal level will only open the door to irresponsibility by others," President Obama contended at a naturalization ceremony for service members in April, "and that includes, for example, the recent efforts in Arizona, which threaten to undermine basic notions of fairness that we cherish as Americans." A month later, however, U.S. District Court judge Susan Bolton encouraged the bishops and the president by blocking enforcement of key tenets of the Arizona law.[27]

As much as he wanted to set immigration reform aside, events were conspiring to compel the president to confront it. A May visit by Mexican President Felipe Calderón was the next detour from Obama's preferred path. "With regard to the United States," Archbishop Rafael Romo Muñoz of Tijuana, head of the Mexican bishops' migration committee, and Bishop John Wester of Salt Lake City, chairman of the U.S. bishops' migration committee, responded to the Calderón-Obama meeting, "it is essential that immigration reform legislation become a priority."[28]

It would not. While Calderón was talking with Obama inside the White House, Representative Gutiérrez and those immigration advocates with whom Obama had met in March were shouting at Obama outside the White House. They joined four young undocumented migrants who had anticipated a DREAM Act, as well as hundreds of other immigration proponents. They were chanting, "Obama, *escuchas, estamos en la lucha* (Obama, listen, we're in the fight)!" Then the police handcuffed them and whisked them off to jail.

In June, Obama invited Colombian Juan Rodríguez, the only DREAM walker who had obtained resident status, to a meeting at the White House. When Rodríguez arrived, the president reached out to shake his hand. But Rodríguez turned away. A visibly angry Obama retorted, "Okay, I get it."

To Catholic immigration proponents, however, he still didn't. In July, Obama finally gave his first speech on immigration, but stopped short of promoting comprehensive immigration reform. He called for tougher border control, stricter workplace verification and, in a nod toward Juan Rodríguez, passage of the DREAM Act. "We should stop punishing innocent young people for the actions of their parents," said the president, "by denying them the chance to stay here and earn an education and contribute their talents to build the country where they grew up."[29]

Coming in the wake of the Arizona law and in the midst of the midterm election campaign, Obama's incremental approach offered little consolation to the Catholic champions of an all-out effort. The Obama speech "takes us practically no closer to the comprehensive reform the Church has long advocated," *America*'s editors grumbled, "than a no doubt vain attempt to pressure Congressional Republicans to go along with the process."[30]

The DREAM Act, attached to a defense authorization bill, fell in the Senate on a virtual party-line vote, 56–43, in September. Then in December, four days after a conference call with reporters by four of the bishops, it failed, 55–41, to overcome a GOP filibuster and obtain a floor vote. Catholic Charities president Rev. Larry Snyder pronounced his organization "deeply disappointed that the Senate rejected the vote on this important piece of legislation."[31]

At the end of November, following the Republican reconquest of the House of Representatives, Obama met with the congressional leaders of both parties to discuss the lame-duck session's legislative agenda. When the subject of the DREAM Act arose, Democratic Senate Majority Leader Harry Reid of Nevada, who owed his reelection in large part to Latino voters, nonetheless informed the president that he would not "waste time" trying to resurrect it.[32]

Yet bolstered by a Gallup poll showing 54 percent of Americans in favor of the DREAM Act, Catholic immigration advocates remained bullish on its prospects. After the outgoing Democratic Congress passed the Earned Income Tax Credit, child tax credits, and an expanded school lunch program, Kathy Saile, the United States Conference of Catholic Bishops' director of social development, boasted that the bishops were "batting a thousand." Kevin Appleby, director of policy and public affairs for the USCCB Office of Migration and Refugee Services, also stayed upbeat. "These issues take time to pass," said the battle-scarred veteran of the immigration wars, "even if the American public is ahead of the public officials."[33]

President Obama concurred. "This is a journey," he consoled his staff after the lame-duck Congress refused to revisit the DREAM Act, "and we will get there." The president compared the quest for immigration reform to the civil rights movement, recalling "how long those battles took." Obama nevertheless told reporters that the failure of the legislation was "maybe my biggest disappointment" of the just-completed congressional session.[34]

So a few days later Obama hosted Rep. Gutiérrez, New Jersey Senator Robert Menendez, and other Hispanic Democratic legislators at the White House. Conceding that the newly elected Republican House would never pass the DREAM Act, Obama solicited suggestions of how he might circumvent Capitol Hill. Gutiérrez and Menendez recommended that the president simply issue an executive order achieving at least some of the goals of the DREAM Act. As the meeting was ending, in a scene captured by White House photographer Pete Souza, erstwhile adversaries Obama and Gutiérrez smiled broadly and embraced.[35]

The smiles would not last. At the same time the Obama administration was pressing for the DREAM Act, it was deporting undocumented aliens at a record rate. Continuing George W. Bush's Secure Communities program, the Obama administration had by August 2011 reached a total of 126,000 deportations in almost three years.

That's when the Department of Homeland Security announced that it would be strengthening the program, by making local cooperation mandatory and by spreading the program throughout the nation by 2013.[36]

The administration's message could not have pleased the over two dozen Guatemalans attending a family reunion with eight former Agriprocessors workers in Postville, Iowa in December. "It was a very emotional moment," Sister Mary McCauley, a Sister of Charity of the Blessed Virgin Mary, related after she greeted the bus at St. Bridget Church. The scene was far different from the one which Sister McCauley had witnessed three years earlier, when ICE raided the Agriprocessors plant. Once again, "this room is filled with tears," she observed, but this time, "for a very different reason."[37]

Testifying before the House Judiciary Committee in January 2011, Coadjutor Archbishop José Gómez of Los Angeles, chair of the United States Conference of Catholic Bishops' Migration Committee, called upon Congress to "de-emphasize the use of workplace raids—in which immigrants are detained and families are separated" in the pursuit of deportation. "This is a short-sighted, bad faith approach," Martin Odom, executive director of the Catholic Legal Immigration Network (CLINIC) complained in speaking about the Secure Communities program, "aimed at securing the highest number of deportations regardless of the desires of communities or the human cost." According to "the Department of Homeland Security's own figures," CLINIC claimed, 79 percent of the Secure Communities deportees had allegedly committed minor offenses—or no offenses at all.

Alison Posner, CLINIC's director of advocacy, worried that crime victims and witnesses would be reluctant to cooperate with police for fear of deportation. "Certainly the bishops acknowledge that the government has the right to pursue this program," the USCCB's Kevin Appleby admitted. "We just wonder if it is the most humane approach."[38]

These criticisms were well-founded. A 2011 study by the University of California-Berkeley's Warren Institute would conclude that 93 percent of those held under Secure Communities were Latino, while only 77 percent of undocumented immigrants were Latino. Eighty-three percent of those arrested were subject to detention, compared to 62 percent of the total number of arrested noncitizens. Of the 52 percent of those arrested under the Secure Communities effort who obtained a hearing, only 24 percent gained access to an attorney, compared to 41 percent of all immigrant court respondents. Only 2 percent of those held would not face deportation, as opposed to 14 percent of all immigrant court respondents.[39]

The administration nonetheless held its ground—for now. ICE spokeswoman Nicole Navas noted that over one-third of those expelled under the Secure Communities effort had felony convictions. "ICE continues to search its records," she added, "and has not found a case where a crime victim or witness has been removed from the country." By the end of the 2011 fiscal year, even as the number of criminal arrests of unauthorized immigrants was declining, immigration authorities had deported an unprecedented 391,953 foreign-born people from the United States, including an "all-time high" of 188,000 convicted criminals. In part because of this record, the president's approval rating among Hispanics would tumble from 78 percent at the genesis of his first term in 2009 to 48 percent by the last quarter of 2011.[40]

Just as it was getting tough on immigration enforcement, however, the administration decided to soften its stance. In an August 18 letter to the members of the Senate, Homeland Security Secretary Napolitano announced that, consistent with a June 17 memo from ICE director John Morton (but over the objections of the ICE agents' union), her department would prioritize candidates for deportation, with criminals at the top of the list. "Individuals present in the U.S. since childhood, minors, the elderly, pregnant and nursing women, victims of serious crimes, veterans and members of the armed services, and . . . individuals with serious disabilities or health problems" would be at the bottom. The new policy would even allow some undocumented immigrants to obtain work permits.[41]

At a September White House meeting, Obama mourned the time he had lost trying to appear like a moderate, and vowed to follow his progressive instincts on same-sex marriage, climate change, poverty, and immigration. "We made a calculated decision not to push hard for it" during hard economic times, Obama said of immigration reform, but he was now willing to change course. So after ICE officials detained Fabian Cervantes following his arrest for driving without a license, they suddenly decided to release him. Cervantes then returned to the aptly named Our Lady of Refuge Catholic Church, the largely Hispanic Brooklyn parish where the pastor, Rev. Michael Perry, had accepted the Mexican carpenter's offer to fix the seventy-year-old structure's broken pews.[42]

"This could keep families together and give hope to young persons who only know America as their home," Bishop John Wester of Salt Lake City said, speaking for his fellow prelates who had just finished criticizing the Secure Communities enhancement. "This is the Barack Obama I have been waiting for," Rep. Gutiérrez said, pausing from blasting the president for the increased deportations during his administration. The president was finally rewarding "the Latinos and immigrant voters who helped put him in office to fight for sensible immigration policies."[43]

To the American Catholic bishops, "sensible immigration policies" continued to mean comprehensive reform. In their October 11 document "Forming Consciences for Faithful Citizenship," the bishops prepared their parishioners for the next year's presidential election by espousing "a temporary work program with worker protections and a path to permanent residency; family reunification policies; a broad and fair legalization program; access to legal protections including due process and essential public programs; refuge for those fleeing persecution and exploitation; and policies to address the root causes of migration." They added, "The right and responsibility of nations to control their borders to maintain the rule of law should be recognized."[44]

The boundary between the United States and Mexico was no barrier in November as Bishops Armando Ochoa of El Paso, Ricardo Ramírez of Las Cruces, New Mexico, and Renato Ascencio Léon of Ciudad Juárez, Mexico concelebrated the twelfth annual border Mass on both sides of the fence dividing the two countries. Among the hundreds attending the service was Betty Hernandez, a mother of three and youth minister at Corpus Christi Church in Anapra, Mexico, who was mourning the death of her neighbor by drug violence a week earlier.[45]

Immigration Reform in 2012

If President Obama had once seemingly forgotten the Latinos on this side of the fence, he was remembering them now. The White House commenced the presidential election year by promoting Catholic Cecilia Muñoz, its highest-ranking Hispanic, from Director of Intergovernmental Affairs to Director of the Domestic Policy Council. Catholic Democratic minority leader Rep. Nancy Pelosi of California lauded Muñoz's "sterling reputation as a powerful voice on behalf of comprehensive, compassionate immigration reform." The liberal group Catholics United also praised the choice, by which "the Obama Administration has signaled how important the faith community is to their governing agenda."[46]

Before joining the administration four years earlier, Muñoz had been an immigration rights lobbyist who once had attended a meeting at the Clinton White House where twice she was asked if she was an American citizen. Formerly an outspoken critic of the mass deportation of irregular immigrants, she had spent much of Obama's first term as the primary defender of such policies against many of her former allies.[47]

At the time of Muñoz's promotion, members of the administration and the faith community were in Salt Lake City, where CLINIC and the USCCB were cosponsoring a conference, "Immigration—A Fifty-State Issue: A Focus on State and Local Immigration Initiatives." Kevin Appleby, the USCCB's director of migration policy, explained the title: "If you have fifty different state policies and untold numbers of local policies on immigration, you're not going to have an effective system," he said in the midst of litigation over Arizona's controversial law. "Instead of putting energy into passing bills that are unconstitutional and build fear in communities, we should put energy into getting our federal delegation to do the right thing and reform the immigration system." Bishop John Wester of Salt Lake City added that the conference "allows us to be part of the solution that we hope will come about once the 2012 elections are over."[48]

If comprehensive immigration reform would have to wait, though, the bishops' critique of existing administration programs would not. At the conference John Sandweg, special counselor to Homeland Security Secretary Napolitano, defended the Secure Communities program as a successful attempt to deport criminals who have committed felonies. To address concerns that the campaign had been overly broad, Sandweg noted that his department had formed a task force to study the issue.

But Sandweg's assurances did not placate many of the conference attendees. In the conference's keynote address, Bishop Wester called upon the administration to adopt the principles of the Utah Compact, an agreement among political, civic, religious, and law enforcement leaders in the bishop's home state. The compact promoted a federal solution to immigration problems, a law enforcement effort directed at felons but not other undocumented aliens, an immigration system which kept families together, a recognition of the economic necessity for business to hire unauthorized aliens, and devotion to the ideal of the U.S. as an inclusive nation. Sandweg "got the message pretty clearly from all the participants," Appleby reported, "that there is a lot of discord in the community—a lot of injustices going on that need to be corrected."[49]

Meanwhile, efforts to revive the DREAM Act were going "terribly," Roger Mahony, the retired cardinal of Los Angeles, lamented in January. So he would be taking his case for the measure not to the enemy territory of Capitol Hill but to the friendly environs of Catholic campuses.[50]

President Obama would also be avoiding Capitol Hill. He continued his election-year offensive in March with the unveiling of a new policy reducing the amount of time that aliens had to spend away from their families while applying for legal status. Rather than having to remain in their home countries, irregular immigrants could return to the United States after obtaining a legal visa if they proved that separation from their families could cause "extreme hardship."[51]

The same month, the Obama administration took Arizona to court over S.B. 1070, that state's restrictive immigration law. The administration argued that by granting state law enforcement officers the authority to enforce federal law, the legislation would violate Article VI, Clause 2—the National Supremacy Clause of the U.S. Constitution. The American Catholic bishops filed an amicus brief in support of the administration, contending that the Arizona measure would undermine religious liberty by forbidding church representatives from assisting undocumented migrants.[52]

Religious liberty was very much on the bishops' minds in April, when they announced their "Fortnight for Freedom," a prayer vigil scheduled to commence in late June and culminate on the Fourth of July. Through primarily identified with USCCB resistance to the administration's requirement that religious institutions provide health insurance coverage to their employees that included contraception, sterilization, and abortion services, the vigil would also target Alabama's new immigration law, which prohibited churches from "harboring" irregular aliens. The statute "makes it illegal for a Catholic priest to baptize, hear the confession of, celebrate the anointing of the sick with, or preach the word of God to, an undocumented immigrant," the prelates complained in "Our First, Most Cherished Liberty: A Statement on Religious Liberty," delivered in April. "An unjust law cannot be obeyed," said the bishops, who would again find themselves in federal court, this time on the opposite side of the administration. "If we face today the prospect of unjust laws, then Catholics in America, in solidarity with our fellow citizens, must not obey them."[53]

A May *Commonweal* symposium on the prelates' pronouncement elicited praise as well as criticism. The document "wisely includes the example of state immigration laws," Douglas Laycock, professor of law at the University of Virginia, asserted. "This is important ... because it shows that serious attacks on religious liberty come from the right as well as the left." But William Galston, a senior fellow at the Brookings Institution, focused on "the most remarkable feature of the bishops' argument—their insistence that if a law is unjust, we must disobey it." Galston found such a formulation disturbingly simplistic. "We must do our best to determine the degree of participation, its proximity to or our remoteness from our agency, and the balance of justice and injustice in the act," Galston countered. "It would be easier to sympathize with the bishops' statement if it displayed some awareness of these moral complexities."[54]

Arizona and Alabama were not the only states whose laws were under scrutiny by Catholic immigration proponents. "Through our ministry we belong to three national networks who do work with immigrant detainees," Sister JoAnn Persch testified in May before the Illinois House of Representatives in opposition to the construction of a privately financed detention center in Crete, Illinois. "As a part of these networks we are always proud to be from Illinois because our legislators have passed humane laws regarding immigration. We are envied because other States are passing inhumane laws." The Illinois assembly then passed another "humane law," preventing the state's detention centers from hiring privately funded staffs.[55]

But passing "humane laws" in the nation's capital was not easy. In June, the president finally took the suggestion of Rep. Gutiérrez and Sen. Menendez to enact much of the DREAM Act without going through Congress. Disregarding the warning by his political advisor David Plouffe that such an "amnesty by fiat" could cost as many non-Hispanic white working-class votes as it would gain Latino votes, Obama issued an executive order permitting undocumented immigrants under the age of thirty-one, who had arrived in the United States before they turned sixteen and had lived in the United States for at least five years, to apply for a two-year exemption from deportation if they were high school graduates, in school, or in the military, and had no criminal records. The president's decision was the product of intense pressure by Latinos and immigration advocates, and sit-ins and hunger strikes by undocumented migrants at Obama campaign headquarters.[56]

"As long as I'm president," Obama vowed amid cries of outrage from congressional Republicans, "I will not give up on this issue." But he did not want to talk much about it either. After his brief statement in the Rose Garden, the president took no questions.[57]

In a June interview with *U.S. Catholic*, Congressman Gutiérrrez faulted Obama for squandering two years of Democratic rule on Capitol Hill, and urged his church to keep the pressure on the president. "For me, it comes down to something fundamental, to my basic values as a Catholic," Gutiérrez said in explaining his passion for immigration reform. After "more illegal immigrants have been deported under President Barack Obama's administration than during any other three-year period in the nation's history," and after "Obama has devoted more resources to 'securing the border' than any of his predecessors," *Commonweal*'s editors lukewarmly welcomed the chief executive's "surprise announcement."[58]

The bishops were more generous. "This important action will

provide protection from removal, and work authorization for a vulnerable group of immigrants," the United States Conference of Catholic Bishops applauded, "who desire to remain in the country and contribute their talents to our communities."[59]

The young immigrants themselves were also willing to forgive Obama for the politics of procrastination. In August, twenty-nine-year-old Erika García awoke early to drive ninety miles to Chicago for a public seminar on the new policy, only to find four thousand people in line by 3 a.m. So she returned to Milwaukee, where she was one of the thousand lucky ones to squeeze into a seminar at St. Adalbert Catholic Church before fire marshals sealed the doors.[60]

"There has been a steady flow of persons coming in looking for, at minimum, a letter from me saying I recognize them as having participated in the life of the parish," said Rev. Mark Hallinan of St. Mary of the Assumption Church on Staten Island, New York. Within the first month of the program, the Obama administration had processed 72,000 cases filed by eager applicants. At that rate, the New York Times estimated in September, at least 200,000 immigrants would have applied by Election Day in November.[61]

At the same time that Obama was delivering his executive order, the Supreme Court was striking down most of Arizona's controversial immigration statute, concluding that the sections of the law which made it a state misdemeanor to violate federal alien-registration requirements or work without proper documentation were unconstitutional intrusions by the state of Arizona on federal power. The decision, authored by Catholic Reagan appointee Anthony Kennedy, also rejected the most inflammatory portion of S.B. 1070, which allowed state and local law enforcement officers to arrest, with probable cause, anyone suspected of crimes which demanded deportation.

But the court unanimously retained the law's provision mandating that state and local police check the immigration status of people they stopped or detained for other reasons if they have "reasonable suspicion" that they are in the country illegally. To Arizona Republican governor Jan Brewer, who signed the law, and the president of the National Council of La Raza, Janet Murguía, who fought it, this tenet was the "heart" of the legislation. Yet its survival did not deter the court's other Catholic Reagan appointee, Antonin Scalia, from acerbically arguing in his dissent to the overall decision that "Arizona contradicts federal law by enforcing applications of the Immigration Act that the president declines to enforce."

The president viewed the decision as mostly positive. "A patchwork of state laws is not a solution to our broken immigration system," Obama said in hailing his Pyrrhic victory.[62]

So did the bishops. Los Angeles Archbishop José Gómez, chairman of the USCCB Committee on Migration, praised the court for the parts of the Arizona law which it overturned while expressing hope that it would reconsider the one it didn't. "We are encouraged that the Court did not rule it constitutional," Archbishop Gómez observed, noting that the majority had preserved the possibility that it would later deem the so-called "show me your papers" proviso unconstitutional. "The U.S. Catholic bishops across the nation will urge their state governments not to pursue laws such as in Arizona," Gómez promised, "but rather to pursue humane reform on the federal level."[63]

To the president's and the bishops' dismay, however, the Supreme Court would not be revisiting the Arizona law anytime soon. In August, a federal appeals court upheld the parts of Alabama's statute which required checks of the immigration status of the state's public school students, rendered contracts with unauthorized entrants unenforceable, made it a state crime for undocumented migrants to apply for jobs or not carry legal identification, prohibited irregular immigrants from obtaining auto or professional licenses, and permitted police to inquire about someone's immigration status.[64]

It was a rare defeat for the expedient alliance of Obama and the

Catholic hierarchy. In October, with a month to go before the election, Los Angeles Police Chief Charlie Beck announced that his office would no longer heed federal requests to detain undocumented immigrants arrested for nonviolent offenses. "This is more evidence that the Secure Communities program is incredibly flawed, and from our perspective cruel," Angelica Salas, executive director of the Coalition for Humane Immigrant Rights of Los Angeles, said in hailing the chief's decision. The Obama administration, which a year earlier had challenged a similar decision in Chicago, this time had no comment.[65]

The Immigration and Customs Enforcement agency also had gratified many undocumented migrants and their Catholic defenders by abandoning its strategy of highly visible, large-scale workplace raids. ICE instead would quietly audit employers' hiring records to detect unauthorized applicants.[66]

Not all the news was good for undocumented entrants. In FY2013, the administration would deport almost as many irregular aliens (360,000), including almost as many convicted criminals (216,000), as it had in the previous fiscal year. Deportation is a "very real problem in our community," said Rev. Dan Reim, a Jesuit priest at Ann Arbor's St. Mary's Student Parish, who successfully petitioned Homeland Security Secretary Janet Napolitano to revoke the order sending one of his parishioners home.[67]

In October, Border Patrol agents met rocks with gunfire, fatally shooting sixteen-year-old José Antonio Elena Rodriguez in the back. The Mexican teenager was at least the fifteenth victim of a Border Patrol shooting in less than two years, and it came after a letter from sixteen members of Congress had prompted a review of the Customs and Border Protection agency's policies regarding the use of force. "When their lives are threatened, when their well-being is threatened, and when they're in danger to suffer great bodily harm," Shawn Moran, vice president at large of the National Border Patrol Council, said in backing up his fellow union members, "the use-of-force policies allow them to defend themselves." The Mexican Embassy in Washington deplored the agents' "disproportionate deadly force," and regretted that not one of the shooters had faced criminal prosecution. "He was carrying nothing but the cellphone I had bought for him," José Antonio's grandmother Taide Elena mourned. "I still can't believe they took his life because he was walking."[68]

An October poll by the Pew Hispanic Center found 69 percent of Latinos planning to vote for the president, while only 21 percent intended to choose former Massachusetts governor Mitt Romney, who remained evasive on immigration issues after advocating "self-deportation" during the Republican primaries. Hispanics by over two-to-one opposed Obama's deportation policies. One in four Hispanic adults, including one in three in the country illegally, personally knew someone who had encountered detention or deportation in the previous year. Most Latinos nevertheless continued to support the chief executive responsible for these unhappy outcomes, either for other reasons or because they considered Romney to be even worse. But Catholics as a whole, divided on immigration as on so many other issues, were evenly split between the two major candidates.[69]

Obama and Romney sparred over immigration in their second October debate. The incumbent assailed Romney's opposition to the DREAM Act and support for the Arizona law; the challenger pledged to do what Obama had not—fix a broken system. Three weeks later, in the November election in which immigration took a back seat to the economy, jobs, education, and health care among Hispanics and non-Hispanics alike, Obama won with a comfortable majority of 71 percent of Latino votes. He expressed his gratitude by announcing that immigration reform would be a priority of his second term. This time, the president insisted, he meant it.[70]

Immigration Reform in 2013

If ever the moment seemed ripe for comprehensive immigration reform, it was in early 2013. President Barack Obama's reelection wrought Republican reassessment. Public opinion polls registered support for the legalization of unauthorized aliens. A struggling economy and improved border security were reducing the flow of undocumented migrants. If not now, the president and Catholic immigration advocates wondered, when?[71]

"If Hispanic Americans perceive that a GOP nominee or candidate does not want them in the United States," said a postelection "autopsy" report by the Republican National Committee following Romney's defeat, "they will not pay attention to our next sentence." Dick Armey, a former congressman from Texas and current "Tea Party" leader, put his party's problem in more colorful terms. "You can't call someone ugly," the report quoted Armey, "and expect them to go to the prom with you."[72]

The son of Cuban immigrants, Marco Rubio had come to symbolize the country's purported shift on comprehensive immigration reform. A darling of his party's right wing, the Florida Republican nonetheless decided to help craft a centrist solution to the divisive dilemma. "Our faith has always been about compassion," the Catholic senator maintained, and on immigration, "it compels you to do something."[73]

Father John Baumann, a Jesuit priest in Chicago, had turned his faith into action in 1972, when he founded what would become People Improving Communities through Organizing (PICO), an interdenominational organization which was now pushing hard for comprehensive immigration reform. In January 2013 the group held a "Separated Families Supper Table" in Washington to spotlight the horrible impact of deportation on the families of "aspiring Americans." Among those in attendance were Rev. Jesus Nieto-Ruiz, pastor of St. Anthony's Catholic Church in Oakland, California, who related the story of one of his parishioners; Alejandra Gómez, a DREAMer who had endured the deportation of her two brothers; and Luis da Silva, whose undocumented status kept him from his father's funeral. "There are millions of families like mine who will sit tonight at a dinner table with missing brothers, sisters, mothers and fathers," said da Silva. "That's why I plan to spend this year working for a roadmap to citizenship for the eleven million aspiring Americans who, also just like me, are ready to take on the responsibilities, privileges, and freedoms of citizenship."[74]

As da Silva was publicly stating the case for comprehensive immigration reform, some of Rubio's senate colleagues were privately laying the groundwork for yet another legislative campaign. "We want to get the old band together," South Carolina Republican Lindsay Graham informed New York Democrat Charles Schumer a few weeks after the 2012 election. Graham and Schumer had collaborated in the aborted 2010 immigration fight, and they agreed to assemble a bipartisan core group to shepherd another bill through the Senate. They also concurred that such a group must include Arizona Republican John McCain, the veteran point person on such matters.

The captains then chose their teams. Schumer selected Catholic Robert Menendez of New Jersey, the party's only Hispanic senator; Catholic Richard Durbin of Illinois, the champion of the DREAM Act; and Michael Bennet of Colorado, where Latinos had helped move the state to the Democratic column in the past two presidential elections.

Because of the division within his party over comprehensive immigration reform, McCain had a tougher chore. Graham, McCain's best friend in the chamber with some of the same bruises from earlier immigration battles, was the easy pick. For the remaining two slots, McCain opted for freshmen Rubio and Mike Lee of Utah. Rubio agreed to join the group only after the four Democrats reluctantly promised to, in his words, "tie a pathway to citizenship to border security and enforcement." Lee insisted on security without citizenship, so McCain replaced him with a fellow Arizonan, Jeff Flake. Schumer and McCain finally had their "Gang of Eight."[75]

Five days after he had advocated immigration reform in his second inaugural address, President Obama welcomed Senator Menendez and the other members of the Congressional Hispanic Caucus to the White House. "I want to make immigration reform one of the top-tier items this year," he told the lawmakers.

"We appreciate your leadership and we're going to need your leadership at certain points," Menendez replied. "But right now, if you put out your bill, they [Republicans] will feel like they're being cornered."

That was not what the president wanted to hear. "After you guys pushed me so hard in not so subtle tones, being critical at times about lacking leadership," Obama protested, "now you're asking me to hold off?"

"I understand why you're upset and how you might feel this way," Menendez empathized with Obama. But "I think the Republicans have come to understand (if they want to be a national party) that they are going to have to deal with this issue. It's really got to be a negotiating process." The senator explained that the Gang of Eight was making progress in formulating its blueprint for comprehensive immigration reform, and they didn't want anything to jeopardize that progress.

Obama promised only to consider Menendez's concerns. That was not good enough for the Gang of Eight. Fearful that Obama might upstage them with a plan of his own, the senators adjusted the timetable for unveiling their outline. Rather than introduce their proposal two days after the president's speech in heavily Hispanic Las Vegas, the Gang of Eight would do so at a press conference the day before. And Schumer and Durbin would urge the president not to match them tit for tat, "If this became 'Obama's immigration reform bill,' that would've been fatal." So Schumer and Durbin "were begging him not to" present his plan.[76]

He wouldn't—at least, not yet. The Gang of Eight held its press conference on Monday, January 28. They proposed a road to citizenship, greater access to work visas for low-skilled and high-skilled immigrants, border protection, and a guest worker program for low-income migrants.

Catholic immigration advocates praised the senators' broad strokes. "Let us welcome the stranger," Sister Simone Campbell, executive director of the Catholic social justice lobby Network, applauded the Gang of Eight's design.[77]

Obama gave his speech on Tuesday, January 29. To the relief of the Gang of Eight, the president did not offer a specific proposal. To their dismay, however, he enunciated a set of principles quite different from theirs, with a shorter route to citizenship and without provisions for border security and guest workers. Senator Rubio criticized the speech's inattention to border enforcement, calling the Obama principles "half-baked and seriously flawed," adding that the president's ideas "would actually make our immigration problems worse."[78]

Obama returned Rubio's fire. "We have done more on border security in the last four years," the president asserted, "than we have done in the previous twenty."[79]

Obama apparently believed that his administration had done enough. In February, someone leaked the administration's specific immigration reform proposal, which said even less about border security than the president's principles had. Following a series of conference calls with the White House, one supporter of comprehensive immigration reform concluded that compromise "was not the message we heard at all." In that case, Rubio maintained, Obama's plan would be "dead on arrival" on Capitol Hill.[80]

While change remained predictably elusive in Washington, it was proving unexpectedly welcome in Rome. In March, the world's Catholics greeted their first Latin American pope, elected by the College of Cardinals to replace the ailing Benedict XVI. "That's a truly historic event, isn't it? " Chicago's Francis Cardinal George marveled as Argentina's Jorge Cardinal Bergoglio, the son of Italian immigrants, became Pope Francis I. "Now almost half the Catholics in the world are from Latin America, including Mexico and the Caribbean."[81]

Within a few days of the announcement of a new pope, there was news of a rapprochement between the president and the Gang of Eight. Graham, who had unfairly blamed Senator Obama for the 2007 bill's defeat, praised President Obama for improving the prospects for a 2013 victory. "He gets it. He's trying to pass a bill," said Graham of the president's low profile. "I think it's true leadership."

To reward the president's deference, the Republican senators surprisingly agreed to Obama's timetable for citizenship for unauthorized aliens—ten years to obtain a green card establishing permanent residence, then three more years to acquire citizenship. The applicants would have to pay a $2,000 fine and back taxes, while learning English and civics. Such a schedule had the political virtue of appearing firm yet flexible by lengthening the wait for permanent residence by two years yet shortening the wait for naturalization by two years.[82]

Catholic immigration advocates also approved. "It is an unusual construction, but it gets them to citizenship in the same time as the Administration plan," Kevin Appleby, director of migration policy for the United States Conference of Catholic Bishops, lauded the compromise. "Most importantly, it eliminates the prospect of a permanent underclass by ensuring that, in time, all will have the opportunity to become Americans."[83]

Having agreed on legalization, the president and the Gang of Eight moved on to border enforcement. Obama and the four Democrats still rejected a so-called "trigger," which would have forced the federal government to secure the border before undertaking legalization, while the four Republicans insisted on it. Obama would win this round as well. Undocumented aliens would obtain temporary legal status within six months of the passage of the law. The Gang of Eight abandoned a trigger for permanent residency in favor of the less stringent requirement that the government apprehend at least 90 percent of those illegally crossing the most porous parts of the border or create a special commission to achieve that target. "It's just a goal," an aide to Senator Schumer admitted. "Because even if we don't achieve it, and the border commission comes into existence, it doesn't delay the path to citizenship."[84]

That was just as the American Catholic bishops had hoped. United States Conference of Catholic Bishops president Timothy Cardinal Dolan of New York advocated "legitimate provisions to secure our country's borders," and the bishops had long equated "leniency" with "legitimacy." Bishop John Wester of Salt Lake City warned that conditioning permanent residency and citizenship for undocumented migrants on border safety would have relegated irregular aliens to a "*de facto* permanent underclass."[85]

After having lost on legalization and border security, the Gang of Eight's Republicans decided not to fight on guest workers. Graham and Schumer had previously agreed to let the heavily Democratic American Federation of Labor-Congress of Industrial Organizations and the predominantly Republican Chamber of Commerce negotiate this provision themselves. When they couldn't produce an agreement, however, Schumer and McCain reluctantly joined the talks along with Richard Trumka, the Catholic head of the AFL-CIO, and Tom Donohue, the Catholic leader of the chamber. In March, the quartet concurred in principle on a compromise in which low-skilled guest workers would receive the higher of the prevailing industry wage or the actual employer wage, while higher-skilled guest workers (e.g., crane operators and electricians) would not be part of the program. The plan would assure that 200,000 janitorial, hospitality, and construction workers could procure visas every year.[86]

Thus did the Gang of Eight reconstruct former Senator Alan Simpson's famous "three-legged stool" of earned legalization, enforcement, and guest workers, albeit again on somewhat wobbly legs. And the public approved of much of it. Sixty-eight percent of Americans in a March 2013 Public Religion Research Institute-Brookings Institution poll believed that the country should provide a path to citizenship and protect the border at the same time, while only 29 percent believed in a border enforcement-only approach. Seventy-four percent of Hispanic Catholics and 62 percent of non-Hispanic white Catholics agreed that "the immigration system should allow immigrants currently living in the U.S. illegally to become citizens provided they meet certain requirements."[87]

To mobilize these members of their church, the American Catholic bishops would be distributing $800,000 to the Catholic Legal Immigration Network (CLINIC), People Improving Communities through Organizing (PICO), and Justice for Immigrants. "These grants represent a distinctly Catholic contribution in promoting comprehensive immigration reform," said Sacramento Bishop Jaime Soto, chairman of the United States Conference of Catholic Bishops' Catholic Campaign for Human Development.[88]

Many Catholics were among the thousands of people, documented and undocumented, who attended the Rally for Citizenship in Washington in April. "We came here eleven years ago because in Guatemala there was no opportunity to even have a house," irregular immigrant Mayra Ragon said to explain why she was at the demonstration with her husband Saul and daughter Camilla. "We came here to find opportunity and to give our daughter a better future."

Twenty-eight congregants from St. Mary's Student Parish in Ann Arbor, Michigan rode a bus for ten hours to attend the rally. Rev. Dan Reim, a Jesuit priest at St. Mary's, explained that they were there in solidarity with the Hispanic members of their church.[89]

With the president, senators from both parties, and so much of the public now open to comprehensive immigration reform, could the House of Representatives be far behind? Congressman Gutiérrez predicted that both houses "will move quickly" to meet this demand. President Obama urged Congress to send him a bill shortly after the late March-early April Easter recess.[90]

Meanwhile, activists on both sides of the country's immigration schism were, in the words of the *New York Times's* Julia Preston, "keeping their powder dry for the fight after legislation is finally introduced." For Catholic immigration advocates, potential stumbling blocks centered, as they always had, on the issues of family reunification and border enforcement. The Obama administration's aggressive deportation policy (which since the George W. Bush administration was counting those seized at the border) had increased the number of removals from 396,906 in FY2011 to 409,849 in FY2012, and continued to break up families. Though the numbers of those apprehended in the country's interior were dramatically declining, and despite the administration's 2010 policy shift to selective deportation, almost half of those removed in 2012, according to the Department of Homeland Security, had no criminal record.[91]

The deportations also appeared to be discouraging young immigrants from applying for the administration's Deferred Action for Childhood Arrivals program, which suspended the deportation of those children of unauthorized entrants who went to college or joined the military. Following a rush when the program began in August 2012, the number of applicants had declined from 113,000 in 2012 to under 15,000 in February 2013. "As we speak, persons are being deported and an untold number of families are being divided," USCCB president Timothy Cardinal Dolan lamented in April. "This suffering must end."[92]

When the Gang of Eight outline became legislation in April, it included a provision which would eliminate visas for foreign siblings of U.S. citizens as well as their married children over thirty years old. The American Catholic bishops feared that this change would lead to even more deportations. "This is an important moment in our country and for the Church," Los Angeles Archbishop José Gómez, chairman of the USCCB Committee on Migration, applauded the Gang of Eight's handiwork. But citing the need to safeguard family unity, he added, "We hope to see the legislation improve and advance."[93]

Fewer visas and more deportations were not the only threats to family unity posed by the Gang of Eight bill. In May, the Democratic chairman of the Senate Judiciary Committee, Patrick Leahy of Vermont, offered an amendment to the measure which redefined the family to include same-sex couples. If the Leahy Amendment passed, however, the senator would coerce his fellow Catholics to choose between the church's devotion to the traditional family and its desire for immigration reform. In other words, it would leave the bishops and many of their followers no choice but to reject the bill. According to Anthony Suárez-Abraham, who headed the Archdiocese of Chicago's Office of Peace and Justice, the bishops went on "high alert" to uncover similar attempts to link gay marriage and immigration reform.[94]

"I think the USCCB would be wrong to walk away," wrote Michael Sean Winters of the liberal National Catholic Reporter, but "I'm not sure that reform can pass without the support of the bishops." Winters would not have to find out, as Catholic Democrat Richard Durbin of the Gang of Eight helped derail the Leahy addition.[95]

While the Senate bill's family visa provisions ran counter to the position of Catholic immigration advocates, its prescriptions for border enforcement alienated most Republicans and most Americans. The legislation called for $4.5 billion in new spending for drones, Border Patrol, fencing, and other security measures. It stipulated that for legalization to proceed, ninety percent of the border must be secure or a commission would be formed. Yet while large majorities of independents and nearly half of Republicans in an April ABC-*Washington Post* poll endorsed a path to citizenship for undocumented aliens, half of these supporters of legalization now believed that it should occur only *after* the border was secure. In an April USA *Today* survey, 71 percent of Americans favored earned legalization, while 80 percent sought "better border control." According to a Pew survey the same month, one in five Mexicans admitted that they would be "inclined to go work and live in the United States without authorization." The challenge for Congress, Texas Republican Senator John Cornyn of Texas posited, was "regaining the public's confidence that the federal government is practically doing its job [on border security]."[96]

According to a May Pew poll, of those who knew of the Senate legislation, Democrats favored it by about three to one, but Republicans disapproved of it by almost two to one. "I can tell you that the bill as currently structured can't pass the House, and I think it's going to struggle to pass in the Senate," Senator Rubio, who had helped write it, admitted in June. Rubio's fellow Republican, Alabama senator Jeff Sessions, was less diplomatic, likening the bill he fervently opposed to a mackerel. "The longer it lays [sic] in the sun," said Sessions, "the more it smells."[97]

So the Gang of Eight solicited amendments to its legislation. Buoyed by a Congressional Budget Office calculation that comprehensive immigration reform would shave almost $200 billion off the federal budget deficit within two decades, Republican senators Bob Corker of Tennessee and John Hoeven of North Dakota, a Catholic, proposed an expensive antidote to the bill's incomplete enforcement provisions. Their $46 billion amendment would double the number of Border Patrol agents, triple the number of border surveillance drones, complete the 700 miles of fencing authorized in 2006, help finance the E-verify system for monitoring hiring at workplaces, and implement a biometric entry and exit tracking system at the country's thirty largest airports. Gang of Eight member Robert Menendez of New Jersey called the CBO numbers a "game changer." Corker, claiming that all of his proposed spending meant that the legislation's target of 90 percent border security was "not a sticking point anymore," hoped that his amendment would be a game changer too.[98]

It was—at least in the Senate. The Senate Judiciary Committee approved the Corker-Hoeven amendment, 13–5, adding about two hundred pages to an already thousand-page bill. But it rejected tougher measures to seal the border, such as Texas Republican senator John Cornyn's attempt to make 90 percent border security a precondition for permanent residency for undocumented entrants. In other words, rather than simply a goal, the 90 percent benchmark would become a mandate, returning the immigration debate to where the Republican members of the Gang of Eight had originally wanted it to go.[99]

The U.S. Catholic bishops hoped that such amendments were merely political theater. "This issue needs to be solved in order for many of the Republican candidates to have a good shot in 2016," the USCCB's Kevin Appleby speculated. "That's why all of them are trying to find some way to support some version of this so that when they run, they'll be able to say that. But the key is trying to stay as (politically to the) right as possible to survive a primary."[100]

But without his amendment, Cornyn would oppose the bill. And Iowa Republican Charles Grassley harbored no presidential ambitions. Grassley would try and fail to amend the bill on the Senate floor to compel the Department of Homeland Security to ensure "effective control" of the border six months before the legalization process could begin. When a party-line vote sank his proposal, Grassley heard ominous echoes of the "empty promises" of Ronald Reagan's Immigration Reform and Control Act of 1986, for which he had cast one of the first votes of his long legislative career.[101]

In addition to their reservations about the bill's border protection tenets, some Republican senators had qualms about its guest-worker ingredients. The Congressional Budget Office predicted that the Senate bill would reduce illegal immigration by only 25 percent because of "people overstaying their visas issued under the new programs for temporary workers." The CBO study thus concluded that the Senate measure would only exacerbate the current illegal immigration climate.[102]

These senators would not have an opportunity to offer amendments on the floor, however, because Senate Majority Leader Harry Reid of Nevada was hurrying his colleagues toward a final vote before the Fourth of July recess. One Republican amendment which succeeded, however, was a proposal by Utah Republican Orrin Hatch to deny Social Security and federal welfare benefits to unauthorized migrants. For Catholic immigration advocates, if the Hatch Amendment was not quite a "poison pill," it was pretty close. "It is a tough pill to swallow, and there is no guarantee it will not get worse later in the process," Appleby lamented. "If the path to citizenship becomes further weakened, there could come a tipping point where the bill becomes unsupportable."[103]

Fourteen Republicans (including half of the chamber's ten Catholics) and two independents joined all fifty-two Senate Democrats (including sixteen Catholics) in passing the Gang of Eight bill on June 27. Loud applause erupted from the packed Senate gallery, where young people chanted "Sí, se puede" (Yes, we can!), and wore blue T-shirts reading "Eleven Million Dreams."[104]

"We came with the hopes of every immigrant—for a better future," said María Barajas, watching the vote on a big screen television in Los Angeles with about two hundred other undocumented migrants. Mrs. Barajas, a wife and mother of two who had crossed into the United States from Mexico with her family thirteen years earlier, hoped that immigration reform would help her fulfill her dream to open a hair salon. "Today is the first step," she added, "toward becoming whole."[105]

The legislation, while frayed, "is a step forward in finally establishing some law and order to our broken system and respecting the rights and family unity of migrants," said Tom Stieritz, director of Catholic Social Action for the Diocese of Cincinnati, speaking for Archbishop Dennis Schnurr. "Echoing the position of our bishops, thousands of Catholics throughout the archdiocese have asked our senators to support such reforms .... By the end of the year, we hope to have an improved immigration system that restores order and promotes human dignity."

But the bishops could always change their minds. "The path to citizenship should be made more affordable and accessible for undocumented immigrants and their families," said Los Angeles Archbishop José Gómez, chairman of the USCCB Committee on Migration. "Our southern border should be a place of mutual support and an extension of hands across boundaries, not a militarized zone," Sacramento Archbishop Jaime Soto, a member of the board of directors of CLINIC, proclaimed. "We oppose the acceleration of border enforcement as a prerequisite for a legalization program that includes citizenship." Archbishop Gómez added, therefore, that the bishops "reserve the right to oppose immigration reform later in the process."[106]

"Later in the process" would mean in the House of Representatives. "Today the Senate did its job," said President Obama as he savored a rare triumph in the immigration wars. "It's now up to the House to do the same."[107]

But the chief executive could do little more than cheer from the sidelines. By swaying "whichever way seemed politically expedient at any given moment," David Martin, Obama's former deputy general counsel at the Department of Homeland Security, would lament, the administration had "lost all credibility on enforcement, despite all the deportations, while letting activists think they could always get another concession if they blamed Obama." When asked the best thing Obama could do to ensure passage of comprehensive immigration reform in the House of Representatives, admissionist Democratic congressman John Yarmuth of Kentucky joked that the president should "oppose it." Republicans were in the majority in the House, and Catholic Speaker John Boehner of Ohio vowed not to permit a vote on immigration reform unless a majority of his party was about to pass it.[108]

Invoking the Democratic president's controversial health care legislation, Republican House leaders emerged from a two-and-one-half-hour, closed-door July meeting with their members determined to avoid "enacting a single, massive, Obamacare-like bill rather than pursuing a step-by-step, common-sense approach to actually fix the problem." In other words, the Senate bill was dead on arrival in the House. "'Comprehensive' has always been a swear word in the House of Representatives," Hispanic Republican Representative Raul Labrador of Idaho, a former immigration attorney, conceded, "but having a step-by-step approach that deals with the issue comprehensively, I don't think that's dead."[109]

In the meeting's acrimonious epilogue, Catholic Steve King of Iowa rejected suggestions of distinguishing the children of the undocumented from their parents. "Once you start down that line," said King, "you're destroying the rule of law." King would later describe some irregular immigrants as drug runners with "calves the size of cantaloupes."

But some more temperate voices spoke in support of DREAM Act-type legislation, while others proposed legalization without citizenship for the undocumented. The Senate and House "will both deal with the topic of immigration," Representative James Lankford of Oklahoma, a member of the House Republican leadership, concluded. "That may be the only common ground they have."[110]

The Republican House majority, wedded to enforcement but wary of legalization, was under less pressure than the Democratic minority to enact a comprehensive statute. In the 232 districts represented by Republicans, Hispanics constituted only 11 percent of the electorate. In the 200 Democratic districts, Latinos were 23 percent of the voters.[111]

Meanwhile, the Democratic and Catholic supporters of the Senate legislation dug in their heels. "Without a path to citizenship, there is not going to be a bill," New York Democratic Senator Charles Schumer of the Gang of Eight asserted. "And to go to conference with various pieces, without a path to citizenship, is a path to a cul-de-sac, to no immigration bill." The U.S. Catholic bishops would also reject legislation, according to Los Angeles Archbishop José Gómez, "should the path to citizenship become inaccessible or eliminated."[112]

"In the end, if there's a bill that doesn't include a path to citizenship but does move the ball forward for illegal immigrants," Aaron Blake of the *Washington Post* wondered, "are Democrats really going to be the ones to halt it when the alternative is nothing?" And were Catholic immigration activists, led by the bishops, really going to follow their pattern of resisting enforcement while insisting upon citizenship?[113]

Time would tell. Network's "Nuns on the Bus" returned in July from their twenty-two-day, fifty-three-city, 6,800-mile trip on which they promoted comprehensive immigration reform to business leaders, government officials, and undocumented aliens. After their 10,000 postcards had helped produce the legislation in the Senate, the sisters prepared to mail 18,000 more to members of the House of Representatives. They would particularly be targeting that body's sixty-one Catholic Republicans. Catholic Democratic representatives Nancy Pelosi of California and Rosa DeLauro of Connecticut praised the nuns' evangelization of the tenets of their church. If the endorsement of the Senate bill by the group's leader, Sister Simone Campbell, served to raise hopes of success in the House, her characterization of the legislation's border provisions as "nuts" threatened to dash them.[114]

"Protecting our borders and creating an earned path to citizenship for the eleven million undocumented immigrants already in this country are not competing interests," the presidents of ninety-three of the nation's 224 Catholic colleges and universities wrote in July to all 163 Catholic members of the House of Representatives, including Speaker Boehner and Minority Leader Pelosi. While the missive's amorphous balance between enforcement and legalization should have heartened congressional optimists, its enthusiastic embrace by the bishops must have soothed the skeptics.[115]

"We have lost a sense of brotherly responsibility," said Pope Francis as he weighed in for the first time on the immigration issue in July, urging a "reawakening of consciences" to combat "indifference" toward migrants. He had just arrived on Italy's island of Lampedusa, which was struggling to absorb the thousands of North African exiles who had not drowned on the way. The pope lamented that when it came to the plight of the world's immigrant population, "We have forgotten how to cry."[116]

"We want to try to pull out all the stops," Kevin Appleby, director of migration policy for the United States Conference of Catholic Bishops said as he announced that the nation's priests would be pressuring the Catholic Republicans in the House and preaching about immigration reform in their churches before Congress returned from its Labor Day recess. The Ignatian Solidarity Network, Faith in Public Life, and the Association of Catholic Colleges and Universities also took up the fight. "It's pretty rare for the Catholics to take an issue like this straight to the pews," President Obama's immigration point person Cecilia Muñoz noted approvingly following a series of White House strategy sessions with Catholic immigration activists. Likening the "recent immigrants from Mexico" to his late Irish grandmother, Bishop Emeritus Robert Banks of Green Bay, Wisconsin took the issue to the congregation at St. Francis Xavier Cathedral on September 8, pleading that "there must be some way to make them legal" without their having "to go back to Mexico."[117]

The next month, as a budget stalemate between the House of Representatives and the president resulted in a partial suspension of the federal government, thousands of citizen and noncitizen supporters of comprehensive immigration reform rallied on the officially closed National Mall to protest the Obama administration's annual deportation average of 400,000 aliens, up 30 percent from the George W. Bush era. Appearing onstage alongside the children of deported parents, Rev. Ted Gabrielli, a Jesuit priest from Dolores Mission Church in Los Angeles, entreated the House to "hear the cries of the children and act now." Catholic Democratic Representatives Luis Gutiérrez of Illinois, Charles Rangel of New York, and Raúl Grijalva of Arizona were among those arrested for intentionally blocking traffic on a street adjacent to the Capitol. "We will go and risk arrest and sacrifice the very freedom that 30,000 people in detention right now do not have," Gutiérrez skewered the White House. The protest was an "enthusiastic demonstration of support for immigration reform," the White House saluted the congressman.[118]

When the sixteen-day partial government shutdown concluded in the middle of October, Democrats on both ends of Pennsylvania Avenue announced that immigration reform remained a legislative priority. "If House Republicans have new and different additional ideas for how we should move forward," President Obama insisted in an October address, "I will be listening." By November, House committees had approved three enforcement bills and two guest worker measures, Speaker Boehner had again ruled out a single comprehensive reform bill, and President Obama and Senator Rubio had agreed to settle for several House measures instead of one. And the bishops, meeting in Washington, had selected Daniel Cardinal DiNardo of Galveston-Houston, described as a "tireless leader on immigration reform," as the USCCB's new vice president. Cardinal DiNardo said of immigration reform, "I think we're at a good time now."[119]

But some House Republicans, still smarting from the media and public opinion battering which they had received during the budget showdown, insisted that they would not be negotiating over immigration with the president who had refused to entertain a delay in implementing health care reform. " I think that what he's done over the last two and a half weeks, he's tried to destroy the

Republican Party," lamented Idaho Republican Raul Labrador, who had once been part of a bipartisan House group searching for an immigration solution.[120]

And some Democrats were still in no mood to strike a deal, either. "We in the House must do something that's comprehensive," said Catholic congressman Rubén Hinojosa of Texas. "We're not going to start over again." Neither were the bishops, who opened their November meeting with a voice vote endorsing the Senate bill and a telephone campaign by Catholic parishioners to members of the House on the feast day of Mother Frances Cabrini, whose ministry to immigrants had helped make her the first American saint. Nor were five members of the interfaith group People Improving Communities through Organizing (PICO), who vowed to fast until Congress legislated a path to citizenship. Unless and until that legislation arrived, immigration activists would continue to obstruct the operations of immigrant detention centers throughout the country.[121]

As the 2013 congressional session ended without any new immigration legislation, the American capital had a familiar feel to it. Most members of the Senate backed comprehensive immigration reform. Most Republican members of the House opposed the Senate bill. And many American Catholics would have to choose between their congressman and their church. "On immigration, we're saying to the House of Representatives, which is dominated by the Republicans, 'You guys have to get your act together,'" said Cardinal Dolan on the first day of the last month of 2013. "And we're not going to let you off the hook." As irresistible Catholic admissionists prepared once again to duel with immovable Republican restrictionists, it didn't have to be this way.[122]

Conclusions

In attempting at various times to please everyone on refugee and immigration matters, President Barack Obama in the end placated virtually no one. Most Republicans on Capitol Hill believed that his policies were too lenient, while many Democrats thought they were too tough. And when not lining up behind the president, Catholic immigration advocates were lashing out at him. So rather than help write a new chapter on immigration reform, the Obama administration in many ways told the same old story.

On refugee issues, Obama won raves from Catholic activists for revoking the policy of incarceration for asylum seekers awaiting decisions on their status, and for granting more asylum claims than his predecessor had. But he earned rebukes for blocking Temporary Protected Status for Haitian exiles, continuing to favor Cuban over Haitian entrants, allowing more deportations of asylum seekers at the border, and authorizing fewer grants of asylum than before 9/11.

On immigration reform, Catholic advocates lauded the closing of the notorious Don Hutto detention center, the reduction of time away from their families for those filing for legal status, the implementation of much of the DREAM Act by executive order, the replacement of workplace raids with auditing of businesses, the escalation of selective deportation, the legal challenges to the restrictionist Arizona and Alabama laws, and the path to citizenship and absence of a border security "trigger" in the 2013 Senate bill. But they lacerated the exclusion of irregular immigrants from the Affordable Care Act; the record number of deportations (augmented by counting border apprehensions); the legal affront to religious liberty embodied in state immigration laws; the failure of legal challenges to Arizona's "show me your papers" provision and Alabama's immigration law; the Senate bill's spending on border enforcement, trimming of family-based visas, and denial of federal benefits; and the inability of the Democratic president and the Democratic

Congress to enact the DREAM Act and comprehensive immigration reform in the first two years of the Obama administration.

By sending mixed signals to his fellow Democrats and to Catholic immigration advocates, Barack Obama in large part forfeited the goodwill with which they had greeted the new administration. As a result, the president sacrificed much of the leverage with which he could have helped move the members of his party (especially the senators) and the leaders of the church (especially the bishops) closer to the center on immigration reform. Then, backed by most of the public, they might have rallied enough House Republicans, including the Catholic Speaker of the House, to vote for a more moderate Senate bill (or bills).

Instead, Congress relegated the president to a supporting role. And Catholic immigration activists continued to espouse positions that appealed to too few members of the Congress, the public, and the church.

6. Conclusion

CONTINUITY AND CHANGE would mark the three-decade odyssey of American Catholics and American presidents on immigration issues between 1981 and 2013. In some ways, church and state remained remarkably consistent in their approaches to immigration. In other ways, however, the leaders of the federal government and the leaders of the Catholic Church contributed to a vastly different political landscape in 2013 than in 1981. Thanks in part to American Catholic leaders and followers who at times discouraged enforcement and encouraged evasion, immigration became a more onerous burden for American presidents.

Continuity

The signs of continuity between the Reagan and Obama administrations were nonetheless prominent and powerful. First, the politicians, the prelates, and the public agreed that the current immigration system was not working. "Recent immigration trends have focused attention on the unenforceable nature of current immigration law and the need for its revision," an internal Reagan administration memo concluded. "We can all agree on two things," said Catholic senator Sam Brownback of Kansas two decades later. "First, the current system is broken, and second, a national solution is desperately needed."[1]

Bishop Joseph Galante of Camden concurred in 2010, "It is clear that current laws are not working." Three years later, and three decades after the introduction of the Reagan comprehensive immigration reform, only 7 percent of Americans responding to a

Public Religion Research-Brookings Institution poll believed that the American immigration system was "generally working," 29 percent thought that it was "working but with some major problems," 40 percent believed that it was "broken but working in some areas," and 23 percent concluded that it was "completely broken."[2]

A second element of continuity from 1981 to 2013 was that the American government, despite fluctuations due to changing world events and public sentiments, generally shared with the Catholic Church a compassionate commitment, in word and deed, to welcoming immigrants. "The Lord Himself chose the stranger—the Samaritan—as the sign of our neighbors," the U.S. Catholic bishops wrote in their April 1980 pastoral "Cultural Pluralism in the United States," adding that "Jesus enjoined us in the great commandment, 'you should love your neighbor as yourself.'" When he accepted his party's nomination for president in July 1980, Ronald Reagan appealed to the convention delegates, "I ask that you trust that American spirit which knows no ethnic, social, political, regional, or economic boundaries." He then asked, "Can we doubt that only a Divine Providence placed this land—this island of freedom—here as a refuge for all these people in the world who yearn to breathe free?"[3]

Thirty years later, the bishops and the president answered Reagan's question in the negative. "Like immigrants now, newcomers in the nineteenth and early twentieth centuries came from different countries than their predecessors," the bishops' Catholic Charities wrote in a 2006 policy paper, and they also "suffered from low wages and dangerous working conditions" in those countries. "We're just a few minutes away from Ellis Island," Barack Obama noted in his second debate with challenger Mitt Romney at Hofstra University in October 2012. "We all understand what this country has become because talent from all over the world [want] to come here."[4]

But they did not just talk about compassion toward outsiders. "The major responsibility for the domestic resettlement of refugees," the 1981 Hesburgh Commission report noted, "has historically rested not with the federal government (responsible for initially accepting the refugees) but with the voluntary associations of private citizens, and state and local governments." From 1975 to 2005, the bishops' Office of Migration and Refugee Services resettled about 900,000 refugees. During the same period, the Catholic Legal Immigration Network was assisting close to 400,000 immigrants per year, helping low-income arrivals find work, connect with their families, avoid persecution, and attain citizenship. "The one organization in civil society to which immigrants tend to belong with greater frequency than the larger population," wrote Michael Foley and Dean Hoge in 2007, "is the local worship community." And since 40 percent of those immigrants were Catholic, the church had an especially important role to play.[5]

So did presidents. Despite the country's rising restrictionism, President Barack Obama in Fiscal Year 2013 authorized admission of the same number of refugees—70,000—as President Ronald Reagan had approved thirty years earlier. This decision, Obama explained, as Presidents Reagan, Bush, Clinton, and Bush had before him, "is justified by humanitarian concerns." Though the numbers of immigrants and refugees rose and fell over the various administrations, Ed Koch, the Jewish mayor of New York from 1978 to 1989, would remember that "two women welcomed the immigrants—Lady Liberty and Mother Church."[6]

A third indication of continuity between 1981 and 2013 was that the presidents repeatedly professed concern about containing the country's boundaries. "This country has lost control of its borders," said Ronald Reagan in October 1983, "and no country can sustain that kind of position."[7]

Three decades later, the president said much the same thing. "In recent years, among some of the greatest impediments to reform were questions about border security," said Barack Obama at the U.S.-Mexican border in May 2011, announcing increases in funding for a fence and Border Patrol agents. "All this contributed to a growing number of undocumented people living in the United States."[8]

The statements of the presidents echoed the sentiments of their constituents. Fifty-five percent of Americans in a 1984 *Newsweek* survey believed that the best approach to illegal immigration was to "arrest and deport" unauthorized entrants. A 2010 Pew poll showed that a plurality of 45 percent of American Catholics sought tighter borders.[9]

Though it ended with amnesty and avoidance, President Ronald Reagan's immigration reform adventure began quite differently. The "original purpose of immigration legislation," the administration reminded itself in a set of talking points in 1983, "was enforcement for border control." An internal George W. Bush administration memo conveyed the president's insistence that "security and enforcement benchmarks ... must be met before other elements" of the 2007 comprehensive immigration reform proposal could be implemented. Reagan's Catholic associate attorney general, Frank Keating, who had argued for comprehensive immigration reform in 1986, reiterated in 2013 that "border security is the indispensable lintel that shoulders the load."[10]

Even without comprehensive immigration reform, the *Washington Post*'s Suzy Khimm would report, Presidents George W. Bush and Barack Obama had made great strides in securing the border. By fiscal year 2011, the federal government was funding 21,444 Border Patrol agents, 651 miles of vehicle fencing, 300 radar and camera towers, and nine drones, and by fiscal year 2012 was detaining as many as 34,000 people per day. According to the Migration Policy Institute, in 2012 alone the Obama administration spent $18 billion on immigration enforcement, more than the combined expenditures by all of the other major arms of federal law enforcement, including the Federal Bureau of Investigation, Drug Enforcement Administration, and Bureau of Alcohol, Tobacco, Firearms, and Explosives.[11]

When Senators Kennedy and McCain introduced their bill in 2006, a majority of Americans believed that the federal government should prioritize border enforcement. The MPI study concluded that it had. "As a result of twenty-five years of investment," said former Clinton administration INS director Doris Meissner, who helped author the report, "the bulwark is fundamentally in place." Even Donald Kerwin, formerly of the Catholic Legal Immigration Network but currently with the MPI, signed onto the report, saluting the federal government's immigration databank as "the largest law enforcement electronic verification system in the world." According to San Diego's Transborder Institute, drug-related violence on the Mexican side of the border was dropping as well. By 2012, following these Bush-Obama measures, pluralities of Americans and Hispanic-Americans placed equal importance on confronting the dilemma of those who had already breached the border and addressing the border itself.[12]

But the numbers could be somewhat misleading, and many restrictionists and admissionists agreed that the border was not yet secure. "A large amount of that spending has nothing to do with immigrants," Mark Krikorian, the executive director of the restrictionist Center for Immigration Studies, said in reacting to the MPI report, noting that the budget figures included all of the funding for the operations of the Customs and Border Protection agency, such as cargo inspections at land and sea ports. "The U.S. border is better controlled than at any time in our history," said Robert Bonner, commissioner of the Customs and Border Protection agency under George W. Bush, approving of the report. But the border was hardly airtight. "The terrain can be quite different depending on what part of the border you are talking about," he explained, "and there are different ways, different tactics really, that need to be brought into play. And this requires almost mile-by-mile analysis." In their own report issued in November 2013, the U.S Catholic bishops acknowledged that the number of unaccompanied minors crossing the border (many of whom were fleeing poverty and violence in Central America) had more than doubled since FY 2011.[13]

Yet like the Reagan administration, the Obama administration wanted little to do with micromanaging the border. For almost a decade, the Department of Homeland Security measured "operational control" of the border. In 2007, the Border Patrol defined "operational control" as "the ability to detect, respond, and interdict border penetrations in areas deemed as high priority for threat potential or other national security objectives." In 2010, the Border Patrol estimated that it had achieved operational control of only about 44 percent of the southwestern U.S. border. The next year, Homeland Security Secretary Janet Napolitano announced that her department was replacing "operational control" with a vaguely defined "border condition index."

But this new metric lasted less than two years. In March 2013 Napolitano told the House Homeland Security Subcommittee on Border and Maritime Security that her department was now using a variety of measures, from apprehensions of irregular immigrants to vacancy rates in Mexican border hotels, to determine control of the border. In October, Kenneth Palinkas, president of the National Citizenship and Immigration Services Council, the union representing the 12,000 U.S. Citizenship and Immigration Services adjudication officers and staff, claimed that the Senate bill would "undermine border security."[14]

The bishops and other Catholic immigration advocates, unlike the presidents and the populace, wanted virtually nothing to do with border security, offering a fourth indication of continuity from 1981 to 2013. Thus did they go from hardly alluding to the border at all (when it wasn't a primary part of IRCA in the 1980s) to a perfunctory reference to national "sovereignty" when it had become a major issue in the 2000s. "The U.S. Catholic bishops have called for reform of our nation's immigration laws for years now, advocating for a new system which balances our heritage as a nation with respect for the rule of law," United States Conference of Catholic Bishops president Timothy Cardinal Dolan of New York and the USCCB Committee on Migration's Archbishop José Gómez of Los Angeles wrote Republican Speaker of the House John Boehner of Ohio in March 2012. "Not only must we re-examine enforcement strategies and policies, Mr. Speaker, we must also revamp other aspects of the system, including legal immigration and family unification policies." They devoted the rest of their letter to stating their opposition to Arizona and Alabama's restrictionist immigration laws and the "human suffering being caused by our flawed immigration laws." The word "border" appeared nowhere in the document.[15]

Nor would it appear in the bishops' postcard campaign to members of Congress in the wake of the 2012 election. But appeals for a "path to citizenship," the preservation of "family unity," job opportunities for "low-skilled immigrants," restoration of "due process protections" for unauthorized entrants, and attention to the "root causes" of immigration would.[16]

"The claim to sovereignty must be addressed," University of Notre Dame theologian Rev. Daniel Groody said in defending the church's position in 2009, "after the needs of distributive justice are met." Three years later, Chicago Auxiliary Bishop John Manz was more succinct. "I don't think it is the Church's role to say you should put up twenty-foot fences," said the bishop, or deploy "more Texas Rangers." At a time when Canada was reassessing its admissionist climate and Mexico was tightening its southeastern border, the American bishops rarely alluded to their country's security.[17]

And sometimes they went further than that, arguing that border enforcement didn't discourage illegal immigration. It encouraged it. The bishops "believe 'enforcement only' will exacerbate the current crisis," Donald Kerwin wrote in 2006. "As evidence, they cite an increase in border control funding between 1993 and 2006 (from $361 million to $1.8 billion) that has been accompanied by roughly a tripling of the country's unauthorized population, from 3.9 million to 12 million."[18]

Seven years later, Bishop Jaime Soto of Sacramento, a member of the board of directors of the Catholic Legal Immigration Network (CLINIC), complained that "the enforcement-only approach has been the default policy for the past two decades. It has only aggravated the problem of irregular immigration." *Boston Globe* columnist James Carroll, a former Catholic priest, concurred. Longing for the days of "circular migration" between Mexico and the United States before the "emphasis on border enforcement since the 1980s put an end to that," Carroll claimed in August 2013 that "the eleven million [undocumented] here today are the unintended consequence of enhanced border security."[19]

These arguments did not sit well with many Catholics. After all, the church hierarchy had once embraced border security—as a bulwark against communist infiltration in the McCarran-Walter Act of 1952, and as a mechanism for protecting native-born laborers in the Immigration and Nationality Act of 1965. "Most people acknowledge obligations toward refugees and asylum seekers . . . but these obligations to outsiders are not commonly thought to cancel out our collective right to protect the national culture or defend the economic interests of existing citizens," wrote political scientist Peter Meilaender in 2007, adding that "to recognize these obligations is neither nativist nor selfish." Yet the bishops merely "pay lip service to the sovereignty of the state," complained Steve Skojec, a parishioner at St. Mary Mother of God Church in Washington, D.C. in 2009, "while placing inordinate weight on the rights of the migrant." In 2011, after Los Angeles Archbishop José Gómez told a group of Catholic business leaders that the United States was not only a "nation of mercy and forgiveness" but also that "I don't like it when our rule of law is flouted," Catholic immigration supporters Deal Hudson and Mark Smith conceded that the archbishop's remarks were "somewhat different from the official statements from the USCCB."[20]

In opening their arms to immigrants, the leaders of the church thus were disaffecting many of their followers, furnishing a fifth similarity between 1981 and 2013. In a 1980 Roper poll, 80 percent of Americans wanted to reduce the number of legal immigrants and refugees. In a 2009 Zogby poll, 78 percent of American Catholics blamed illegal immigration on lax enforcement; 69 percent thought that immigration levels were too high; 69 percent believed that native-born Americans would do virtually any job if it paid well enough; 64 percent espoused enforcement efforts which would send undocumented immigrants home; and only 23 percent backed earned legalization. In a 2011 Gallup poll, 78 percent of Americans opposed any increase in legal immigration. "The area in which the Church carries significant authority is of a different type," Chester Gillis explained in 2003. "This is due, in part, to the fact that American Catholics are (by and large) no longer an immigrant community"—and had not been for over a generation.[21]

According to a 1986 Lilly Foundation study, only 39 percent of Catholic adults believed that "the Catholic bishops should take a stand on some political issues such as the arms race or the American economic system." Auxiliary Bishop Robert Donnelly of Toledo estimated that "less than one percent of the people in the Church" in 1992 typically read the bishops' pastoral letters. The liberal *America* editor Rev. Thomas Reese, whose 1992 book *A Flock of Shepherds* examined the role of the United States Catholic Conference, concluded that "both on the left and the right, we have an anti-clericalism. The one thing that the two groups agree on is that the bishops do not know what they are doing."[22]

But the bishops *were* aware of the diminished level of commitment of many parishioners. "I would agree that often we are not in the same ballpark as our people," Joseph Cardinal Bernardin of Chicago conceded in October 1992.[23]

And that was well before the church's sexual abuse scandal, which erupted in Bernard Cardinal Law's Boston in 2002 and engulfed eleven thousand priests in 95 percent of the country's dioceses. As the scandal unfolded, the church unraveled. Weekly Mass attendance plummeted for a time from 52 percent of Catholics in 2000 to 35 percent in 2003, and donations by Catholics temporarily dipped by half between 2002 and 2004.[24]

University of Notre Dame historian Scott Appleby concluded in 2004 that "no previous generation of American Catholics inherited so little of the content and sensibility of their faith from their parents as have today's youth." Seventy percent of American Catholics indicated that the views of their bishops were not important factors to consider when they voted. No wonder that only a third of American Catholics in that presidential election year said they even occasionally cast faith-based votes.[25]

If many lay Catholics were not listening to their clergy, perhaps it was because there was nothing to hear. According to a 2010 Pew poll, about two-thirds of churchgoing Catholics never recalled hearing about immigration from their parish priests. And virtually all of those who didn't attend Mass never heard about it at all.[26]

In their 2011 open letter to the nation's undocumented community on the Feast of Our Lady of Guadalupe, the nation's thirty-three Latino bishops, including Archbishop José Gómez of Los Angeles, acknowledged this deepening discord between prelate and parishioner. They lamented that many of their fellow Catholics would not welcome their plea for "just, humane, and effective immigration reform." In 2013, the court-ordered release of documents demonstrating a cover-up of prior clerical sexual abuse in the Archdiocese of Los Angeles led Archbishop Gómez to relieve his retired predecessor, outspoken immigration activist Roger Cardinal Mahony, of all public duties.[27]

And not all Catholics stayed in the church. "Catholicism has experienced the greatest losses as a result of affiliation changes," a 2008 survey by the Pew Center on Religion and Public Life discovered. "While nearly one in three Americans (31 percent) were raised in the Catholic faith, today fewer than one in four (24 percent) describe themselves as Catholic."[28]

These defections would have been even more severe if not for a sixth ingredient of continuity from the 1980s that carried into the new century, the emergence of Latinos as the largest and fastest-growing cohort of new American Catholics. The annual influx of 650,000 legal newcomers from Asia and Latin America, when added to the thousands of those entering the country illegally, was surpassing the heyday of European immigration that took place from 1820 to 1920. A 1978 *Our Sunday Visitor* survey found that religion was "very important" to 64 percent of Hispanic Catholics, a number ten points higher than for all U.S. Catholics. In November 1982, the American Board of Catholic Missions agreed to fund the National Catholic Rural Life Conference's Southwest Project, which identified as one of its two most important goals "addressing the problem of securing greater participation of Hispanics within the Church, and of the need to become aware of, and active on, the concerns of Hispanics." In their December 1983 pastoral "Hispanic Presence: Challenge and Commitment," the bishops promised to broaden their outreach to the Latino community. Four years later came their National Pastoral Plan for Hispanic Ministry, and the creation of regional and diocesan offices of Hispanic Ministry. The appointment of additional Latino bishops soon followed.[29]

President Reagan similarly recognized the burgeoning Hispanic contribution to the United States. "If this issue is handled with care, we can solidify our support not only among the Hispanics but also use the immigration issue as an opportunity to demonstrate compassion and outreach," administration pollster Richard Wirthlin suggested in 1981. "We need to develop a comprehensive Hispanic Strategy document which would include the strong support for, and natural ties between, Hispanics and conservative issues," Latino White House aide Henry Zuñiga urged in 1982, citing the president's opposition to a national identification card as a way to help reverse declining Hispanic support for the administration.[30]

"Mr. President, you and your campaign organization have spent a lot of time trying to increase your support among Hispanic voters, yet you continue to support the controversial immigration bill [without anti-discrimination language]," a reporter queried Reagan during the 1984 campaign. "I think that if we take every precaution we can in that immigration bill to make sure that there is no discrimination," Reagan responded, "I think we can protect against that." Reagan would cave to Hispanic and Catholic groups on anti-discrimination language in IRCA, and in his second term he would appoint Hispanic Lauro Cavazos as his Secretary of Education.[31]

The 2008 Pew poll found that while Protestants outnumbered Catholics by over two to one (55 percent to 21 percent) among native-born Americans, Catholics outnumbered Protestants by almost two to one (46 percent to 24 percent) among foreign-born Americans. By 2012, Hispanics comprised over one-third of the American Catholic faithful, roughly offsetting the European-American exodus. And Hispanics continued to exhibit greater religiosity than other Catholics. A 2011 National Catholic Reporter study found that Latino Catholics from the millennial generation were more likely to agree that "being Catholic is an important part of who I am" than non-Hispanic Catholics.[32]

These realities were apparent to Catholic immigration supporters and detractors alike. Archbishop Gómez unabashedly admitted that his fellow Latinos offered fertile ground for an American Catholic revival. "One thing immigrants do for the American Catholic Church is they enrich the church," said John Garvey, president of the Catholic University of America. "They're keeping the Catholic Church fresh and the churches full." Dave Gibson, writing on the conservative Catholic website Examiner.com, detected a connection between the departure of Catholics after the clerical sex scandal and the recruitment of Catholics through illegal immigration.[33]

Like Reagan, Republican George W. Bush actively courted the Hispanic vote, winning two-fifths in his 2004 re-election bid. Bush rewarded these voters by appointing Alberto Gonzales as the first Latino Attorney General. Democrat Barack Obama wooed Latinos even more ardently, garnering two-thirds of the Latino vote in 2008. Obama rewarded these voters by appointing Sonia Sotomayor as the first Latino Supreme Court Justice.[34]

While Latino Catholics were not lacking in attention from their church and their government, they remained by no means easy to please. In 1991, Timothy Matovina noticed several major differences between Hispanic and other American immigrant groups. The geographical proximity of their home countries, the perpetual cycle of their immigration, their widespread failure to overcome poverty, their frequent encounters with racism based on skin color, their syncretic Catholicism, and the modern church's acceptance of cultural diversity separated these newcomers from those of different cultural and generational origins.[35]

In 2008, Catherine Wilson was still uncovering six components of a distinctive "religious identity politics" in the Latino Catholic community. Their attachment to sacred symbols like the cross, their embrace of totems of Catholic devotionalism like novenas and feast days, their humanization of God, their commitment to the communal nature of the church, their reliance on the Spanish language as the medium of their religious message, and their promotion of social action combined to forge a largely separate Latino profile within the American church and society. In their 2009 comparison of Italian-Americans and Polish-Americans with Mexican-Americans, Richard Alba, Albert Raboteau, and Josh DeWind concluded that, unlike the other two groups, Mexican-Americans "kept their distance from the European-American-dominated Church—for instance, worshipping at home altars and preserving their veneration of the Virgin of Guadalupe."[36]

In addition to these signposts of separation between Hispanics and other Americans, there still existed formidable fissures within the Latino Catholic community as well. One source of division was the variation of status among Latino immigrants, as delineated by David Badillo. "Temporary workers" were those holding jobs for a specific time; "recurrent migrants" were those who regularly traversed the border; and "settled migrants" were those who lived in the United States permanently, whether legally or illegally. Badillo added that income level, geographical location within the U.S., degree of fluency in English, and extent of formal education also served to divide Hispanic-Americans, especially among Cuban-Americans, Mexican-Americans, and Puerto Ricans.[37]

A seventh link between 1981 and 2013 was the aggressive lobbying of the bishops. Unlike traditional lobbyists, who raised money to win access, votes, and elections, the American Catholic hierarchy relied heavily on arguments which were hard to challenge and numbers which were hard to ignore. The bishops' conference has "a unique role in this town," said Frank Monahan, who headed their government liaison office throughout most of this period, because the church "has a well-developed set of social policies and a history of dealing with those policies that's highly respected." In addition, "we're the largest religion—there are so many Catholics out there around the country." In the Archdiocese of Chicago in 2013, the Office for Immigrant Affairs and Immigration Education, Priests for Justice for Immigrants, and Sisters and Brothers of Immigrants issued a statement by Francis Cardinal George promoting comprehensive immigration reform; organized a joint press conference, a 100,000-postcard campaign, and visits to Illinois Congressmen; and scheduled rosaries, prayer, and fasting at individual parishes.[38]

Not everyone appreciated the bishops' political activism, however. In 1980, the Abortion Rights Mobilization filed suit against the United States Catholic Conference, accusing the bishops of violating the restriction on political campaign activity in section 501 of the Internal Revenue Code. The Supreme Court dismissed the lawsuit in 1990. But in 2012 Citizens for Responsibility and Ethics in Washington sued the United States Conference of Catholic Bishops on the same grounds.[39]

The Catholic hierarchy's constant political activism on behalf of refugees and immigrants nevertheless belied an eighth reality which tethered 1981 to 2013. When compared to their other major concerns, especially abortion, immigration reform was not a high political priority for the prelates or their pope. In the 1974 Declaration on Abortion, issued by the Vatican Congregation of the Faith, Pope Paul VI proclaimed, "In the course of history, the Fathers of the Church, her Pastors, and Doctors have taught the same doctrine—the illicitness of abortion." The Holy Father added that "a Christian can never conform to a law which is in itself immoral, and such is the case of a law which would admit in principle the licitness of abortion." On the other hand, Joseph Cardinal Bernardin of Chicago would posit that even nuclear war, which the cardinal had denounced in the pastoral "The Challenge of Peace" approved by the bishops' liberal majority in 1983 and which he had aligned with abortion as violations of a "consistent ethic of life" later that year, was a subject about which the hierarchy had offered only "providential judgments" open to "criticism, debate, and questioning."[40]

Three decades later, in their 2011 statement "Forming Consciences for Faithful Citizenship," the bishops divided six "current and fundamental problems" between those "involving opposition to intrinsic evils" and those "raising serious moral questions." Abortion, euthanasia, human cloning and "destructive research on human embryos" were in the former category; "the failure to repair a broken immigration system" was in the latter. While the "unjust immigration system" was not an "optional concern," and Catholics must not "dismiss or ignore Church teaching" on the issue, "choices about how best to respond" to it were matters of "principled debate and decision."[41]

A conservative majority of the bishops (just short of the required two-thirds consensus) voted to accept the draft of a pastoral entitled "The Hope of the Gospel in Difficult Economic Times" at their November 2012 meeting. "Some matters before our Catholic conscience are bedrock principles of human dignity and the common good," the document said, again citing "the protection of human life," this time alongside "the nature of marriage as given to us by God." Then, echoing Cardinal Bernardin, the statement added, "Some things are of a more prudential nature, such as how best to allocate public funds to assist those who are in need of assistance."[42]

While the bishops in 2012 eviscerated Alabama's restrictive immigration law as "unjust" and went to court to stop Arizona's, they had never declared federal immigration statutes illicit or unconstitutional, as they had branded *Roe v. Wade* since 1973. From 1981 to 2013, they had worked instead to modify the existing federal laws. In her study of the Sanctuary movement, Susan Bibler Coutin claimed that its participants sought only to "reinterpret" U.S. immigration law, and its Tucson border workers, by interviewing Central American exiles, even contended that "we are carrying out the 1980 Refugee Act, whereas the INS is not." At no time after 1973, however, did prolife Catholic activists assert that they were in any way implementing the Supreme Court's abortion decision. "Are the American immigration laws imperfect? Certainly," wrote Philip Lawler on the conservative website *CatholicCulture.Org* in 2011. "But are they so fundamentally wrong that it is a moral act to defy them? The bishops have not made the case to justify such a claim."[43]

"There is no single authentic Catholic position on immigration" as there is on abortion, Archbishop José Gómez of Los Angeles, himself a Mexican immigrant, admitted in 2011. Gómez cited a poll showing that Hispanic Catholics elevated abortion and traditional marriage well above immigration as their primary political preoccupations. While other Catholics considered immigration more important than abortion, they still placed it far behind jobs and the economy. The church hierarchy had been so insistent on the primacy of the abortion issue that when Pope Francis said little about it in the early days of his papacy, he was, in his words, "reprimanded for that." So indelibly etched was the church leaders' abortion posture that their liberal Democratic immigration reform ally Senator Charles Schumer of New York proudly included them alongside evangelical Christians, agricultural growers, and the U.S. Chamber of Commerce as "very conservative" components of his diverse 2013 coalition.[44]

Yet the bishops and many other Catholic immigration advocates remained almost as unyielding in their public stand on immigration as their church was in its stance on abortion, displaying a ninth and final connection between 1981 and 2013. "Some years ago, I was arrested a few times on criminal charges, for blocking the doors of abortion clinics," Lawler recalled in 2011. "I feel no remorse for these crimes; in fact I am proud of what I did because it was done for a just cause." He then contrasted his practice of civil disobedience to abortion laws with his church's advocacy of civil disobedience to immigration laws. "At the time," Lawler remembered, "I would have welcomed statements of support for our blockades from the U.S. bishops."[45]

When USCCB president Timothy Cardinal Dolan pronounced the bishops "all-in" on comprehensive immigration reform in early 2013, Michael Sean Winters of the liberal National Catholic Reporter appeared to put "life" issues and immigration on the same plane. "The issue for the whole body of bishops," Winters asserted, "is whether or not they will put the same emphasis and energy behind the campaign for immigration reform that they have put into the [2012] effort to overturn the HHS [Department of Health and Human Services] contraception mandate."[46]

"On the legal question, do you think there should be penalties against abortion doctors?" John McCormack of the conservative Weekly Standard asked Sister Simone Campbell, leader of Network, the national Catholic social justice lobby, which had sent its "Nuns on a Bus" on a nationwide tour during the 2012 presidential campaign to protest House Republican budget cuts. "That's beyond my pay grade," said Sister Campbell, separating herself from the hierarchy. "I don't know."

When questioned about her views on immigration, however, she lined up behind the bishops. Sister Campbell then confessed that the recalcitrance on their side had at times been counterproductive. When the next immigration reform proposal arrived on Capitol Hill, she promised in early 2013, things would be different. "We want to amend it, yes, but we want to pass it. We don't want to nitpick it to death," she vowed. "That's what we did in 2007." And, she might have added, long before then.[47]

Alan Simpson would recall that the most hostile witness he encountered in immigration committee hearings in the 1980s and 1990s was a Catholic priest, Monsignor Salvador Alvarez, who savaged the senator's "racist" guest worker plan. "Public interest advocates perpetually doubt their right to take less than an absolutist position," Philip Schrag of the Committee to Preserve Asylum learned from his alliance with Catholic and other refugee activists in 1996. They thus stand their ground "even when it is clear that advocating an absolutist position will result in worse legislation than seeking a compromise." When asked to identify the "political opponents" of the 2007 comprehensive immigration reform legislation, Catholic Secretary of Commerce Carlos Gutierrez included those ostensible supporters of the bill who "would demand that they get 100 percent of what they want out of a comprehensive bill."[48]

A Catholic nun, Sister Lily Butler, was one of ten protesters arrested for blocking the street outside a New York City immigrant detention center in August 2013. At an October 2013 forum, when California Democratic representative Xavier Becerra, a Catholic, compared permanent residence without citizenship to "slavery," Catholic Republican representative Mario Díaz-Balart of Florida cautioned that while he shared Becerra's passion for comprehensive immigration reform, "We can't draw lines in the sand."[49]

Yet Catholic immigration proponents did exactly that—for over thirty years. By approaching the citizenship-only extreme, supporters of comprehensive immigration reform were unwittingly playing into the hands of their adversaries. As Marc Rosenblum observed, the opponents of comprehensive immigration reform generally united in favor of border enforcement and worker verification, and against legalization and visa revisions. The proponents, however, divided among business groups, who wanted more work-based visas and legalization but opposed worker verification; labor unions, who resisted work-based visas but sought worker verification and legalization; and religious (including Catholic) and civil liberties organizations, who advocated family-based visas and legalization but opposed border enforcement and worker verification.[50]

The more the bishops and other immigration interests stood firm, the further they advanced their opposition's "divide and conquer" strategy. Catholic immigration advocates commenced their lobbying effort aimed at the 1996 House bill allied with business interests in favor of splitting the legislation between its legal and illegal immigration provisions. After the business lobbyists abandoned the plan to divide the bill in return for higher quotas on employment-based visas, Catholic interests further fractured the coalition by prioritizing family reunification.[51]

"Are you disturbed by the fact that many advocates of unlimited immigration are business leaders [who are] looking for cheap labor [and] refuse to grant immigrants labor rights?" Laura Sheahen of the Catholic conservative website *Beliefnet* queried Washington's Theodore Cardinal McCarrick about the alliance in favor of the Kennedy-McCain comprehensive immigration reform bill in 2006. "Very much so," McCarrick replied. Los Angeles Archbishop José Gómez belatedly attempted to close the gap within the admissionist forces in his speech to Catholic business leaders in 2011.[52]

But the gap remained. Thomas Donohue, the Catholic president of the U.S. Chamber of Commerce, broke with the bishops of his church in August 2013 when he expressed the willingness of his organization to accept a "path to legality" for unauthorized aliens. "You get a path to citizenship," he explained, "but it might come a little later." Yet the bishops and other Catholic immigration advocates were unwilling to wait. "A minority of House Republicans could be the rock on which immigration reform founders," Rutgers University political scientist Ross Baker opined in October 2013, but given the divisions within the ranks of its supporters, "the power of the wave that propels it might be less than a tsunami."[53]

Catholic admissionists were often less malleable than those for whom they purported to speak. "We don't need citizenship, only permanent residency," admitted Jorge Mújica in August 2013, seven years after he helped organize the Chicago protest which sparked the nationwide demonstrations against the Sensenbrenner enforcement-only bill. "For many undocumented people, citizenship is not a priority," Oscar Chacon, executive director of the admissionist National Alliance of Latin American and Caribbean Communities, conceded in November. "What the undocumented population needs is to be able to live here, work here, and travel."[54]

A 2013 Pew Research Center survey found that almost two-thirds of Mexicans eligible for citizenship had not become naturalized, while a majority of Latinos and a plurality of Asian-Americans believed that living and working in the country legally were more important than attaining citizenship. According to the Department of Homeland Security, over twenty-five years after the passage of the Immigration Reform and Control Act, 60 percent of those granted amnesty under the law had chosen the permanent legal residency that their Catholic "representatives" refused over the citizenship that their Catholic "representatives" demanded. "I think if we stick with the message of citizenship or nothing," said Alejandra Saucedo, an undocumented immigrant from Argentina, "we could end up with nothing."[55]

Greater pliability on immigration issues would have advanced the political interests of irregular immigrants without compromising the theological mission of the church. "One happy characteristic ... of social justice is that it is ideologically neutral. It is as open to people on the left as on the right or in the center," wrote Catholic conservative Michael Novak in 2000. "The virtue of social justice allows for people of good will to reach different—even opposing—practical judgments about the material content of the common good (ends) and how to get there (means). Such differences are the stuff of politics."[56]

"I devoutly believe that one can be a conservative and be a good Christian, and that one can be a progressive and be a good Christian," Catholic liberal E.J. Dionne concurred in 2008. "Ideally, the Catholic Church's role in politics is to cause discomfort, to encourage questions, to challenge narrowly ideological views. Oddly, a Church that is seen as dogmatic has often had a moderating effect on politics." On immigration and refugee issues, however, the church remained doggedly dogmatic.[57]

Change

Despite all these similarities between 1981 and 2013, the latter struggles for refugee and immigration reform in some important ways bore little resemblance to the former, to the discredit of the bishops and the detriment of the presidents. First, immigration issues became much more visible. "A paucity of data," Jimmy Carter's comptroller general Elmer Staats complained in 1980, "makes a thorough analysis of the impact of illegal aliens on the United States impossible." By 2013, there was no such problem, as about forty organizations representing all sides of the immigration question spewed forth endless statistics in countless reports. Kathleen Arnold divides today's prominent immigration scholars into "conservative" restrictionists such as Lawrence Auster, Samuel Huntington, Peter Skerry, and George Borjas; "moderate" admissionists like Rogers

Brubaker, Victor Nee, and Richard Alba; "progressive" admissionists like Alejandro Portes and Rubén Rumbaut, and "alternative" open borders proponents such as Saskia Sassen and Yasemin Soysal (with whom Arnold sympathizes).[58]

Illegal immigration's brighter spotlight was due in large part to irregular immigrants' newfound bravery and even brazenness. In the 1980s, with the exception of many Central Americans who spoke on behalf of the Sanctuary movement, unauthorized entrants warily lurked in "the shadows" of American life, fearing apprehension and deportation. In the 2000s, despite higher expulsion rates, increasing numbers of the undocumented were fearlessly exposing themselves to mainstream society. In 2006, millions of unauthorized aliens spilled onto city streets throughout the country to protest passage of the House immigration bill the year before. The "breadth, intensity, and public militancy" of these demonstrations, according to Gary Gerstle, "had no precedent in American history."[59]

By 2012, an undocumented migrant from the Philippines, Pulitzer Prize–winning journalist Jose Antonio Vargas, was appearing on the cover of *Time* alongside other irregular aliens and above the provocative headline, "We are Americans—Just Not Legally." In his story inside the magazine, entitled, "Not Legal, Not Leaving," Vargas approvingly quoted Gaby Pacheco, whose parents had illegally brought her to the U.S. from Ecuador when she was seven. "For many [undocumented] people," she explained her unabashed openness, "coming out is a way of saying you're not alone."[60]

"It was surreal," Vargas would marvel several months later when he testified alongside Homeland Security secretary Janet Napolitano and Immigration and Customs enforcement officer Chris Crane in a hearing on immigration reform before the Senate Judiciary Committee. "I was sitting next to the people whose job it is to deport me," he told the *New York Post*. "And they were smiling and shaking my hand."[61]

Not only had many of these unauthorized exiles ostentatiously emerged from "the shadows," but the church was eager to greet them when they did. In their open letter to the nation's undocumented community in 2011, the Latino Catholic bishops noted the menial work, low wages, and family division which characterized their experience in the United States, saluting the immigrants as a "revitalizing force" for their adopted country. Rather than being "treated as criminals because you have violated current immigration laws," the letter continued, the undocumented underclass should be "receiving our thanks."[62]

In some respects this heightened visibility accelerated the pursuit of immigration reform by humanizing its potential beneficiaries and heightening its urgency. "Collectively, these [undocumented] activists have turned immigration reform into a full-fledged movement," attorney Raul Reyes approved in USA Today in December 2013. But the greater presence of irregular immigrants ultimately lengthened the odds against achieving reform. The 2006 demonstrations against the House enforcement-only bill, replete with provocative slogans and Mexican flags, inspired the backlash that helped prevent a reconciliation of the House and Senate bills. The July 2013 arrests of the "Dream Nine," the young Mexican immigrants who protested the American immigration system by crossing and recrossing the U.S.-Mexican border, and the September 2013 demonstration by seven unauthorized entrants who chained themselves to the White House fence to denounce the administration's deportation policy, divided their fellow immigration advocates between those who believed they were helping, and those who thought they were hurting, the cause of reform. Marc Rosenblum had noted in 2011 that individuals make easier targets than "the system," and some undocumented migrants seemed to be inviting such blowback."[63]

A second major change between 1981 and 2013 was the growing partisanship in the nation's capital. In the 1980s the bishops faced little risk of appearing partisan because the immigration issue bridged the political divide. In the mid-term election year of 1986, the Simpson-Mazzoli bill passed overwhelmingly with sixty-two Republican and 168 Democratic votes in the House. "We knew that enacting an immigration reform bill would require a bipartisan effort," Senator Simpson and Congressman Mazzoli would remember twenty years after. "We held unprecedented joint House-Senate hearings – not just in Washington but all over the country. We heard from all sides and points of view." Simpson joked at the time that he was receiving Christmas cards addressed to "Simpson Mazzoli."[64]

In the midterm election year of 2010 there was no immigration reform bill on which to vote. "We knew Obama wasn't going to do much [on immigration] because we have a Congress that doesn't want to," Bishop Manz would recall.[65]

The president was more blunt. "We're going to punish our enemies and we're gonna reward our friends on issues that are important to us," Obama told the Spanish-speaking radio network Univision in the heat of the 2010 election season. "Then it's going to be harder."[66]

"I probably should have used the word 'opponents' instead of 'enemies,'" Obama would apologize. But it didn't seem to matter. Those Republican foes of comprehensive immigration reform whom the bishops lamented and the president chastised regained control of the House of Representatives in 2010 and helped devise a party platform two years later which advocated a double fence on the border and a federalization of Arizona's punitive immigration law. But there was no Ronald Reagan to prod the two parties to cooperate, and there were no Alan Simpson and Romano Mazzoli to show them how.[67]

An unpopular president, as George W. Bush had become by 2007, and as Barack Obama had become by 2011, could not easily appeal over the heads of a Congress which was completely, in Bush's case, and partly, in Obama's case, in the hands of the other party. But a still-popular president like Reagan could enact comprehensive immigration reform, even in an election year in which his party would lose control of both houses of Congress.[68]

The task facing Barack Obama was even more imposing as Congress became even more ideological. *National Journal* found that in the 111th Congress, which met during Obama's first two years, the most conservative Democratic senator was more liberal than the most liberal Republican senator, and the situation was almost identical in the House of Representatives. Before the 2010 Republican takeover of the House of Representatives, there were fifty-four moderate "Blue Dog" Democrats in the House. Following the election and two retirements, that number had dwindled to twenty-four. In the previous two Congressional elections, the number of moderate Republicans had declined so dramatically that by 2012, two-thirds of House Republicans would identify themselves as members of the conservative House Study Committee, and there would be no GOP equivalent to the Democrats' Blue Dog Coalition. "Washington, D.C. is a place where bipartisanship is always lauded," Congressman Gutiérrez ruminated in 2013, "but never rewarded."[69]

In many ways the politicians' ideological rigidity mirrored the constituents who elected them. Between 1998 and 2012, according to a survey by the Kaiser Foundation and the *Washington Post*, the number of Democrats and Republicans identifying themselves as "definitely partisan" rose from less than half to over two-thirds. In the 2012 presidential election, President Obama won only 6 percent of Republican votes, while Governor Romney earned only 7 percent of Democratic votes. Catholic parishes often reflected this fragmented polity. "Because of the ideological polarization of cable television news, talk radio, and the Internet, Americans can now get their information from entirely partisan sources," Michael Gerson, former speechwriter for President George W. Bush, surmised. "They can live, if they choose to, in an ideological world of their own creation, viewing anyone outside that world as an idiot or criminal, and finding many who will cheer their intemperance." And they could, as Bishop David O'Connell of Trenton, New Jersey did in 2013, portray the highly contested path to citizenship for the undocumented as a lofty "principle," while decrying the "political and partisan brushes" which were creating "the polarization and delay in resolution" of the immigration impasse.[70]

The poisoned partisan atmosphere of 2013 helped elicit a third change: a metamorphosis in the terms of the debate. For the bishops and the president, the Reagan era was responsible in its clarity and refreshing in its candor. "We have advocated . . . a meaningful amnesty provision," Santa Fe Archbishop Robert Sanchez said in presenting the bishops' position in 1976. "They [Hispanics] should be looking at that [which] should be [of] the greatest appeal to them," President Reagan contended in 1984, citing the "very generous amnesty [and] that all the way up to 1982, we're willing to give these people permanent residency."[71]

"Mr. Smith, as the Chief Law Enforcement Officer of the country, are you entirely comfortable with an amnesty plan," a reporter asked Reagan's attorney general in 1981, "that particularly would reward some six million people for breaking our laws in coming here illegally?" William French Smith replied, "Yes, I am. . . . We have from three to six million people here [illegally] . . . so we have to recognize the fact that those people are here and, in large measure, they are going to stay here."[72]

The absence of enforcement of the worker verification tenets of the Immigration Reform and Control Act by Reagan and subsequent presidents would then transform "amnesty" from an explanation to an epithet. In his testimony before the Hesburgh Commission in 1980, Rev. John Paul Szura of the Catholic Theological Union joined his church's chorus in favor of "amnesty" for the undocumented. Yet he presciently suggested "that we closely examine our choice of words in certain areas so that we no longer call it granting 'amnesty' when the person has done nothing wrong; and that the United States not close its doors on immigrants rather than open them more widely."[73]

The word "amnesty" indeed began to disappear from the tongues and pens of admissionists during the George W. Bush administration. Mark Krikorian, the executive director of the restrictionist Federation for American Immigration Reform (FAIR), noticed in September 2001 that Bush administration officials were employing the terms "normalization" and "earned adjustment" when they really meant "amnesty." These terms would soon publicly give way to "legalization" and "earned legalization," even while privately an administration document spoke of "amnesty plus."[74]

The bishops followed suit. "We try to argue in the best sense of the word for a path to citizenship," Bishop Manz would note in 2012, "not an amnesty." When announcing his "DREAM" executive order, President Obama assured Americans that "this is not amnesty." The bishops and the president were still endorsing amnesty but, based on the incomplete implementation of IRCA, they had chosen to attach conditions (such as military service and college education) and call it something else.[75]

The abandonment of the term "amnesty" was a significant admission by immigration advocates that their opponents had successfully put them on the defensive. They wasted valuable time and effort debating the description "amnesty" instead of defending the merits of comprehensive immigration reform. "You pay a fine, you're on probation, you secure the border, you get the employer verification system up and running, you're at the back of the line, you can't receive any government benefits during this time," Wisconsin Catholic Republican congressman Paul Ryan said in defending his support for comprehensive immigration reform in 2013. "That's not amnesty," Ryan protested, even though the 1986 law, which contained several similar provisions, actually was.[76]

Just as "amnesty" was exiting the vocabulary of immigration advocates, the word "illegal" was undergoing a similar transformation. In between his governorship and his presidency, Ronald Reagan delivered a series of radio commentaries on a variety of issues. He discussed immigration only once, in November 1977. Citing a report that apple growers had to import foreign workers when they didn't attract enough domestic applicants, Reagan said that the situation "makes me wonder . . . about the illegal alien fuss." He skeptically inquired, "Are great numbers of our unemployed really victims of the illegal alien invasion or are those illegal tourists actually doing work our people won't do?"[77]

Within the next three decades, however, the word "illegal" gradually vanished from the parlance of immigration supporters inside and outside of the White House and the Catholic hierarchy. In January 2005, President George W. Bush justified his call for comprehensive immigration reform by describing the "millions of hard working men and women condemned to fear and insecurity in a massive, undocumented economy." The conservative magazine *The American Enterprise* noted that "never before has a prominent U.S. politician, let alone a president, rationalized illegal immigration that baldly. Bush's remarks placed illegal aliens on the same level as legal immigrants as seekers of opportunity."[78]

President Obama's statements would achieve the same result. "Our journey is not complete until we find a better way to welcome the striving, hopeful immigrants who still see America as a land of opportunity," he intoned in his second inaugural address in January 2013, "until bright young students and engineers are enlisted in our workforce rather than expelled from our country." Thus did the president seem to equate those who entered the country illegally to find work with those who did so legally to go to school.[79]

The adjective "illegal" would also depart from the language of Catholic immigration advocates, including the bishops. Los Angeles Archbishop José Gómez, chairman of the United States Conference of Catholic Bishops Committee on Migration, praised the Gang of Eight's January 2013 legalization provisions for allowing "immigrants and their families to come out of the shadows and into the light." Catholic Charities Maine Refugee and Immigration

Services of Portland, Maine; Catholic Community Services Family Immigration Services of Mount Vernon, Washington; and the bishops' Catholic Legal Immigration Network (CLINIC) joined about fifty other organizations in sending a letter to President Obama advocating a legal "framework for ensuring the future success of all immigrants—those who enter the country through traditional means as well as those who may become legal residents through a legalization program." They added that "to ensure the success of immigration reform, a vibrant integration program is essential." In some ways, such integration had already begun, in word if not in deed.[80]

Many of those who pressed for such a change were well-intentioned. "Because the United States requires all within its bounds to be known to government officials, the category 'illegal alien' connotes not only criminality but anarchy," Susan Bibler Coutin regretted in 1993. "In contrast to the arborescent metaphors used to refer to the 'rooted,' illegal aliens are compared to uncontrollable, even chaotic bodies of water. Those who write about illegal aliens use such phrases as 'steady stream,' 'shut off the flood,' 'wet' versus 'dry' labor, and 'the trickle of illegal crossers became a torrent.' The Border Patrol's expression for legalizing immigrants is to 'dry them out.'"[81]

So rather than "illegal aliens," immigration advocates came to prefer the term "undocumented workers," recognizing their contributions to the American economy. It was not "illegal," after all, to seek a better life for one's family, especially when most native-born Americans refused to accept the low-paying, physically taxing jobs which these new arrivals selflessly filled.[82]

Even the word "undocumented" carried its own stigma, however, perniciously consigning these newcomers to an underappreciated and undercompensated underclass. Thus they became simply "immigrants." But the new nomenclature did not just magnanimously join unauthorized with authorized immigrants. It made it easier to demonize opponents of illegal immigration by unfairly tying them to opposition to legal immigration.

"Along with Dolls and Stuffed Animals, Making Time for Immigration Activism" was the title of a July 2013 *New York Times* story by Fernanda Santos depicting an Arizona teenager who became an activist following the arrest of her parents in a workplace immigration raid. "I wanted there to be justice for my parents and justice for the fathers and mothers," the girl explained, "whose only crime was work." Actually, that was not her parents' only crime. "Her parents are criminals, technically speaking, having pleaded guilty to impersonation for falsifying a Social Security number to secure employment," the otherwise sympathetic article conceded, which was "a felony in this state." After reading the account, *Washington Post* columnist Esther Cepeda concluded that "any real shot at an immigration compromise—one that codifies who gets to stay and who must leave—will depend on accurately separating perception from reality." And neither side enhances the prospects for such a deal, she added, "when they pretend that eleven million people are all angels and devils."[83]

Some Catholics viewed "immigrants" through the same Manichean lens. "Do we really believe that America is one nation under God, made up of every other people?" Archbishop Gómez asked in his 2013 book *Immigration and the New America: Renewing the Soul of Our Nation.* "Or is America instead a nation that is essentially white, Anglo-Saxon, and Protestant, but *permits* the presence of people of other races, colors, and religions?" Rev. Richard Wilson, pastor of New Bedford's Our Lady of Guadalupe Parish at St. James Church, claimed that those parishioners who offered sanctuary to undocumented aliens "have a deeper faith." Those who didn't, Rev. Mark Fallon of Catholic Charities in New Bedford contended, preferred the "cheap exit" favored by the "cable news racists who want to target them [undocumented entrants] and put a label on them and treat them as criminals." Catholic Democratic congressman Joe

Garcia of Florida, the son of Cuban refugees, urged his church's clergy to "speak from the pulpit" in favor of the 2013 Senate bill to "deflate these phony arguments about the fear of the stranger, the fear of the traveler, and this fear of the outsider." Colorado's bishops obliged, entreating their congregants to reject the "manifestations of xenophobia and racism" of those opposed to comprehensive immigration reform.[84]

"We believe in immigration. We want to be compassionate and helpful to people who have been here a long time," said Alabama Republican senator Jeff Sessions, a leading opponent of the 2013 Senate bill, confronting these critics. "But a nation has not only a right but also a responsibility to establish a responsible level of immigration that promotes assimilation, self-sufficiency, and rising wages." When not lobbying against comprehensive immigration reform, Mark Krikorian, now the executive director of the Center for Immigration Studies, was teaching a class, sponsored by Catholic Charities, which prepared legal immigrants for their citizenship exams. "The United States needs more people, and we need them to be legal so they can pay taxes," said Alfredo Mesa Moreno, a twenty-nine-year-old field scientist from Spain who hoped to become an American citizen in 2014. "But with this [2013 Senate comprehensive immigration reform] law, it can be like a call for immigrants to come here illegally." Mesa added, "I guess it's complicated," more complex than some of those who dropped the descriptor "illegal" appeared to acknowledge.[85]

USA Today's Tom Krattenmaker worried in August 2013 that his fellow religious liberals were falling into the same trap as had ultimately ensnared the Religious Right. "Don't play the 'God' card too fast and loose; don't give blind allegiance to one political party or ideology; don't use language and tactics that dehumanize political opponents and turn them into enemies," Krattenmaker warned. "Don't reflexively assign malign intentions to everything the other side is trying to do."[86]

A fourth change from the earlier era was the attitude of Hispanics toward illegal immigration. In a 1983 survey, 46 percent of Hispanics, and 50 percent of Hispanic citizens, wanted the country to admit fewer immigrants, while only 15 percent of all Hispanics and 12 percent of Hispanic citizens wanted to admit more. While 74 percent of Latinos supported amnesty for irregular immigrants, 61 percent backed greater border enforcement and 60 percent endorsed employer sanctions. In 1987, polls showed that California Hispanics approved of the restrictionist Proposition 187 all the way up to the vote itself, when they narrowly—and unsuccessfully—opposed it, by 48 percent to 46 percent.[87]

A decade later, James Davidson, Andrea Williams, Richard Lamanna, Jan Stenftenegel, Kathleen Maas Weigert, William Whalen, and Patricia Wittberg concluded that the younger generations of Latinos were more sympathetic to illegal immigration than their parents and grandparents. Another decade later, those offspring were coming of age—and repudiating the restrictionism of their elders. According to a Pew Hispanic Center survey, Mexican immigrants in 2011 were more likely to be female (47 percent versus 45 percent), older (median age of thirty-eight versus twenty-nine), better educated (41 percent with at least some high school versus 25 percent), and in the country longer (71 percent for more than ten years versus 50 percent) than in 1990. According to the 2011 *National Catholic Reporter* study, 65 percent of Hispanic millennials strongly agreed with the bishops on immigration reform.[88]

Or were the bishops agreeing with the Hispanic millennials? The sympathy of Catholic clergy for the plight of the friends and relatives of many of their congregants was the natural reaction not just of a church that had become more Latino, but of a church that was becoming less Latino. Adopting a stance toward immigration reform which was heavy on reconciliation and light on retribution was not only a gesture toward those Latinos who entered their churches, but it was an effort to keep them from leaving.

Between 1981 and 2013, both sides of the U.S.-Latin American border were experiencing the growth of Protestant alternatives to the faith of their elders. As late as 1996, Catholics comprised 81 percent of all Latin Americans. By 2010, however, that figure had descended to 70 percent. In the meantime, Protestants rose from 4 percent to 13 percent of that region's population, potentially steering the church toward its first Latin American pope three years later. While 69 percent of first-generation Latinos in the United States in 2012 were Catholic, 41 percent of the second generation and 60 percent of the third generation were not. Although over two-thirds of Latinos in the United States were Catholic in 2012, a Gallup Poll found them less religious than Protestant Hispanics, and the Pew Forum on Religion and Public Life estimated that only about half of Latinos would be Catholic by 2030. As of 2012, only 15 percent of new Catholic priests being ordained in the United States were Hispanic. At the very time that the Catholic hierarchy was turning more noticeably than ever toward these newest Americans, many of them, attracted to evangelical and charismatic denominations, were turning away.[89]

Perhaps these young Hispanics were seeking solace from the plight that their parents and grandparents were facing—a stagnant economy, which offered a fifth and final deviation from the example of the 1980's. By 1986, when immigration reform became law, the country had climbed out of the throes of the 1981–1982 recession, and was in the midst of a robust recovery, a powerful magnet luring unauthorized and authorized immigrants alike. By 2013, when immigration reform was but a DREAM, the country was still suffering the aftershocks of the 2008–2009 recession, a lethal deterrent which stymied the wages of native-born unskilled workers, cost the jobs of immigrant unskilled workers, and brought the migration of 12 million undocumented Mexicans over four decades almost to a standstill.[90]

In 2000, 700,000 Mexicans lawfully and unlawfully arrived in the United States. In 2010, that number dwindled to 140,000. The nation's unauthorized population, which had climbed from 8.4 million in 2000 to 12 million in 2007, dipped to 11.1 million in 2009, and remained at that level through 2011. Meanwhile, the Hispanic-American birth rate was declining by almost one-fifth from 2007 to 2011. Although illegal immigration to the United States would rise again as unemployment began to fall, there were now more Americans entering Mexico than there were Mexicans entering the United States. A faltering U.S. economy, alongside a Mexican economy growing at 4 percent per year and exporting more manufactured goods than all of the rest of Latin America, was achieving what presidents from Reagan to Obama had failed to achieve: a virtual halt to illegal immigration.[91]

The Verdict

Throughout over three decades of change and continuity, the Catholic power structure and many of its followers, by admirably endeavoring to put principle ahead of politics, at times exaggerated the former at the expense of the latter. The motives of these immigration advocates were noble. Their words were heartfelt. But the results were too often the opposite of what they intended, inviting backlash instead of winning converts.

In this latest act in the longstanding drama of American Catholics, these determined defenders appeared more Catholic than American. While they may have been winning points in heaven, they were losing votes in Congress. The more they entered the arena of national politics, they less they seemed willing to play. "Religious values will not be accepted as part of the public morality unless they are shared by the community at large," Mario Cuomo, the Catholic former Democratic governor of New York wrote in 2004, reprising his famous speech at the University of Notre Dame twenty years earlier. "The plausibility of achieving that consensus is a relevant consideration in deciding whether or not to make the effort to impose those values officially." Cuomo was defending his support for abortion rights, which his church unconditionally opposed. But he could have been expressing his support for comprehensive immigration reform, which his church prudentially promoted.[92]

"Tiring of the messy trade-offs of politics is understandable, but it's no answer to our discontent, for history has issued a sure warning that the alternatives to democratic discord are far worse," *Commonweal*'s editors, otherwise sympathetic to the bishops' immigration views, asserted in 2013. "The nation's current political impasse calls for a renewed commitment to the practice of politics, not to Christian detachment. . . . There is no need to choose between fidelity to Christ and our secular democratic hopes." The hopes for immigration reform need not have fallen victim to litmus tests, whether administered by the Republican Right or the Catholic Left.[93]

"Comprehensive" immigration reform, whether passed in parts or as a whole, meant just that—rigid restrictionists (such as most House Republicans during the George W. Bush and Barack Obama administrations) would have to agree to the legalization they didn't want, while adamant admissionists (such as Catholic activists and many House and Senate Democrats during the same time period) would have to submit to the border and interior enforcement they didn't want and to sacrifice the citizenship most unauthorized immigrants didn't seek. Presidents Reagan through Obama were willing to varying degrees to split the difference between these two camps. But despite progress in both houses in 1986 and in the Senate in 2006 and 2013, both sides largely held fast.

In the midst of the debate over the Senate's comprehensive immigration reform bill in late May 2013 came word of the death of Rev. Andrew Greeley, the renowned sociologist, novelist, columnist, and commentator who had moved from the right to the left flank of the church. Greeley had lived long enough to see the hierarchy veer in the opposite direction, from the stirring liberalism of Pope

John XXIII to the stern conservatism of Pope Benedict XVI. Comprehensive immigration reform, with its theological appeal to social justice and its pragmatic promise of larger congregations, was one of the few causes which united both camps, in the pulpits if not in the pews. At Father Greeley's funeral, Chicago's conservative Francis Cardinal George mused that while the two of them did not agree on many issues, they had attended the opera together several times. "He said it's the most Catholic of the operas," Cardinal George recalled of *La Traviata*, Greeley's favorite, "because in the end ... everyone is forgiven."[94]

Americans also believe in forgiveness, and their nation's history is rife with second chances and second acts. But the church's doctrine and the country's documents teach that forgiveness has its limits, and absolution has a price. However erratically and inadequately, American presidents from 1981 to 2013 generally accepted these grim realities—at the border, in the workplace, and on Capitol Hill. Catholic immigration advocates generally denied them.

In her testimony before Congress in 1995, former Texas Democratic congresswoman Barbara Jordan, chair of the federal Commission on Immigration Reform, asserted that American immigration law should preserve and promote the "national interest." The Catholic organization Justice for Immigrants, founded by the bishops in 2005, contended that citizenship for undocumented aliens would preserve and promote the "common good." Despite many instances of cooperation and collaboration toward common objectives, three decades of conflict between American presidents and Catholic immigration advocates ultimately showed that the "national interest" and the "common good" were not always the same thing.[95]

Notes

Notes to the Introduction

1. Elizabeth Rolph, *Immigration Policies: Legacy From the 1980's and Issues from the 1990's* (Santa Monica, Calif.: Rand, 1992); Saskia Sassen, *Losing Control? Sovereignty in an Age of Globalization* (New York: Columbia University Press, 1992); Frank Bean, ed., *At The Crossroads: Mexico and U.S. Immigration Policy* (Lanham, Md.: Rowman and Littlefield, 1997); Peter Schuck, *Citizens, Strangers, and In-Betweens* (Boulder, Colo.: Westview Press, 1998); James Gimpel and James Edwards, *The Congressional Politics of Immigration Reform* (Boston: Allyn and Bacon, 1999); Debra DeLaet, *U.S. Immigration Policy in the Age of Rights* (Westport, Ct.: Greenwood Press, 2000); Nicolas Laham, *Ronald Reagan and the Politics of Immigration* (Westport, Conn.: Praeger, 2000); Cheryl Shanks, *The Politics of American Sovereignty* (Ann Arbor, Mich.: University of Michigan Press, 2001); Hugh Davis Graham, *Collision Course: The Strange Convergence of Affirmative Action and Immigration Policy in America* (New York: Oxford University Press, 2002); Roger Daniels, *Guarding the Golden Door: American Immigration Policy and Immigrants Since 1882* (New York: Hill and Wang, 2004); Mae Ngai, *Impossible Subjects: Illegal Aliens and the Making of Modern America* (Princeton, N.J.: Princeton University Press, 2004); Marc Rosenblum, *The Transnational Politics of U.S. Immigration Policy* (La Jolla, Calif.: Center for Comparative Immigration Studies, University of California, San Diego, 2004); Otis Graham, *Immigration Reform and America's Unchosen Future* (Bloomington, Ind.: AuthorHouse, 2008); Kathleen Arnold, *Immigration After 1996: The Shifting Ground of Political Inclusion* (University Park, Pa.: Penn State University Press, 2011); Philip Kretsedemas, *The Immigration Crucible: Transforming Race, Nation, and the Limits of the Law* (New York: Columbia University Press, 2012).

2. Felix Podimattam, *The Struggle for Justice and Responsible Disobedience* (Bangladorem, India: Rego and Sons, 1998); Daniel Groody, *Border of Death, Valley of Life* (Lanham, Md.: Rowman and Littlefield, 2002); Gioacchino Campese and Pietro Ciallella, eds., *Migration, Religious Experience, and Globalization* (New York: Center for Migration Studies, 2003); David Badillo, *Latinos and the New Immigrant Church* (Baltimore: Johns Hopkins University Press, 2006); Daniel Groody and Gioacchino Campese, eds., *A Promised Land, A Perilous Journey* (Notre Dame, Ind.: University of Notre Dame Press, 2008); Patrick Bascio, *On the Immorality of Illegal Immigration* (Bloomington, Ind.: Indiana University Press, 2009); Donald Kerwin, ed., *And You Welcomed Me: Migration and Catholic Social Teaching* (Lanham, Md.: Lexington Books, 2009); Ben Daniel, *Neighbor* (Louisville, Ky.: Westminster John Knox Press, 2010); Timothy Matovina, *Latino Catholicism* (Princeton, N.J.: Princeton University Press, 2011); Todd Scribner and Kevin Appleby, eds., *On "Strangers No Longer": Perspectives on the Historic U.S.-Mexican Catholic Bishops' Pastoral Letter on Migration* (New York: Paulist Press, 2013).

3. Donald Kerwin, "'They' Are 'Us,'" *America*, November 19, 2001, 15–16.

4. Lawrence J. McAndrews, *Broken Ground: John F. Kennedy and the Politics of Education* (New York: Routledge, 2012), 24–25.

5. "Immigration Bureau/Department," *Manuscript Collection, United States Conference of Catholic Bishops*, at http://archives.lib.cua.edu/ncwccfm#IMM; "National Catholic Rural Life Conference," at http://www.ncrlc.com/page.aspx?ID=7; "Bishops' Committee for Hispanic Affairs," *Texas State Historical Association*, at http://www.tshaonline.org/handbook/online/articles/46millionici; Kerwin, "'They' Are 'Us,'" 16; Michael Warner, *Changing Witness: Catholic Bishops and Public Policy* (Grand Rapids, Mich.: Erdman's, 1995), 2; "A Short History of the USCCB," *The Fifth Column*, March 29, 2011, at http://skellmeyer.blogspot.com/2011/03/short-history-of-usccb-html, 1.

6. "The Chinese Exclusion Act (1882): Brief Overview," n.d., at http://www.lehigh.edu/~ineng/VirtualAmericana/chines.

7. Donna Gabbacia and Maddalena Marinari, "American Immigration Policy," in *Companion to Lyndon B. Johnson*, Mitch Lerner, ed. (Hoboken, N.J.: Wiley-Blackwell, 2012), 220; Philip Schrag, *A Well-Founded Fear: The Congressional Battle to Save Asylum in America* (New York: Routledge, 2000), 21–26; David Kennedy, Lizabeth Cohen, and Mel Piehl, *The Brief American Pageant* (New York: Wadsworth, 2012), 512; Donald Kerwin, "The Natural Rights of Migrants and Newcomers," in *A Promised Land, A Perilous Journey, in Migration, Religious Experience, and Globalization*, ed. Groody and Campese, 199; Kennedy, Cohen, and Piehl, *The Brief American Pageant*, 646.

8. Gabbacia and Marinari, "American Immigration Policy," 220.

9. Kennedy, Cohen, and Piehl, *The Brief American Pageant*, 714; "Immigration Act of 1990," U.S. Citizenship and Immigration Services. "IIRIRA 96-A Summary of the New Immigration Bill," *Visalaw.com*, November 3, 1996, 1.

10. Kerwin, "The Natural Rights," 202–3; Tom Head, "Comparing 2006 House and Senate Immigration Reform Bills—H.R.4437 and S. 2611," *About.com*, *Civil Liberties*, *New York Times*; Ashley Parker and Jonathan Martin, "Senate, 68 to 32, Passes Overhaul for Immigration," *New York Times*, June 28, 2013, sec. A, 1, 18.

11. William Chip and Michael Scaperlanda, "The Ethics of Immigration: An Exchange," *First Things*, May 4, 2008, 1.

12. Daniel, *Neighbor*, 17–19; William O' Neill, "Christian Hospitality with the Stranger," in *And You Welcomed Me: Migration and Catholic Social Teaching*, ed. Kerwin, 149.

13. Daniel, *Neighbor*, 20; United States Catholic Conference, "Welcoming the Stranger Among Us: Unity in Diversity," November 15, 2000, at http://usccb.org/pcmrt/bpsstatement,html, 2; Daniel, *Neighbor*, 23.

14. D. Paul Sullins, "Introduction," in *Catholic Social Thought*, ed. D. Paul Sullins and Anthony Blasi (Lanham, Md.: Rowman and Littlefield, 2009), 15–17.

15. United States Catholic Conference, "Welcoming the Stranger Among Us," 2; "Bishops' Committee for Hispanic Affairs," *Texas State Historical Association*.

16. United States Catholic Conference, "Welcoming the Stranger Among Us," 2; Todd Scribner, "Negotiating Priorities: The National Catholic Welfare Conference and U.S. Migration Policy in the Post–World War II World, 1948–1952," *American*

Catholic Studies 121 (Winter 2010), 61–86; Jeffrey Togman, *The Ramparts of Nations: Institutions and Immigration Policies in France and the United States* (Westport, Conn.: Praeger, 2002), p. 35; Ira Mehlman, "John F. Kennedy and Immigration Reform," *The Social Contract* 1 (Summer 1991), 1–2.

17. Michael Blume, "Migration and the Social Doctrine of the Church," in Campese and Ciallella, eds., 63; Mehlman, "John F. Kennedy and Immigration Reform,"5; Togman, *The Ramparts of Nations: Institutions and Immigration Policies*, 37; Graham, *Collision Course: The Strange Convergence*, 64.

18. Blume, "Migration and the Social Doctrine of the Church," 63; David Bovee, *The Church and the Land: The National Catholic Rural Life Conference and American Society* (Washington, D.C.: The Catholic University of America Press, 2010), 322–23.

19. Dominique Peridans, "What Are They Thinking? A Look at Roman Catholic 'Doctrine' on Immigration," *Center for Immigration Studies*, October 2012, at http://www.cis.org.

20. United States Catholic Conference, "Political Responsibility," September 1995, in *Pastoral Letters and Statements of the United States Catholic Bishops, Volume VI, 1989–1997*, Patrick W. Carey, ed. (Washington, D.C.: United States Catholic Conference, 1998), 732–33.

21. United States Conference of Catholic Bishops, "The Catholic Church's Teaching on Immigration Enforcement," January 2011, at http:// www.usccb.org/issues-and-actions/human-life-and-dignity/immigration/church, 1; Chip and Scaperlanda, "The Ethics of Immigration: An Exchange," 1; Mark Zwick and Louise Zwick, *Mercy Without Borders* (New York: Paulist Press, 2010), 192–93.

22. Olivia Ruiz Marrujo and Alberto López Pulido, "Dismantling Borders of Violence: Migration and Deportation Along the U.S.-Mexico Border," *U.S. Catholic Historian* 28 (Fall 2010), 143.

23. Bascio, *On the Immorality of Illegal Immigration*, 2; Badillo, *Latinos and the New Immigrant Church*, 198.

24. Daniel, *Neighbor*, 41–42.

25. Peridans, "What Are They Thinking?"

26. Chip and Scaperlana, "The Ethics of Immigration: An Exchange," 2; Laura Sheahen, "When Did We See You a Stranger: Cardinal Theodore McCarrick on Immigration," *Beliefnet*, April 2006, at http://www.beliefnet.com/Faiths/Christianity/2006/04/; Reuven Brenner, "Our Muddled Masses," *First Things*, January 2010, 1.

27. "Welcome, Stranger," *America*, April 8–15, 2.

28. Podimattam, *The Struggle for Justice and Responsible Disobedience*, 26–27; Daniel Groody, "Crossing the Divide: Foundations of a Theology of Migration and Refugees," in *And You Welcomed Me*, Kerwin, ed., 10.

29. Podimattam, *The Struggle for Justice and Responsible Disobedience*, 2–4.

30. Eduardo Moisés Penalver, "Are Illegal Immigrants Pioneers?" *Commonweal*, May 5, 2006, 9; John F. Kavanaugh, "Amnesty?" *America*, March 10, 2008, 2; Chip and Scaperlanda, "The Ethics of Immigration: An Exchange," 5.

31. Daniel T. Griswold, "Immigration and the Welfare State," *Cato Journal* 32 (Winter 2012), 159–60, 170.

32. United States Conference of Catholic Bishops, "Why Don't Unauthorized Migrants Come Here Legally?" 2012, at http://www.usccb.org/issues-and-action/human-life-and-dignity/immigration/whydo, 2–3; Alan Gomez, "An Immigration Food Fight," *USA Today*, March 18, 2013, sec. A, 2.

33. Mia Crosthwaite, "Jesus in the Disguise of an Illegal Alien," *National Catholic Reporter*, September 12, 2003, 1.

34. "Now We're Talking," *International Herald Tribune*, January 30, 2013, 6.

Notes to Chapter 1

1. Michael Teitelbaum, "Right versus Right: Immigration and Refugee Policy in the United States," *Foreign Affairs*, Fall 1980, 21; Roger Daniels and Otis Graham, *Immigration, 1882–Present* (Lanham, Md.: Rowman and Littlefield, 2001), 79.

2. "Statement of the Most Reverend Robert F. Sanchez, Archbishop of Sante Fe, on Behalf of the United States Catholic Conference before the Subcommittee on Immigration and Naturalization of the Senate Committee on the Judiciary Concerning S. 3074," March 17, 1976, Series VII, Box 93, Folder: Miscellaneous, Select Commission on Immigration, 1979–83, Center for Migration Studies-American Committee for Italian Migration Archives, New York, N.Y., 6; "Convention Relating to the Status of Refugees, Geneva, July 28, 1951, and Protocol Relating to the Status of Refugees, New York, 31 January 1967," at http://untreaty.un.org/cod/avl/ha/prsr/prsr.html; National Conference of Catholic Bishops, "Resolution on the Pastoral Concern for People on the Move," November 8–11, 1976, United States Catholic Conference Papers, United States Catholic Conference Archives, Washington, D.C., 19–20; Teitelbaum, "Right Versus Right," 21.

3. Roger Daniels, *Guarding the Golden Door: American Immigration Policy and Immigrants Since 1882* (New York: Hill and Wang, 2004), 205; "We Were Poor in Cuba, but," *Time*, May 18, 1981, 25.

4. United States Catholic Conference, "Resolution on Cuban and Haitian Refugees," May 1980, in *Pastoral Letters of the United States Catholic Bishops, Volume IV, 1975–1983*, Hugh Nolan, ed. (Washington, D.C.: United States Catholic Conference, 1984), 378.

5. Norman Zucker, "The Conundrum of American Immigration and Refugee Policy: The 1980's and Beyond," *Brookings Institution*, November 18, 1981, Series VI, Box 361, Folder: 1982 Immigration Bill, Romano Mazzoli Papers, University of Louisville Archives, Louisville, Ky., 3–5.

6. Letter from Rev. John McCarthy to William Casey, November 20, 1980, Frank Hodsoll Files, Box 12, Folder: Immigration and Refugees [Task Force] [1], Ronald Reagan Presidential Papers, Ronald Reagan Presidential Library, Simi Valley, Calif., 1–2.

7. Memorandum from Attorney General William French Smith to President Ronald Reagan, June 26, 1981, Series VIII, Box 94, Folder: Miscellaneous, Simpson-Mazzoli, 1977–81, CMS-ACIMA, 1

8. John Donohue, "The Uneasy Immigration Debate," *America*, March 20, 1982, 207.

9. *Select Commission on Immigration and Refugee Policy, Second Semi-Annual Report to Congress*, October 1980, Box 123, Folder: [SCIRP—Second Semiannual Report to Congress, 1980], Theodore Hesburgh Papers, University of Notre Dame Archives, Notre Dame, Ind., 53, 103, 105,109,122, 123, 180, 184, 49.

10. "Executive Summary," *United States Immigration and the National Interest: Final Report of Select Commission on Immigration and Refugee Policy*, March 1981, Series VI, Box 361, Folder: August 1981 Judiciary Committee, RMP, ULA, xxi–xxiv.

11. Memorandum from Attorney General William French Smith to President Ronald Reagan, June 26, 1981.

12. Ronald Reagan, "Statement on United States Immigration and Refugee Policy," July 30, 1981, *Public Papers of the President of the United States: Ronald Reagan, Book II, July 1-December 31, 1981* (Washington, D.C.: U.S. Government Printing Office, 1982), 677.

13. Donohue, "The Uneasy Immigration Debate," 207.

14. "United States Catholic Conference Position on S. 2222," Series VIII, Box 95, Folder: Miscellaneous, Simpson-Mazzoli, Undated, CMS-ACIMA; Memorandum from "EG" to Red Caveney, May 29, 1981, Frank Hodsoll Files, Box 1, Folder: Immigration [8],RRPP, RRPL; "VOLAG Meeting," June 26, 1981, Frank Hodsoll Files, Box 1, Immigration [8], RRPP, RRPL; "Testimony of Bishop Anthony J. Bevilacqua, Chairman, Ad Hoc Committee on Migration and Tourism, National Conference of Catholic Bishops, to the House Subcommittee on Immigration, Refugee, and International Law," October 28, 1981, Series VIII, Box 94, Folder: Miscellaneous, Simpson-Mazzoli, 1982, CMS-ACIMA, 1–3.

15. "Statement of Donald G. Hohl, Associate Director, Migration and Refugee Services, United States Catholic Conference," January 25, 1982, Series VIII, Box 94, Folder: Miscellaneous, Simpson-Mazzoli, 1982 January-June, CMS-ACIMA, 5–7, 4.

16. Mary Thornton, "Hill Chairmen Propose New Immigration Bill," *Washington Post*, March 18, 1982, sec. A, 4.

17. "Statement of His Excellency Anthony J. Bevilacqua, Chairman, Committee on Migration and Tourism, National Conference of Catholic Bishops/ United States Catholic Conference, Before Joint Hearings of the Senate Subcommittee on Immigration and Refugee Policy and the House Subcommittee on Immigration Refugee and International Law," April 1, 1982, Series VIII, Box 94, Folder: Miscellaneous, Simpson-Mazzoli, 1982, January-June, CMS-ACIMA, 5–6.

18. Letter from Msgr. Daniel Hoye, "Dear Senator," June 17, 1982, Series VIII, Box 94, Folder: Miscellaneous, Simpson-Mazzoli, 1982, January-June, CMS-ACIMA, 1–2.

19. "Summary of the Immigration Reform and Control Act of 1982 (S. 2222) as Passed by the Full Senate," *United States Catholic Conference Office of Migration and Refugee Services*, August 17, 1982," August 17, 1982, Series VIII, Box 94, Folder: Miscellaneous, Simpson-Mazzoli, 1982, July-August, CMS-ACIMA, 1–2.

20. "Summary of the Immigration Reform and Control Act of 1982 (H.R. 6514) as Reported to the Full House by Judiciary Committee, September 26, 1982," October

26, 1982, Series VIII, Box 94, Folder: Miscellaneous, Simpson-Mazzoli, 1982, CMS-ACIMA, 2–3.

21. Letter from Msgr. Daniel Hoye, "Dear Congressman," September 10, 1982, Series VIII, Box 94, Folder: Miscellaneous, Simpson-Mazzoli, 1982, CMS-ACIMA, 2.

22. Memorandum from James Michael Hoffman, January 7, 1983, United States Catholic Conference Office of Migration and Refugee Services, January 7, 1983, Series VIII, Box 94, Folder: Miscellaneous, Simpson-Mazzoli, 1983, CMS-ACIMA, 1.

23. Letter from Rev. John McCarthy to Rep. Romano Mazzoli, United States Catholic Conference Office of Migration and Refugee Services, July 1, 1983, Series VI, Box 362, Folder: 1982–1984 Immigration Letters, RMP, ULA.

24. "Recognizing Refugees," *America*, January 13, 1985, 1.

25. Betsy Cooper and Kevin O'Neill, "Policy Brief," *Migration Policy Institute Policy Analysis* 3 (August 2005), 4.

26. "Issue Paper: Legal Status of Cubans and Haitians," n.d., Frank Hodsoll Files, Box 12, Folder: Immigration and Refugees [Task Force] [9], RRPP, RRPL, 1–8.

27. "VOLAG Meeting," June 26, 1981, Frank Hodsoll Files, 1–2.

28. "Subject: Immigration and Refugee Policy Cabinet Meeting," July 1, 1981, Frank Hodsoll Files, Box 12, Folder: Immigration and Refugees [General] [18], RRPP, RRPL, 1.

29. Gregory Jaynes, "Haitian Freighter Seized by Customs after Breakdown near Florida," *New York Times*, October 29, 1981, sec. A, 22; Memorandum from George Bush to William Clark, March 26, 1982; Memorandum from Michael Guhin to William Clark, April 2, 1982, Robert Kimmitt Files, Box 5, Folder: Legal-Immigration [2], RRPP, RRPL.

30. Memorandum from William Clark to the Vice President, April 6, 1982, Robert Kimmitt Files, Box 5, Folder: Legal-Immigration [2], RRPP, RRPL.

31. Letter from Alan Nelson to Kenneth Cribb, April 9, 1982, Richard Williamson Files, Box 3, Folder: Immigration/Refugees [2], RRPP, RRPL, 1.

32. Justice Department, "For Immediate Release," June 14, 1982, Richard Williamson Files, Box 3, Folder: Immigration/Refugees [2], RRPP, RRPL, 1.

33. Letter from Rev. John Roach to President Ronald Reagan, April 7, 1982, Jack Burgess Files, Box 3, Folder: Catholic Miscellaneous [3] OA 9747, RRPP, RRPL.

34. Memorandum from Elizabeth Dole to Edwin Meese, James Baker, and Michael Deaver, November 2, 1982, Morton Blackwell Files, Box 7, Folder: Catholic Strategy (1 of 3), OA 12450, RRPP, RRPL.

35. Draft Letter from Ronald Reagan to Rev. John Roach, attached to Letter from John Mackey to Stephen Galesbach, November 5, 1982, Morton Blackwell Files, Box 7, Folder: Catholic Strategy (1of 3), OA 12450, RRPP, RRPL.

36. Michael Kennedy and Barry Bearak, "We're Not Going to Hurt You," *Los Angeles Times*, December 5, 1987, sec. A, 13.

37. "The Golden Door," *Wall Street Journal*, July 9, 1986, 22.

38. Lou Cannon and John Goshko, "Reagan to Bar Immigration of Cubans via Third Countries," *Washington Post*, August 12, 1986, sec. A, 10.

39. Memorandum from Philip Brady to Vice President George Bush, September 9, 1986, Office of Chief of Staff Philip D. Brady Files, Stack G, Folder: Cuban/Nicaraguan Immigration [5] [OA/ID 1453–006], George Bush Vice Presidential Papers, George Bush Presidential Library, College Station, Tex.

40. Kennedy and Bearak, "We're Not Going to Hurt You," 13–14.

41. John Bolt, "Use of Bishop in Prison Riot Was Officials' 'Last Resort,'" December 8, 1987, sec. A, 16; Agustín Román and Enrique San Pedro, "In Defense of Cuban Prisoners in the Atlanta Federal Penitentiary," December 21, 1986, in Timothy Matovina and Gerald Poyo, eds., *Presente! U.S. Latino Catholics from Colonial Origins to the Present* (Maryknoll, N.Y.: Orbis Books, 2000), 234–38.

42. Arnold Burns, "The New Policy for Cuban Detainees," *Miami Herald*, December 13, 1987, sec. C, 5.

43. Alfonso Chardy, "Immigration Agreement Criticized," n.d., sec. A, 1, Office of Chief of Staff, Philip D. Brady Files, Stack G, Folder: Cuban/Nicaraguan Immigration [2] [OA/ID 14831–003], GBVPP, GBPL.

44. Carlos Harrison, "U.S.-Cuban Agreement Bolstered," December 25, 1987, sec. A, 1.

45. "Recognizing Refugees," *America*, 1; Cooper and O'Neill, "Policy Brief," 4.

46. John Crewdson, "U.S. Returns Illegal Immigrants Who Are Fleeing Salvador War," *New York Times*, March 2, 1981, sec. A, 1, 14.

47. Jeremiah Baruch, "Half-Open Door," *Commonweal*, July 15 1983, 390.

48. Mark Gibney, "Seeking Sanctuary," *Commonweal*, May 18, 1984, 296.

49. Oscar Oliva, " Testimony of a Salvadoran Refugee," Box 4, Folder: Testimony—Sanctuary Refugees, Chicago Religious Task Force on Central America Records, Wisconsin Historical Society, Madison, Wis., 1–2.

50. Karen Herrling, "Harboring: Overview of the Law," *Catholic Legal Information Network*, October 2007, at http://cliniclegal.org/sites/default/files/finalharboring1031, 1; Susan Hansen, "Convicted Nun Scores Bishops on Sanctuary," *National Catholic Reporter,*May 16, 1985, 5; Peter Applebome, "Sanctuary Movement: New Hopes After Trial," *New York Times*, May 6, 1986, sec. A, 20; Mark Starr and Joseph Cincotti, "Sanctuary of Salvadorans," *Newsweek*, July 11, 1983, 27.

51. "Emergency Guest Worker Status," n.d., James Warner Files, Box 1, Folder: Immigration-Guest Worker Proposal, OA 18328, RRPP, RRPL.

52. Draft Letter from Chicago Religious Task Force on Central America to Joseph Cardinal Bernardin, July 1983, Box 1, Folder: Agendas, 1982–83, CRTFCAR, WHS, 1–4.

53. Archbishop John Roach, "Statement on U.S. Policy in Central America," July 22, 1983, in *Pastoral Letters of the United States Catholic Bishops*, Nolan, ed., 582.

54. Charles Mohr, "Reagan Receives Bishops' Protest," *New York Times*, March 10, 1983, sec. A, 7.

55. Richard Maslin, "Message of John Paul," *New York Times*, March 10, 1983, sec. A, 8.

56. Archbishop James Hickey, "U.S. Catholic Conference Testimony on Central America," *Origins*, March 24, 1983, 1–2.

57. Letter from Rev. Joseph Bernardin to Robert Reilly, April 23, 1984, Robert Reilly Files, Box 1, Folder: Cardinal Bernardin, OA 12418, RRPP, RRPL; Gibney, "Seeking Sanctuary," 296.

58. Bruce Buursma, "Cardinal Rips U.S. Policy," *Chicago Tribune*, January 17, 1984, sec. 1, 1–2.

59. Letter from Robert Reilly to Rev. Edmund Szoka, January 10, 1984, Robert Reilly Files, Box 1, Folder: Bishop Letter on Central America 1/10/84, OA 12418, RRPP, RRPL.

60. "For Immediate Release," Archdiocese of Chicago, February 24, 1984, Box 1, Folder: Agendas-1984, CRTFCAR, WHS.

61. Mary Engel, "Support Reaffirmed for Sanctuary Movement," *Albuquerque Journal*, February 28, 1984, sec. B, 8.

62. Faith Ryan Whittlesey, "White House Outreach Working Group on Central America," April 4, 1984, and August 8, 1984, Robert Reilly Files, Box 14, Folder: Outreach—Working Group on Central America," OA 13516, RRPP, RRPL, 1–4.

63. "Talking Points for Luncheon with Cardinals and Archbishops," April 18, 1984, Robert Reilly Files, Box 6, Folder: President's Luncheon with and Briefing of U.S. Catholic Cardinals, 4/18/84, OA 12421, RRPP, RRPL, 1–2; Liz Armstrong, "Bishops Back Reagan on Pro-Life, Tuition Tax Credits; Hit Other Policies," *National Catholic News Service*, April 19, 1984, 1–2.

64. James Reel, "Sanctuary Leaders Renew Defense of Asylum Seekers," April 5, 2002, at http://natcathorg/NCR_Online/archives2/2002b/040502i.htm, 2; Aaron Bekemeyer, "The Acme of the Catholic Left: Catholic Activists in the U.S. Sanctuary Movement," B.A. thesis, April 2012, University of Michigan, at http://deepblue.lib.umich.edu.bitstream/handle/2027.4219, 65.

65. "Sister Darlene Nicgorski's Statement on the Verdict," no date, Box 4, Folder: Darlene Nicgorski, CRTFCAR, WHS, 3.

66. Bekemeyer, "The Acme of the Catholic Left," 54.

67. Reel, "Sanctuary Leaders Renew Defense of Asylum Seekers," 2; Applebome, "Sanctuary Movement: New Hopes After Trial," 20.

68. Russell Chandler, "Mahony's Style: Making Waves, Friends," *Los Angeles Times*, February 17, 1986, sec. A, 3; Hector Tobar, "Father Luis Olivares, Voice for the Poor, Dies of AIDS," *Los Angeles Times*, March 20, 1993, at http://articles.latimes.com/1993-03-20/local/me-13086_1_father-luis-olivares; George Volsky, "U.S. Churches Offer Sanctuary to Aliens Facing Deportation," *New York Times*, April 8, 1983, sec. A, 16; Dean Peerman, "Should Churches Provide Sanctuary?" *Christian Century*, April 27, 1983, 387.

69. Susan Hansen, "Convicted Nun Scores Bishops on Sanctuary," *National Catholic Reporter*, May 16, 1986, 5.

70. Timothy Byrnes, *Catholic Bishops in American Politics* (Princeton, N.J.: Princeton University Press, 1991), 5; Charles Austin, "More Churches Join in Offering Sanctuary for Latin Refugees," *New York Times*, September 21, 1983, sec. A, 18; "Bishop Assails Arrests of Sanctuary Activists," *New York Times*, December 10, 1984, sec. B, 13; Archbishop John Roach, "Statement on U.S. Policy in Central America," July 22, 1983, in *Pastoral Letters of the United States Catholic Bishops*, Nolan, ed., 582; Maria Cristina Garcia, *Seeking Refuge: Central American Migration to Mexico, The United States, and Canada* (Berkeley: University of California Press, 2006), 105.

71. Hugh Lacey, "Sanctuary: A Christian Obligation," February 3, 1985, n.d., no number, Box 1[Additions], Folder: Articles About Sanctuary, 1985–1989, CRTFCAR, WHS; David Bauman, "'Sanctuary' Vows to Keep Sheltering Illegal Aliens," *USA Today*, January 16, 1985, sec. A, 3; Don Lattin, "Franciscans in Seven States Open Arms to 'Illegals,'" March 22, 1985, n.p., Box 1[Additions], Folder: Articles About Sanctuary, 1985–1989, CRTFCAR, WHS.

72. Ann Crittenden, *Sanctuary: A Story of American Conscience and Law in Collision* (New York: Weidenfeld and Nelson, 1988), 201.

73. Letter from David Clennon to Rev. Theodore Hesburgh, May 11, 1985, Box 4, Folder: 5/19/85, Notre Dame, Duarte, CRTFCAR, WHS, 1–3; Mark Rising, "Please Read Before Voting," n.d., Box 4, Folder: Sanctuary by Denomination: Roman Catholic, CRTFCAR, WHS; Bekemeyer, "The Acme of the Catholic Left,"58.

74. Miriam Davidson, "Sanctuary Movement under Fire," *Christian Science Monitor*, October 22, 1985, 18.

75. Rael Jean Isaac, "Sanctuary Scoundrels," *American Spectator*, April 1986, 22.

76. Lattin, "Franciscans in Seven States Open Arms to 'Illegals'"; Davidson, "Sanctuary Movement under Fire," 20; Memorandum from Renny Golden, n.d., Box 1, Folder: Agendas-1984, CRTFCAR, WHS.

77. Isaac, "Sanctuary Scoundrels," 22.

78. Susan Bibler Coutin, *The Culture of Protest: Religious Activism and the U.S. Sanctuary Movement* (Boulder, Colo.: Westview Press, 1993), 113; Isaac, "Sanctuary Scoundrels," 22.

79. David Simcox, "The Other Side of Sanctuary," *Chicago Tribune*, January 3, 1986, sec. 1, 19.

80. David Bovee, *The Church and the Land: The National Catholic Rural Life Conference and American Society* (Washington, D.C.: The Catholic University of America Press, 2010), 218–19.

81. Colman McCarthy, "Motley's Crew and the Church," *Washington Post*, July 14, 1985, sec. F, 2.

82. David Kirp, "Is the Sanctuary Movement Being Persecuted?" *Christian Science Monitor*, December 31, 1985, 11.

83. "Outreach Committee Report," July 29, 1986, Box 1, Folder: Agendas, 1986–87, CRTFCAR, WHS, 1.

84. "State of the Movement," January 1987, Box 1, Folder: Analysis of CRTF Work-Position Papers, CRTFCAR, WHS, 1–2.

85. Dan Schanche and J. Michael Kennedy, "Sanctuary Movement Encouraged by Pope," *Los Angeles Times*, September 14, 1987, sec. B, 1, 8; "Papal Aide Denies Speech Endorsed Sanctuary Group," *Los Angeles Times*, September 15, 1987, sec. C, 5.

86. Bekemeyer, "The Acme of the Catholic Left," 5.

87. Crittenden, *Sanctuary: A Story of American Conscience*, 358.

88. "Statement by Honorable Elliott Abrams, Assistant Secretary of State for Human Rights and Humanitarian Affairs, Before the Committee on the Judiciary Subcommittee on Immigration, Refugees, and International Law, House of Representatives," April 12, 1984, John Roberts Files, Box 28, Folder: Immigration and Naturalization [7], RRPP, RRPL, 2–4.

89. Crittenden, *Sanctuary: A Story of American Conscience*, 299.

90. Dean Peerman, "Opposing Deportation of Salvadoran Refugees," *Christian Century*, March 14, 1984, 271; Crittenden, *Sanctuary: A Story of American Conscience*, 88.

91. "An Interview with Senator DeConcini," *Monday*, March 24, 1986, Box 8, Folder: Moakley-DeConcini, CRTFCAR, WHS, 1, 3, 4.

92. McCarthy, "Motley's Crew and the Church," 2.

93. *Congressional Record*, October 9, 1986, 30074.

94. "Subject: Adjudication of Asylum Claims in South Texas," n.d., National Security Council, Nancy Bearg Dyke Subject Files, Stack G, Folder: Refugees, Central America [OA/ID CF 1480] [3 OF 3], GBVPP, GBPL, 1–4; Memorandum from Arnold Burns to Alan Nelson, June 23, 1987, Kenneth Cribb Files, Box 2, Folder: Immigration-Miscellaneous, RRPP, RRPL; "Equal Treatment of Refugees from El Salvador and Nicaragua," July 24, 1987, Series VII, Box 363, Folder: 1986–1988 Subcommittee on Immigration, 100th Congress, RMP, ULA, 1–2.

95. Cheryl Shanks, *Immigration and the Politics of American Sovereignty* (Ann Arbor: University of Michigan Press, 2001), 214, 224; Linda Chavez, "GOP Can Learn From Reagan on Immigration," *Crisis*, September 30, 2011, at http://www.crisismagazine.com/2011/gop-can-learn-from-reagan-on-immi, 1; Memorandum from Joe Ghoughassian to Martin Anderson and Ed Gray, March 4, 1981, Martin Anderson Files, Box 4, Folder: Immigration and Refugee Policy, President's Task Force on [1], RRPP, RRPL, 2–3.

96. "Testimony on H.R. 892 by Rev. Msgr. George G. Higgins, Secretary for Research, United States Catholic Conference, Before the Subcommittee on Immigration, Citizenship, and International Law, U.S. House of Representatives," March 13, 1975, Series VIII, Box 94, Folder: Miscellaneous, Simpson-Mazzoli, 1983, CMS-ACIMA, 2–3.

97. George Gallup, "Majority Favors Law Against Hiring Illegal Aliens," November 30, 1980, attached to Memorandum from Frank Hodsoll to James Baker, April 30, 1981, Elizabeth Dole Files, Box 5, Folder: Immigration [2 of 4], RRPP, RRPL; Memorandum from "Dan" to "Ron," November 26, 1980, Series VI, Box 361, Folder: 1980–1981 Immigration Subcommittee, 1 of 3, RMP, ULA, 3.

98 Teitelbaum, "Right versus Right," 21, 23–24.

99. "Will the U.S. Shut the Door on Immigrants?" *U.S. News and World Report,* April 12, 1982, 49; "Opening the Golden Door," *Commonweal,* February 13, 1981, 61.

100. *Select Commission on Immigration and Refugee Policy, Second Semi-Annual Report to Congress,* "THP, UNDA," 50, 51, 134–35, 129, 128–129.

101. Letter from Michael Semler to Martin Anderson and attached, May 20, 1981, Martin Anderson Files, Box 4, Folder: Immigration and Refugee Policy, President's Task Force on [1], RRPP, RRPL; "Opening the Golden Door," *Commonweal,* 69.

102. Ronald Reagan, "Excerpts from an Interview with Walter Cronkite of CBS News," March 3, 1981, *Public Papers of the Presidents of the United States: Ronald Reagan, 1981*(Washington, D.C.: U.S. Government Printing Office, 1982), 201.

103. Memorandum from Joe Ghoughassian to Ron Frankum, February 11, 1981, Frank Hodsoll Files, Box 11, Folder: Immigration and Refugees [General] [11], RRPP, RRPL, 3; Memorandum from Donna Alvarado to Ed Gray and Frank Hodsoll and attached Talking Points, February 23, 1981, Frank Hodsoll Files, Box 12, Folder: Immigration and Refugees [Task Force] [2], RRPP, RRPL, 2–4.

104. "Proposed Illegal Immigration Policy Package," "Annex A," and "Annex B," attached to Memorandum from Frank Hodsoll to James Baker, April 30, 1981, Frank Hodsoll Files, Box 9, Folder: Immigration and Refugee Policy Development [1], RRPP, RRPL, 5–6, 8, 9, 1, 1.

105. Martin Anderson, *Revolution: The Reagan Legacy* (Palo Alto, Calif.:Hoover Institution Press, 1988), 273; Memorandum from Craig Fuller, June 30, 1981, RRPP, RRPL; Memorandum from Craig Roberts to Don Regan, July 22, 1981, RRPP, RRPL, 1–2; Memorandum from William Niskanen to Craig Fuller, June 30, 1981, RRPP, RRPL, 1; and Memorandum from Terrel Bell to Craig Fuller, June 30, 1981, Margaret Tutwiler Files, Box 7, Folder: Immigration 1981[2] OA 10587, RRPP, RRPL; Anderson, *Revolution: The Reagan Legacy,* 273, 276.

106. Memorandum from Richard Wirthlin to James Baker, Edwin Meese, and Michael Deaver, June 18, 1981, Frank Hodsoll Files, Box 10, Folder: Immigration and Refugees [7], RRPP, RRPL, 1-2; Memorandum from Fred Fielding to Martin Anderson, July 1, 1981, Elizabeth Dole Files, Box 5, Folder: Immigration [4 of4], RRPP, RRPL, 2; Anderson, *Revolution: The Reagan Legacy,* 277.

107. Ronald Reagan, "Statement on United States Immigration and Refugee Policy," July 30, 1981, *Public Papers of the Presidents of the United States: Ronald Reagan, 1981,* 676–77.

108. "Catholic Rural Life Conference Endorses Campbell's, Libby's Boycott," *NCRLC News,* November 20, 1981, Series 12, Box 1, Folder: Press Releases, 1975–1987, National Catholic Rural Life Conference Records, Marquette University Archives, Milwaukee, Wis., 1–2.

109. Thornton, "Hill Chairmen Propose New Immigration Bill," 4.

110. Letter from Msgr. Daniel Hoye, "Dear Congressman," December 2, 1982, Series VI, Box 361, Folder: 1982 RLM's H.R. 7357 December, 2 of 2, RMP, ULA, 1–2.

111. Thornton, "Hill Chairmen Propose New Immigration Bill,"4; "Press Release from Bishop Anthony J. Bevilacqua," November 17, 1982, Series VI, Box 361, Folder: 1982 RLM's H.R. 7357, December, 2 of 2, RMP, ULA.

112. Memorandum from James Robinson to Most Rev. Archbishops, Bishops, and Other Interested Persons, United States Catholic Conference, November 17, 1982, Series VIII, Box 94, Folder: Miscellaneous, Simpson-Mazzoli, 1982, CMS-ACIMA, 1–4; Memorandum from Rev. Joseph Cogo to the Members of the Northeast Italian Apostolate Committee, June 3, 1982, Series VIII, Box 94, Folder: Miscellaneous, Simpson-Mazzoli, 1982, January-June, CMS-ACIMA, 1–2.

113.Letter from Rev. Theodore Hesburgh to Rep. Thomas O' Neill, October 6, 1982, Series VII, Box 361, Folder: 1982 Immigration Bill, October-November, RMP, ULA.

114. Hoye, "Dear Congressman," December 2, 1982, 1–2.

115. Memorandum from James Robinson to Most Reverend Archbishops, State Catholic Conference Directors, and Other Interested Persons, December 3 1982, CMS-ACIMA.

116. Robert Pear, "What the House Said in Not Voting an Immigration Bill," *New York Times*, December 27, 1982, sec. B, 12 ; Letter from Rep. Romano Mazzoli to Bishop Thomas Kelly, January 4, 1983, Series VI, Box 362, Folder: 1982–1984 Immigration Letters, RMP, ULA.

117. Pear, "What the House Said in Not Voting an Immigration Bill," 12.

118."Dissenting Views of Congressman F. James Sensenbrenner, Jr. on H.R. 6514," October 7, 1982, Series VIII, Box 94, Folder: Miscellaneous, Simpson-Mazzoli, 1982, CMS-ACIMA, 1.

119. Memorandum from James Michael Hoffman, January 7, 1983, United States Catholic Conference Office of Migration and Refugee Services, 1.

120. "Immigration Reform," *Congress and the Nation, Volume VII, 1985–1988* (Washington, D.C.: Congressional Quarterly, 1990), 717; Letter from William French Smith to Peter Rodino, September 27, 1983, Series VI, Box 362, Folder: 1982–1984 Immigration Letters, RMP, ULA, 1–2.

121. Carl Rowan, "Tip O' Neill Goofs on Immigration," *Washington Post*, n.d., n.p., Series VI, Box 362, Folder: 1983 Immigration, RMP, ULA.

122. Letter from Rep. Romano Mazzoli to Rev. Theodore Hesburgh, September 27, 1983, Series VI, Box 362, Folder: 1982–1984 Immigration Letters, RMP, ULA, 1–2.

123. Letter from Rep. Romano Mazzoli to Rev. Theodore Hesburgh, August 10, 1984, Series VI, Box 362, Folder: 1983–1984 Immigration Letters, RMP, ULA, 1–2.

124. Memorandum from Richard Wirthlin to James Baker, Michael Deaver, Frank Fahrenkopf, Paul Laxalt, Ed Rollins, and Stuart Spencer, July 26, 1984, Michael Deaver Files, Box 65, Folder: [Reagan-Bush 1984] Attitudes on Immigration, Prepared by Reagan-Bush [1984] [1], RRPP, RRPL, 4,6.

125. "Who Killed Immigration Reform?" *San Diego Tribune*, October 17, 1984, sec. B, 8.

126. Letter from Mother Teresa to President Ronald Reagan, October 20, 1984, John Roberts Files, Box 27, Folder: Immigration and Naturalization [1], RRPP, RRPL, 1.

127. Memorandum from Linda Chavez to Ralph Bledsoe, June 27, 1985, and Memorandum from Ralph Bledsoe to Al Kingon, June 26, 1985, Ralph Bledsoe Files, Domestic Policy Council, Box 51, Folder: WG on Immigration Reform [1985–1986] [1

of 4], Box 50, RRPP, RRPL; Memorandum from Max Friedersdorf and M. B. Oglesby to Ronald Reagan, July 11, 1985, Frederick McClure Files, Box 2, Folder: Immigration Reform [2] OA 14863, RRPP, RRPL, 1.

128. "Minutes, Domestic Policy Council," July 11, 1985, Frederick McClure Files, Box 2, Folder: Immigration Reform [3], OA 14863, RRPP, RRPL, 1–4; Memorandum from Edwin Meese to the President, n.d., Ralph Bledsoe Files, Box 51, Folder: WG on Legal Immigration Reform [1985–1986] [2 of 4], OA 18792, RRPP, RRPL; Memorandum from Max Friedersdorf and M. B. Oglesby to the President, July 11, 1985, Frederick McClure Files, Box 2, Folder: Immigration Reform [2], OA 14863, RRPP, RRPL, 1–2.

129. "Attorney General's Testimony on H.R. 3080," September 6, 1985, RRPP, RRPL, Latin Affairs Directorate, National Security Council: Records, Box 6, Folder: Immigration, 91170, RRPP, RRPL, 3.

130. "Immigration Reform," *Congress and the Nation, Volume VII*, 1985–1988 718; Robert Pear, "Administration Reported Set to Back New Immigration Bill," June 14, 1985, at http://www.nytimes.com/1985/06/14/us/administration-report.

131. Catherine Walsh, "How Should We Control Our Borders? An Interview with Congressman Romano Mazzoli," *St. Anthony Messenger*, October 1986, 17; Bovee, *The Church and the Land*, 324.

132. Letter from Sen. Alan Simpson to President Ronald Reagan, January 29, 1986, Frederick McClure Files, Box 2, Folder: Immigration Reform [3], OA 14863, RRPP, RRPL, 1–2.

133. Letter from Rep. Peter Rodino to President Ronald Reagan, January 24, 1986, Frederick McClure Files, Box 2, Folder: Immigration Reform [3], OA 14863, RRPP, RRPL; Ronald Reagan, "Address Before a Joint Session of Congress on the State of the Union," February 4, 1986, *Public Papers of the Presidents of the United States: Ronald Reagan, Book I, 1986, January 1–June 27, 1986* (Washington, D.C.: U.S. Government Printing Office, 1988), 125–30; October 9, 1986, 29987; Walsh, "How Should We Control Our Borders?" 17.

134. Memorandum from Linas Kojelis to Frederick Ryan, February 19, 1985, Ralph Bledsoe Files, Box 51, Folder: WG on Legal Immigration Reform 91985–19860 [1 of 4], RRPP, RRPL; Frank Moan, "Immigration Reform: Three Missing Ingredients," *America*, March 22, 1986, 288; Judith Cummings, "Los Angeles Archbishop Leads Drive to Aid Hispanic Catholics," *New York Times*, June 15, 1986, 1.

135. "Immigration Reform," *Congress and the Nation, Volume VII*, 1985–1988, 718.

136. *Congressional Record*, October 9, 1986, 29989, 29992, 30063; *Congressional Record*, October 15, 1986, 31573, 31576.

137. Evan Wyloge, "The Immigration Reform and Control Act: What It Is, Why It Matters," *Latino America*, n. d., at http://asu.news21.com/archive/2009/the_first_immigration _amnesty/, , 1; "Key Votes," *Congress and the Nation, Volume VII*, 1985–1988, 957; "Immigration Reform," *Congress and the Nation, Volume VII*, 1985–1988, 720.

138. Cooper and O'Neill, "Policy Brief," 4; Bob Secter, "Immigration Measure Clears House 230 to 166: Prospects Brighten for Congressional Approval of Reform Package Feared Dead Two Weeks Ago," *Los Angeles Times*, October 10, 1986.

139. Ronald Reagan, "Remarks on Signing the Immigration Reform and Control Act of 1986," November 8, 1986, *Public Papers of the Presidents of the United States: Ronald Reagan, Book II, 1986, June 29–December 31, 1986* (Washington, D.C.: U.S. Government Printing Office, 1988), 1524.

140. Donald Kerwin, "Immigration Reform and the Catholic Church," *Migration Information Service*, May 1, 2006, 3.

141. Peter Applebome, "The Papal Visit: At San Antonio Stop, A View of Church's Future," *New York Times*, September 13, 1987, 1.

142. Jennifer Kingson and Sarah Lyall, "Ideas and Trends: How Some American Catholics See John Paul II's Visit," *New York Times*, September 20, 1987, 1; Nicholas Laham, *Ronald Reagan and the Politics of Immigration Reform* (Westport, Ct.: Praeger, 2000), 205, 218; Romano Mazzoli and Alan Simpson, "Enacting Immigration Reform, Again," *Washington Post*, September 15, 2006, 2.

143. Memorandum from Charles Smith to Charles Hobbs, October 20, 1986, Jan Mares Files, Box 1, Folder: Immigration Legislation Memo 10/20/86, OA 19369, RRPP, RRPL, 7–8.

144. Hugh Davis Graham, *Collision Course: The Strange Convergence of Affirmative Action and Immigration Policy in America* (New York: Oxford University Press, 2002), 186–87.

145. Cooper and O'Neill, "Policy Brief," 5–7.

146. Otis Graham, *Unguarded Gates: A History of America's Immigration Crisis* (New York: Rowman and Littlefield, 2004), 109; Otis Graham, "Failing the Test: Immigration Reform," in *The Reagan Presidency*, ed. Hugh Davis Graham and Elliot Brownlee (Lawrence, Kans.: University of Kansas Press, 2003), 274.

147. "Legal Immigration Reform Plan," May 1988, Philip Brady Files, Box 1, Folder: Immigration and Naturalization Service [2], OA 18346, RRPP, RRPL, 3.

148. National Conference of Catholic Bishops, United States Catholic Conference, "Statement of Principles for Legal Immigration Policy," September 13, 1988, White House Office of Records Management Subject File- Immigration, Scanned, Stack G, Box 3, Folder: IM Immigration [144106CV-12859], GBVPP, GBPL, 1.

149. William French Smith, *Law and Justice in the Reagan Administration* (Stanford, Calif.: Hoover Institution, 1991), 200.

Notes to Chapter 2

1. Electronic interview of Douglas Wead by author, June 25, 2011.

2. Memorandum from Blair Dorminey to Peter Rodman, February 13, 1989, National Security Council, Latin American Directorate Files, Box 1, Folder: Central America-Immigration Issues, 1/20/89–12/31/89 [OAA/ID CF00189] [1 of 2], George Bush Presidential Papers, George Bush Presidential Library, College Station, Tex.

3. Doug Bandow, "Refugees Deserve a Better Welcome," *Wall Street Journal*, February 13, 1989, sec. A, 14.

4. "The Central American Refugee Problem," Handwritten Notes by Nancy Bearg Dyke from Meeting with Robert Pastorino, March 9, 1989, National Security Council, Nancy Bearg Dyke Subject Files, Stack G, Folder: Refugees, Central America [OA/ID CF01480] [2 of 3], GBPP, GBPL.

5. Bandow, "Refugees Deserve a Better Welcome."

6. Morton Kondracke, "Borderline Cases," *The New Republic*, April 10, 1989, 8–9.

7. Christopher Marquis, "Large Exile Community in Miami Strongly Opposes Deportations," *Miami Herald*, June 10, 1989, n.p., National Security Council, Nancy Bearg Dyke Subject Files, Stack G, Folder: Refugees, Central America [OA/ID CF01480] [2 of 3], GBPP, GBPL.

8. "INS Chief Resigns; Under Fire in Justice Dept. Audit," *Los Angeles Times*, June 26, 1989, 1–2.

9. Memorandum from David Pacelli to Brent Scowcroft, June 27, 1989, attached to "Talkers for Interview with the Miami Herald," and Memorandum from David Pacelli to Nancy Bearg Dyke, June 28, 1989, National Security Council, Nancy Bearg Dyke Subject Files, Stack G, Folder: Refugees, Central America [OA/ID CF01480] [2 of 3], GBPP, GBPL.

10. Memorandum from Blair Dorminey to Nancy Bearg Dyke, June 27, 1989, National Security Council, Nancy Bearg Dyke Subject Files, Stack G, Folder: Refugees, Central America [OA/ID CF01480] [2 of 3], GBPP, GBPL, and "Prepared Statement of Michael G. Kozak, Acting Assistant Secretary, Bureau of Inter-American Affairs, Department of State, before the Subcommittee of the Committee of the Judiciary, United States Senate," June 21, 1989, 2; National Security Council, Nancy Bearg Dyke Subject Files, Stack G, Refugees, Central America [OA/ID CF01480] [1 of 3], GBPP, GBPL.

11. John Goshko, "Quayle Expresses Caution on Plan to Disband Contras," *Washington Post*, August 22, 1989, sec A, 15.

12. Memorandum from Blair Dorminey to Nancy Bearg Dyke, et al., August 22, 1989, National Security Council, Blair Dorminey Files, OA/ID CF00232, Stack G, Folder: Nicaragua, Deportations to [OA/ID CF00232], GBPP, GBPL.

13. "Refugee Asylum," *Congress and the Nation, Vol. VIII, 1989–1992* (Washington, D.C.: Congressional Quarterly, 1993), 756.

14. Letter from Alan Nelson to Robert Gates, December 11, 1989, National Security Council, Latin American Directorate File, Box 1, Folder: Nicaragua, July–December 1989 [1] [OA/ID CF00192–009], GBPP, GBPL,1.

15. "Remarks by the President at American Cardinals Dinner," December 12, 1989, Public Liaison, Office of, Leigh Ann Metzger Files, Stack G, Folder: Catholics [OA/ID 06888–016], GBPP, GBPL, 2.

16. Letter from Bernard Cardinal Law to President George Bush, January 10, 1990, White House Office of Records Management Subject File—Immigration, Unscanned, Box 10, Folder: IM Immigration [100745–104911], GBPP, GBPL, 1.

17. Letter from James Budeit to Bernard Cardinal Law, February 6, 1990, WHORM Subject File—Immigration, Unscanned, Box 10: Folder: IM Immigration [100745–104911], GBPP, GBPL.

18. Letter from Thomas Melady to Philip Brady, December 27, 1991, Public Liaison, Office of, Leigh Ann Metzger Files, Stack G, Folder: Catholics [OA/ID 06888–016], GBPP, GBPL, 1–2.

19. Robert Kahn, "INS Gets Tough: Don't Drop in on U.S. Unannounced," *National Catholic Reporter*, n.d., n.p., and Mary McCann, "Religious Group Calls for End of Refugee Detention," n.d., 2, Box 6, Folder: General, Chicago Religious Task Force on Central America Records, Wisconsin Historical Society, Madison, Wis.

20. McCann, "Religious Group Calls for End of Refugee Detention,"1; Brian Jaudon, "INS Renews Border Crackdown," *Sojourners*, n.d., Box 6, Folder: General, CRTF-CAR, WHS.

21. "Adjudication of Asylum Claims in South Texas," n.d., National Security Council, Nancy Bearg Dyke Subject Files, Stack G, Folder: Refugees, Central America [OA/ID CF 01480] [3 of 3], GBPP, GBPL, 1.

22. Memorandum from Samuel Berger, Maria Echaveste, John Hilley, Bruce Reed, and Chuck Ruff to President Bill Clinton, n.d., White House Office of Records Management Files, Bruce Reed Files, Box 115, Folder: Immigration [1], William Jefferson Clinton Presidential Papers, William Jefferson Clinton Presidential Library, Little Rock, Ark., 1; "Immigration Debate: Research Paper Topics," *Congressional Quarterly Press*, at http://debates.cqpress.com/immigration/ImmigrationP; Aaron Bekemeyer, "The Acme of the Catholic Left: Catholic Activists in the U.S. Sanctuary Movement," B.A. thesis, University of Michigan, April 2012, 94.

23. Edward Brett, *The U.S. Catholic Press on Central America* (Notre Dame, Ind.: University of Notre Dame Press, 2003), 123–57.

24. Letter from Archbishop Theodore McCarrick to President George Bush, September 24, 1991, Public Liaison, Office of, Leigh Ann Metzger Files, Stack G, Folder: Roman Catholic Church [OA/ID 07162–025], GBPP, GBPL.

25. "Statement of Ambassador Robert Gebhard, Deputy Assistant Secretary of State for Inter-American Affairs, before the House Judiciary Committee Subcommittee on International Law, Immigration and Refugees," November 20, 1991, WHORM Subject File, Immigration, Scanned, Box 5, Stack G, Folder: IM Immigration [288376–289762], GBPP, GBPL, 2–3.

26. Letter from Archbishop Daniel Pilarczyk to President George Bush, November 20, 1991, WHORM Subject File, Immigration, Scanned, Box 5, Stack G, Folder: IM Immigration [288376–289762], GBPP, GBPL.

27. "Throwing People Back is No Good," *America*, March 7, 1992, 183; Letter from Princeton Lyman to Archbishop Daniel Pilarczyk, n.d., WHORM Subject File, Immigration, Scanned, Box 5, Stack G, Folder: IM Immigration [288376–289762], GBPP, GPBL.

28. George Bush, "White House Statement on Haitian Migrants," May 24, 1992, *Public Papers of the President of the United States: George Bush, 1992–1993, Book I, January 1–July 31, 1992* (Washington, D.C.: U. S. Government Printing Office, 1993), 818; "Throwing People Back Is No Good," *America*, 183.

29. Letter from Rep. Joseph Moakley to Raymond Davisson, September 7, 1992, Legislative Correspondence, Box 38, Folder: IM/245: Final 1997, Congressman John

Joseph Moakley Papers, Suffolk University Law Library, Boston Mass.; "Throwing People Back Is No Good," *America*, 183.

30. "Statement of Ambassador Gebhard, before House Judiciary Committee," WHORM Subject File, 7.

31. George Bush, "Interview with Tom Randles, WTVT-TV Miami," November 20, 1991, *Public Papers of the Presidents of the United States: George Bush, Book II, 1991, July 1–December 31, 1991* (Washington, D.C.: U.S. Government Printing Office, 1992), 1494.

32. Memorandum from Jane Leonard to Leigh Ann Metzger, May 7, 1992, and attached Letter from Bernard Cardinal Law to President George Bush, February 10, 1992, Public Liaison, Office of, Jane Leonard Files, Stack G, no folder, GBPP, GBPL.

33. Letter from Sholom Comay to President George Bush, April 16, 1992, WHORM Subject File, Immigration, Scanned, Box 4, Stack G, Folder: IM Immigration [230511CU-236743], GBPP, GBPL; "Appendix A—Digest of Other White House Announcements," *Public Papers, Book I, 1992–1993*, 1223.

34. George Bush, "Remarks at a Question-and-Answer Session with Mount Paran Community School in Marietta," May 27, 1992, *Public Papers, Book I, 1992–1993*, 831.

35. Memorandum from Roger Porter to Ronald Kaufman, October 5, 1992, and attached "President Bush's Response to USCC," September 30, 1992, 21–23, White House Office of Political Affairs, Ron Kaufman Files, Stack G, GBPP, GBPL.

36. George Bush, "Question-and-Answer Session in Miami," October 23, 1992, *Public Papers of the Presidents of the United States: George Bush, Book II, 1992–1993, August 1, 1992–January 20, 1993* (Washington, D.C.: U.S. Government Printing Office, 1993), 1942.

37. "Immigration," in *The Gallup Poll: Public Opinion, 1992*, George Gallup, ed. (Wilmington, Del.: Scholarly Resources, 1993), 33.

38. "Conclusions, 1989 Texas Immigration and Border Study," attached to Memorandum from Daniel Levin to Brent Scowcroft, April 16, 1990, National Security Council Files, Virginia Lampley Subject Files, Box 2, Stack G, Folder: Immigration, 1989–1990, [OA/ID CF 00707], GBPP, GBPL, 12–13.

39. United States Catholic Conference Administrative Board, "Relieving Third World Debt: A Call for Co-Responsibility, Justice, and Solidarity," September 1989, in *The Pastoral Letters of the United States Catholic Bishops, Vol. VI, 1989–1997*, Patrick Carey, ed. (Washington, D.C.: United States Catholic Conference/National Conference of Catholic Bishops, 1998), 80,96; Teresa Kane, "Challenges Facing U.S. Catholics: The Next Ten Years," *Commonweal*, November 17, 1989, 623.

40. Memorandum from the Domestic Policy Council to President George Bush, February 15, 1990, WHORM Subject File, Immigration, Scanned, Box 2, Stack G, Folder: IM Immigration [114106CV-128597], GBPP, GBPL, 3–6.

41. Letter from Paul Simon, "Dear Friend," March 27, 1989, Box 1 [Additions], Folder: M2004–170, Affiliates, CCIRP, 1989, CRTFCAR, WHS; "Immigration Reform," *Congress and the Nation, Vol. VIII*, 753–54.

42. Letter from the United States Department of Justice to Rep. Thomas Foley, September 19, 1990, WHORM Subject File, Immigration, Scanned, Box 3, Stack G, Folder: IM Immigration [176422GU-187202 CU], GBPP, GBPL, 1.

43. Letter from Bernard Cardinal Law to John Sununu, September 27, 1990, WHORM Subject File, Immigration, Scanned, Box 3, Stack G, Folder: IM Immigration [176422 CU-187202CU], GBPP, GBPL.

44. Memorandum from Roger Porter to President George Bush, 22 October 1990, WHORM Subject File, Immigration, Scanned, Box 3, Stack G, Folder: IM Immigration [176422CU-187202CU], GBPP, GBPL, 2.

45. Memorandum from Roger Porter to President George Bush, October 25, 1990, WHORM Subject File, Immigration, Scanned, Box 3, Stack G, Folder: IM Immigration [176422CU-187202CU], GBPP, GBPL, 1; Memorandum from Charles Kolb to David Demarest, November 8, 1990, and attached "The Immigration Act of 1990," 1, WHORM Subject File: IM Immigration [176422CU-187202CU], GBPP, GBPL; Philip Martin, "U.S. Immigration Patterns and Policies," *University of California-Berkeley*, February 26, 2012, at http://migrationfilesucdavis.edu/uploads/files/2012/ciip, 8.

46. Christopher Jencks, "Who Should Get In? Part II," *New York Review of Books*, December 20, 2001, 11; Hugh Davis Graham, *Collision Course: The Strange Convergence of Affirmative Action and Immigration Policy in America* (New York: Oxford University Press, 2002), 124.

47. Memorandum from Roger Porter to President George Bush, October 25, 1990, WHORM Subject File, Immigration, Scanned, Box 3, Stack G, Folder: IM Immigration [176422CU- 187202CU], GBPP, GBPL.

48. "Unemployment Rate," *Portal Seven*,1990 and 1991, at http://portalseven.com/employment/unemployment_rate_for; Memorandum from Roger Porter to President George Bush, May 22, 1992,WHORM Subject File, Immigration, Scanned, Box 6, Stack G, Folder: IM Immigration [321563–32983255], GBPP, GBPL, 1–2.

49 Handwritten note from President George Bush to Roger Porter and Samuel Skinner, May 27, 1992, WHORM Subject File, Immigration, Scanned, Box 6, Stack G, Folder: IM Immigration [321563–32983255], GBPP, GBPL.

50. Porter to Kaufman, October 5, 1992, and attached USCC questionnaire, 21–22.

Notes to Chapter 3

1. Bill Clinton and Al Gore, *Putting People First* (New York: Times Books, 1992), 119–20.

2. Bill Clinton, "Statement by the President on the Situation in Haiti," March 2, 1993, *Public Papers of the Presidents of the United States: William J. Clinton, Book I, 1993, January 20–July 31, 1993* (Washington, D.C.: U.S. Government Printing Office, 1994), 231.

3. Bill Clinton, "Remarks at a Town Meeting in Detroit," February 10, 1993, *Public Papers, Book I, 1993*, 84.

4. Bill Clinton, "Exchange with Reporters, Prior to Discussions with Secretary General Manfred Woerner of the North Atlantic Treaty Organization," March 2, 1993, *Public Papers, Book I, 1993*, 230.

5. Joan Biskupic, "Court, 8–1, Upholds Return of Haitians," *Washington Post*, June 22, 1993, sec. A, 1, 13.

6. Colin Powell, *My American Journey* (New York: Random House, 1995), 572.

7. Tom Morgenthau, "America: Still a Melting Pot?" *Newsweek*, August 9, 1993, 25.

8. "Bishops Warn Against Anti-Immigrant Views," *Christian Century*, December 8, 1993, 1232–33.

9. Bill Clinton, "Exchange with Reporters Prior to Discussions with Prime Minister Andreas Papandreou of Greece," April 22, 1994, *Public Papers, Book I, 1994, January 1 to June 30, 1994* (Washington, D.C.: U.S. Government Printing Office, 1995), 754.

10. Bill Clinton, "Remarks Announcing the Appointment of William H. Gray III as Special Advisor on Haiti and an Exchange with Reporters," May 8, 1994, *Public Papers, Book I, 1994*, 860–61.

11. Larry Berman and Emily Goldman, "Clinton's Foreign Policy at Mid-Term," in *The Clinton Presidency: First Appraisals*, ed. Colin Campbell and Bert Rockman (Chatham, N.J.: Chatham, 1996), 310; Taylor Branch, *The Clinton Tapes: Wrestling History with the President* (New York: Simon and Schuster, 2009), 168; Bill Clinton, "Remarks Announcing Additional Economic Sanctions Against Haiti," June 10, 1994, *Public Papers, Book I, 1994*, 1064.

12. Bill Clinton, "Address to the Nation on Haiti," September 15, 1994, *Public Papers of the Presidents of the United States: William J. Clinton, Book II, 1994, July 1 to December 31, 1994* (Washington, D.C.: U. S. Government Printing Office, 1995), 1559; Branch, *The Clinton Tapes: Wrestling History with the President*, 191.

13. John Murrin, Paul Johnson, James McPherson, Alice Fahs, Gary Gerstle, Emily Rosenberg, and Norman Rosenberg, *Liberty, Equality, Power: A History of the American People* (New York: Thomson Wadsworth, 2008), 1002.

14. "Good News and Bad News from Congress," *America*, November 7, 1998, 5; Roger Daniels, *Guarding the Golden Door: American Immigration Policy and Immigrants Since 1882* (New York: Hill and Wang, 2004), 211.

15. Bill Clinton, *My Life* (New York: Alfred A. Knopf, 2004), 463, 467.

16. Branch, *The Clinton Tapes: Wrestling History with the President*, 176.

17. Steven Greenhouse, "U.S. Will Return Refugees to Cuba in Policy Switch," *New York Times*, May 3, 1995, 1, 14; "Press Briefing by Attorney General Janet Reno, General John Sheehan, Commander in Chief of the United States Atlantic Command, and Undersecretary of State for Political Affairs Peter Tarnoff," May 2, 1995, Freedom of Information Act File #2006-0460-F, Box 7, Folder: Cuba—U.S. Migration Policy [OA/ID 415], William Jefferson Clinton Presidential Papers, William Jefferson Clinton Presidential Library, Little Rock, Ark., 3–4.

18. Branch, *The Clinton Tapes: Wrestling History with the President*, 530.

19. "All Grown Up: Elián González, Survivor of Raft Journey from Cuba, Turns Eighteen," *NBC News*, December 7, 2011.

20. Clinton, *My Life*, 905; Daniels, *Guarding the Golden Door*, 211.

21. "Immigration," *Congress and the Nation, Volume IX, 1993–1996* (Washington, D.C.: Congressional Quarterly, 1998), 712.

22. Memorandum from Diana Yin to Thomas Epstein, June 10, 1993, FOIA File #2006–0460–F, National Security Council, Boorstin, Robert, Speechwriting, Box 5, Folder: Immigration—Key Policy Issues [OA/ID 414], WJCPP, WJCPL, 1–2.

23. Ann Devroy and Michael Arnold, "Clinton Escalates Fight on Illegal Immigration," *Washington Post*, July 28, 1993, sec A, 1, 12; "Remarks by the President, the Vice President, and the Attorney General During Immigration Policy Announcement, "FOIA File # 2006–0460–F, National Security Council, Boorstin, Robert, Speechwriting, Box 4, Folder: Immigration—INS [Immigration and Naturalization Service] (Agency) [OA/ID 414], WJCPP, WJCPL, 2.

24. Memorandum from Leon Panetta to Vice President Al Gore, July 12, 1993, FOIA File # 2006–0460–F, National Security Council, Boorstin, Robert, Speechwriting, Box 5, Folder: Immigration—Key Policy Issues [OA/ID 414] WJCPP, WJCPL, 3.

25. "Immigration," *Congress and the Nation, Volume IX, 1993–1996*, 712.

26. "Immigration Debate," *America*, 9 October 1993, 3.

27. Patrick McConnell, "Hunting A Way In," *Los Angeles Times*, March 10, 1997, sec. B, 1; Philip Schrag, *A Well-Founded Fear: The Congressional Battle to Save Political Asylum in America* (New York: Routledge, 2000), 229; Karen Manges Douglas and Rogelio Saenz, "The Criminalization of Immigrants and the Immigration-Industrial Complex," *Daedalus* 142 (Summer 2013), 205; Memorandum from Samuel Berger, Maria Echaveste, John Hilley, Bruce Reed, and Chuck Ruff to President Clinton, n.d., White House Office of Records Management Subject File—Bruce Reed, Box 115, Folder: Immigration [1], WJCPP, WJCPL, 1; "Is Secure Communities Keeping Our Communities Secure? Hearing Before the Subcommittee on Immigration Policy and Enforcement of the Committee on the Judiciary, House of Representatives, 112th Congress, 1st Session," November 30, 2011, at http://judiciaryhouse.gov/hearings/printers/112th/112–69, 1.

28. Schrag, *A Well-Founded Fear*, 229; "White House Staffing Memorandum," September 30, 1996, WHORM Subject File—Bruce Reed, Box 115, Folder: Immigration [1], WJCPP, WJCPL, 3.

29. Warren Strobel, "Clinton's Trip Leaves Promises to Keep," *Washington Times*, May 12, 1997, sec. A, 1, 18.

30. Handwritten note by Bruce Reed, n.d., WHORM Subject File—Bruce Reed, Box 115, Folder: Immigration [2], WJCPP, WJCPL.

31. Berger, Echaveste, Hilley, Reed, and Ruff to President Clinton, WHORM Subject File, 1.

32. George Anderson, "Keeping out the Immigrant," *America*, July 17–24, 2000, 9.

33. George Anderson, "Immigrants in Detention," *America*, January 15, 2000, 1–2.

34. "Refugees at Risk," *America*, September 10, 2001, 1; Daniels, *Guarding the Golden Door*, 211; United States Catholic Conference, "Welcoming the Stranger Among Us: Unity in Diversity," November 15, 2000, at http://nccbuscc.org/mrs/unity.shtml, 14.

35. Devroy and Arnold, "Clinton Escalates Fight on Illegal Immigration," 14.

36. Kathleen Arnold, *American Immigration after 1996* (University Park, Pa.: Penn State University Press, 2011), 35, 13; "Administration Policy on Illegal Immigration

Executive Summary," July 1993, Domestic Policy Council, Carol Rasco Issue Papers, Box 125, Folder: Immigration [OA/ID 8506], WJCPP, WJCPL, 1; Bill Clinton, "Remarks and an Exchange with Reporters on Immigration Policy," July 27, 1993, *Public Papers, Book I, 1993,* 1194.

37. Morgenthau, "America: Still a Melting Pot?" 18; "Remarks by the President, the Vice President, and the Attorney General during Immigration Policy Announcement," July 27, 1993, *Public Papers, Book I, 1993,* 1.

38. "Immigration Debate," *America,* 3; Mario Cuomo, "Immigration is a Source of Our Strength," *USA Today,* July 19, 1993, n.p., FOIA Files # 2006–0460–F, Box 7, Folder: Immigration—Editorials [OA/ID 4/14], WJCPP, WJCPL.

39. Memorandum from Stephen Warnath to Carol Rasco, August 10, 1994, WHORM Subject File—Bruce Reed, Box 115, Folder: Immigration [3], WJCPP, WJCPL.

40. Memorandum from Rahm Emanuel and Ron Klain to Leon Panetta, September 29, 1994, WHORM Subject File—Bruce Reed, Box 115, Folder: Immigration [1] WJCPP, WJCPL.

41. "Skittish on Immigration," *Atlanta Constitution,* October 4, 1994, sec A, 18; Emanuel and Klain to Panetta, WHORM Subject File.

42. James Torrens, "An Interview with Cardinal Mahony," *America,* January 28, 1995, 7.

43. Bill Clinton, "Teleconference Remarks and a Question-and-Answer Session with the National Council of La Raza," July 19, 1995, *Public Papers of the Presidents of the United States: William J. Clinton, Book II, 1995, July 1–December 31, 1995* (Washington, D.C.: U.S. Government Printing Office, 1996), 1120.

44. "Talking Points for Meeting with Senator Bob Dole," January 20, 1995, FOIA File #2007–0088–F, WHORM Subject File—Melanne Verveer, Box 3, Folder: Catholic [Folder 1] [2] [OA/ID 20024]. WJCPP, WJCPL, 1.

45. Bill Clinton, "Address Before a Joint Session of Congress on the State of the Union," January 24, 1995, *Public Papers of the Presidents of the United States, Book 1, 1995, January 1–June 30, 1995* (Washington, D.C.: U. S. Government Printing Office, 1996), 81; "Administration Policy on Illegal Immigration," July 1993, Domestic Policy Council, 6; Bill Clinton, "Remarks on the Immigration Policy Initiative and an Exchange with Reporters," February 7, 1995, *Public Papers, Book I, 1995,* 167.

46. "Immigration," *Congress and the Nation, Volume IX, 1993–1996,* 718.

47. Bill Clinton, "Statement on the Commission on Immigration Reform," September 12, 1995, *Public Papers, Book I, 1995,* 1352.

48. "Immigration," *Congress and the Nation, Volume IX, 1993–1996,* 723–24.

49. "Immigration under Fire," *America,* September 30, 1995, 4.

50. "Message of Pope John Paul II for World Migration Day, 1996," July 25, 1995, 2.

51. "Immigration," *Congress and the Nation, Volume IX, 1993–1996,* 723–24; "Hurricane Mitch," *History Channel,* at http://www.history.com/topics.

52. Hugh Davis Graham, *Collision Course: The Strange Convergence of Affirmative Action and Immigration Policy in America* (New York: Oxford University Press, 2002), 120, 126–27; Otis Graham, *Immigration Reform and America's Unchosen Future* (Bloomington, Ind.: Author House, 2008), 272.

53. Christopher Jencks, "Who Should Get In? Part II," *New York Review of Books*, December 20, 2001, 14; "Immigration," *Congress and the Nation, Volume IX, 1993–1996*, 724–27.

54. Hugh Davis Graham, *Collision Course: The Strange Convergence*, 129; Otis Graham, *Immigration Reform and America's Unchosen Future*, 273.

55. Otis Graham, *Immigration Reform and America's Unchosen Future*, 128; Hugh Davis Graham, *Collision Course: The Strange Convergence*, 187.

56. Hugh Davis Graham, *Collision Course: The Strange Convergence*, 187.

57. "Fortress North America: The New Immigration Law," *America*, May 9, 1998, 3–4; "Churches, Lawyers, INS Helping Immigrants Know Rights," *America*, May 15, 1999, 5; David Bovee, *The Church and the Land: The National Catholic Rural Life Conference and American Society* (Washington, D.C.: The Catholic University of America Press, 2010), 324; Anderson, "Immigrants in Detention," 1.

58. George Anderson, "Keeping Out the Immigrant," 9; Arnold, *American Immigration After 1996*, 38.

59. "AFL-CIO, Bishops to Collaborate on Amnesty, Immigration," *America*, April 1, 2000, 4; Otis Graham, *Immigration Reform and America's Unchosen Future*, 275.

60. "Bishops' Meeting at a Glance," *America*, December 2, 2000, 4; United States Catholic Conference, "Welcoming the Stranger Among Us: Unity in Diversity."

61. Hugh Davis Graham, *Collision Course: The Strange Convergence*, 187; Jeffrey Passel and Robert Suro, "Rise, Peak, and Decline, 1992–2004," n.d., Todd Braunstein Files, Box 3, Folder: Immigration Files, Federalism EO—Immigration [2], George W. Bush Presidential Papers, George W. Bush Presidential Library, Dallas, Tex., 4.

62. Letter from Rev. Fred Kammer to President Bill Clinton, February 25, 1994, FOIA File #2007–0088–F, WHORM Subject File, Box 1, Folder: ME-074973 [OA/ID 23559], WJCPP, WJCPL.

63. Letter from President Bill Clinton to Rev. Fred Kammer, May 3, 1994, FOIA File # 2007– 0088–F, WHORM Subject File, Box 1, Folder: ME-074973 [OA/ID 23559], WJCPP, WJCPL.

64. Letter from Rev. William Keeler to President Bill Clinton, March 28, 1994, FOIA File, # 2007–0088–F, WHORM Subject File, Box 1, Folder: ME-074973 [OA/ID 23559], WJCPP, WJCPL.

65. Letter from President Bill Clinton to Rev. William Keeler, April 18, 1994, FOIA File # 2007–0088–F, WHORM Subject File, Box 1, Folder: ME-074973 [OA/ID 23559], WJCPP, WJCPL.

66. Letter from Rev. John Ricard to Rep. Willis Archer, January 13, 1995, FOIH File # 2007–0088–F, WHORM Subject File, Box 1, Folder: WE-101102 [OA/ID 12161], WJCPP, WJCPL.

67. Branch, *The Clinton Tapes: Wrestling History with the President*, 369; Letter from Donna Shalala to Rep. Willis Archer, March 1, 1995, Domestic Policy Council, Carol Rasco Issue Papers, Box 127, Folder: Welfare-NGA [OA/ID 8506], WJCPP, WJCPL.

68. Handwritten Notes by Melanne Verveer, n.d., FOIA File # 2007–0088–F, WHORM Subject File, Box 5, Folder: Clinton Presidential Records, National Security Council,

WJCPP, WJCPL; Memorandum from Marilyn DiGiacobbe to Ruby May, April 18, 1995, FOIA File # 2007–0088–F, WHORM Subject File, Box 3, Folder: Gearan, Mark—Catholics, Press Guidance for Cardinal Hickey Meeting [OA/ID 4940], WJCPP, WJCPL.

69 "Benefits and Legal Immigrants," September 23, 1995, Domestic Policy Council, Carol Rasco Issue Papers, Box 127, Folder: Welfare Reform [5] [OA/ID 8506], WJCPP, WJCPL, 2.

70. "Welfare Reform Delayed in Senate," Catholic Charities *Action Alert*, June 19, 1995, FOIA File # 2051–0088–F, WHORM Subject File, Box 3, Folder: Verveer, Melanne—Catholic [Folder 2] [1] [OA/ID 20024], WJCPP, WJCPC, 6.

71. Ibid., 6.

72. Ibid., 6.

73. Letter from Rev. Fred Kammer to President Bill Clinton, June 1, 1995, FOIA File #2007–0088–F, WHORM Subject File, Box 1, Folder: WE–118564 [OA/ID 12162], WJCPP, WJCPL.

74. Letter from Rev. John Ricard to Sen. Robert Dole, June 28, 1995, FOIA File # 2007–008–F, WHORM Subject File, Box 3, Folder: Verveer, Melanne-Catholic [Folder 2] [1] [OA/ID 20024], WJCPP, WJCPL; Letter from Sr. Catherine McNamee to President Bill Clinton, October 12, 1995, FOIA File #2007–0088–F, WHORM Subject File, Box 1, Folder: WE–143275 [OA/ID 143275] WJCPP, WJCPL.

75. "Benefits and Legal Immigrants," Domestic Policy Council, 1.

76. Ibid., 4.

77. Memorandum from Bruce Reed and Rahm Emanuel to President Bill Clinton, September 22, 1995, Domestic Policy Council, Carol Rasco Issue Papers, Box 127, Folder: Welfare Reform [2] [OA/ID 8506], WJCPP, WJCPL, 4–5.

78. Letter from Rev. Anthony Pilla to President Bill Clinton, November 29, 1995, FOIA File #2007–0088–F, WHORM Subject File, Box 1, Folder: WE–141971 [OA/ID 12162], WJCPP, WJCPL, 1.

79. Letter from Rev. Anthony Pilla to President Bill Clinton, July 26, 1996, FOIA File #2007–0088–F, WHORM Subject File, Box 1, Folder: WE–178672 [OA/ID 12162] , WJCPP, WJCPL.

80. "Statement by President Clinton on Welfare Reform Legislation," July 31, 1996, Domestic Policy Council, Carol Rasco Issue Papers, Box 127, Folder: Welfare—NGA [OA/ID 8506], WJCPP, WJCPL, 2, 4.

81. Letter from Rev. Fred Kammer and Rev. Joseph Sullivan to President Bill Clinton, August 9, 1996, FOIA File #2007–0088–F, WHORM Subject File, Box 1, Folder: WE–183956 [OA/ID 02163] WJCPP, WJCPL; "On File," *Origins Online*, April 4, 1996, at http://www.originsonline.com.

82. Letter from President Bill Clinton to Rev. Anthony Pilla, August 20, 1996, FOIA File # 2007–0088–F, WHORM Subject File, Box 1, Folder: WE–178673 [OA/ID 02162], WJCPP, WJCPL, 1.

83. "Catholic Health Association Pledges to Address Welfare Reform Provisions Jeopardizing Coverage to Legal Immigrants," August 8, 1996, FOIA File #

2007–0088–F, WHORM Subject File, Box 5, Folder: Clinton Presidential Records, Public Liaison, Herman, Alexis/Moy, Ruby—Catholics for a Free Choice [OA/ID 6275], WJCPP, WJCPL.

84. "Statement by the Press Secretary," August 23, 1996, Domestic Policy Council, Carol Rasco Issue Papers, Box 127, Folder: Welfare-NGA [OA/ID 8506], WJCPP, WJCPL.

85. Letter from Diana Aviv, John Frederickson, Cecilia Munoz, Sharon Daley, and Karen Narasaki, December 10, 1996, FOIA File, #2007–0088–F, WHORM Subject File, Box 1, Folder: FI004–199176 [OA/ID 12133], WJCPP, WJCPL, 1.

86. "Clinton Meets with Religious Leaders," *Christianity Century*, January 22, 1997, 71.

87. Peter Edelman, "The Worst Thing Bill Clinton Has Done," *Atlantic Monthly*, March 1997, 6.

88 Letter from President Bill Clinton to Diana Aviv, 12 March 1997, FOIA File, #2007–008-F, WHORM Subject File, Box 1, Folder: FI 004-199176 [OA/ID 12133], WJCPP, WJCPL.

89. Memorandum from Diana Fortuna to Bruce Reed and attached "Draft Talking Points," March 20, 1997, FOIA File #2007–0088–F, WHORM Subject File, Box 1, Folder: FI 004–199176 [OA/ID 12133], WJCPP, WJCPL, 1–2.

90. John Raffa, "Budget Act Restores Assistance Due to Legal Immigrants," *Palm Beach Sun Sentinel*, August 24, 1997; Letter from Kathy Thornton and Mary Elizabeth Clark to President Bill Clinton, March 22, 1999, FOIA File # 2007–0088–F, WHORM Subject File, Box 1, Folder: WE–298948 [OA/ID 14114], WJCPP, WJCPL.

91. Letter from Rev. Fred Kammer to President Bill Clinton, November 3, 2000, FOIA File #2007–0088–F, WHORM Subject File, Box 5, Folder: Clinton Presidential Records, Public Liaison—Shea, Maureen—Catholic Charities [1] [OA/IS 20946], WJCPP, WJCPL; "Statement by President Bill Clinton," September 21, 2000, FOIA File #2007–0088–F, WHORM Subject File, Box 5, Folder: Clinton Presidential Records, Public Liaison—Shea, Maureen—Catholic Charities [1] [OA/ID 20946], WJCPP, WJCPL.

Notes to Chapter 4

1. George W. Bush, *Decision Points* (New York: Random House, 2010), 301.

2. Bush, *Decision Points*, 301; Andrew Wroe and Jon Herbert, "Introduction," in *The George W. Bush Presidency: A Tale of Two Terms*, ed. Andrew Wroe and Jon Herbert (Edinburgh: Edinburgh University Press, 2009), 4; David Frum, *The Right Man* (New York: Random House, 2003), 36.

3. June Hopkins and Anthony Cupaluolo, "For Better or Worse?" *Policy and Practice of Public Human Services* 09 (June 2001), 24–25; James Guth, "Bush and Religious Politics," in *Ambition and Division: Legacies of the George W. Bush Presidency*, ed. Stephen Schier (Pittsburgh: University of Pittsburgh Press, 2009), 90.

4. Marc Rosenblum, "U.S. Immigration Policy Since 9/11: Understanding the Stalemate Over Comprehensive Immigration Reform," *Migration Policy Institute*, 2011, 3;

"Immigration," *Congress and the Nation, 2001–2004* (Washington, D.C.: Congressional Quarterly, 2006), 589.

5. Rosenblum, "U.S. Immigration Policy Since 9/11," 3; George W. Bush, "Remarks and a Question-and-Answer Session with Students at Crawford Elementary School and an Exchange with Reporters in Crawford, Texas," August 23, 2001, *Public Papers of the President of the United States: George W. Bush, Book II, 2001, July 1–December 31, 2001* (Washington, D.C.: U.S. Government Printing Office, 2003), 101.

6. Otis Graham, *Immigration Reform and America's Unchosen Future* (Bloomington, Ind.: Author House, 2008), 323.

7. Bush, *Decision Points*, 301.

8. "Vatican at U.N. Conference on Racism," *America*, September 10, 2001, 4.

9. Claire Schaeffer-Duffy, "Immigrant Plight Spurs Bishops to Ask for Meeting with Ashcroft," *National Catholic Reporter*, December 14, 2001, 3.

10. "Refugees on Hold," *America*, 11 March 2002, 3.

11. Schaeffer-Duffy, "Immigrant Plight Spurs Bishops," 3.

12. United States Conference of Catholic Bishops, "Living with Faith and Hope after September 11," November 14, 2001, at http://www.usccb.org/sdwp/sept11.shtml, 2; Schaeffer-Duffy, "Immigrant Plight Spurs Bishops," 1–2.

13. Schaeffer-Duffy, "Immigrant Plight Spurs Bishops," 1; "Refugees on Hold," 2.

14. Jeffrey Jones, "Americans' Views of Immigration Growing More Positive," Gallup News Service, July 10, 2006, at http://www.gallup.com/poll/23623/Americans-Views-Immigration-Growing-More-Positive, 2; Schaefer-Duffy, "Immigrant Plight Spurs Bishops," 1–2.

15. "Haitians in Detention," *America*, August 26–September 2, 2002, 3.

16. "Haitians in Detention," 1.

17. George W. Bush, "The President's News Conference," November 7, 2002, *Public Papers of the Presidents of the United States: George W. Bush, Book II, 2002, July 1–December 31, 2002* (Washington, D.C.: U.S. Government Printing Office, 2005), 2051.

18. Thomas Reese, "Refugees in Danger," *America*, September 8, 2003, 3.

19. Reese, "Refugees in Danger," 3; Kathleen Bishop, "U.S. Adopts New Policy for Hearings on Political Asylum for Some Aliens," *New York Times*, December 20, 1990, sec. B, 18; Aaron Bekemeyer, "The Acme of the Catholic Left: Catholic Activists in the U.S. Sanctuary Movement, 1982–1992," B.A. Thesis, University of Michigan, 2012,, 94.

20. Reese, "Refugees in Danger," 3.

21. "Bishops Issue Call to Political Responsibility," *National Catholic Reporter*, October 24, 2003, 2.

22. George W. Bush, "Remarks Following Discussion with President Mikheil Saakashvili of Georgia and an Exchange with Reporters," February 25, 2004, *Public Papers of the Presidents of the United States: George W. Bush, Book I, 2004, January 1–June 30, 2004* (Washington, D.C.: U.S. Government Printing Office, 2007), 267.

23. "Message of Holy Father John Paul II for the World Day of Migrants and Refugees, 2005, at http://vatican.va/holyfather/johnpaulii/messages/migration/documents/hfjp-ii-m, 2.

24. "Good and Bad Immigration Reform," *America*, June 6–13, 2005, 3.

25. "Immigration Reform," *America*, n.d., at http://americamagazine.org/, 1; "Testimony of Most Rev. Thomas Wenski, Bishop of Orlando, Florida, before the House Subcommittee on Immigration, Citizenship, Refugees, Border Security, and International Law on Comprehensive Immigration Reform," May 22, 2007, 10.

26. "U.S. Policy on Haitian Migrants 'Totally Immoral,'" *America*, April 16– 23, 2007, 7.

27. "Protection for Haitians," *America*, April 20–27, 2009, 5; Marc Lacey, "Meager Living of the Haitians is Wiped Out by Storm," *New York Times*, September 11, 2008, 5.

29. Carl Hulse, "Immigrant Surge Rooted in Law to Curb Child Trafficking," *New York Times*, July 7, 2014; "Refugees and Asylees in the U.S.," *Migration Policy Institute*, at http://www.migrationpolicy.org/article/refugees-and asylees.

30. Gary Gerstle, "Minorities, Multiculturalism, and the Presidency of George W. Bush," in *The Presidency of George W. Bush*, Julian Zelizer, ed. (Princeton, N.J.: Princeton University Press, 2010), 277; Robert Draper, *Dead Certain: The Presidency of George W. Bush* (New York: Free Press, 2007), 32–33.

31. George W. Bush, "Remarks in Signing the Enhanced Border Security and Visa Entry Reform Act," May 14, 2002, *Public Papers, Book II, 2002*, 794.

32. "Other Matters Approved by U.S. Bishops," *America*, November 25, 2002, 6; J. Kevin Appleby, "Toward Immigration Reform," *America*, March 19, 2007, 1.

33. Appleby, "Toward Immigration Reform," 1; Interview of Bishop John Manz by author, September 20, 2012.

34. Joe Feuerherd, "Advocates Oppose Proposal For INS," *National Catholic Reporter*, September 6, 2002, 1; Arthur Jones, "The Lobbying Game," *National Catholic Reporter*, June 3, 2003, 3; Memorandum from Ryan Bounds through Karl Zinsmeister to the President, n.d., Thomas Von Der Heydt Files, Box 1, Folder: Immigration—A Timeline (2001–2008), George W. Bush Presidential Papers, George W. Bush Presidential Library, Dallas, Tex., 2.

35. George W. Bush, "Satellite Remarks to the League of United Latin American Citizens," July 8, 2004, *Public Papers of the Presidents of the United States: George W. Bush, Book II, 2004, July 1–December 31, 2004* (Washington, D.C.: U.S. Government Printing Office, 2007), 1250; George W. Bush, "Remarks in a Discussion in Hudson, Wisconsin," August 18, 2004, *Public Papers, Book II, 2004*, 1718.

36. "Immigration Reform and the Bush Proposal," *America*, March 8, 2004; Verghese J. Chirayath, "The Immigration President?" *America*, May 24–31, 2004, 6.

37. Paul Srubas, "Woman Becomes U.S. Citizen after Facing Deportation," *Green Bay Press-Gazette*, November 3, 2013, sec. A, 4.

38. "Presidential Debate in Tempe, Arizona," George W. Bush and John Kerry, October 13, 2004, *Public Papers, Book II, 2004*, 2993.

39. Frank Newport, "Americans Worried about Immigration Oppose Bush Plan," *Gallup Poll, 2004* (Wilmington, Del.: Scholarly Resources, 2006), 14–15.

40. George W. Bush, "The President's News Conference," January 26, 2005, *Public Papers of the Presidents of the United States: George W. Bush , Book I, 2005, January 1–June 30, 2006* (Washington, D.C.: U. S. Government Printing Office, 2009), 85.

41. Patricia Zapor, "Church Organizations Launch Campaign to Aid Immigrants," *Catholic News Service*, May 10, 2005,1–3.

42. Ibid.

43 Ibid.

44. "Immigration," *Congress and the Nation, 2005–2008* (Washington, D.C.: Congressional Quarterly, 2010), 688.

45. "Bishop Says House-Passed Immigration Reform Bill Would Hurt the Nation," *Catholic News Service*, December 19, 2005, 1.

46. "Immigration," *Congress and the Nation, 2005–2008*, 688.

47. George W. Bush, "Interview with Foreign Print Journalists," March 27, 2006, *Public Papers of the Presidents of the United States, Book I, 2006, January 1–June 30, 2006* (Washington, D.C.: U. S. Government Printing Office, 2010), 583.

48. "Immigration Reform," *America*, February 6, 2006, 1.

49. Patricia Zapor, "Diverse Group Pushes Bush to Support Comprehensive Immigration Law," *Catholic News Service*, March 23, 2006,1–2.

50. "Immigration," *Congress and the Nation, 2005–2008*, 688; "Bishops' Chairman Analyzes Immigration Bill," *America*, April 17, 2006, 7.

51. "Bishops' Chairman Analyzes," *America*, 7.

52. Richard John Neuhaus, "Who Speaks for the Church?" *First Things*, June 15, 2007, 1; Bill O'Reilly, "The Catholic Church Gets Political on Illegal Immigration," *Fox News*, March 8, 2006; Zapor, "Diverse Group Pushes," 1–2.

53. Patricia Zapor, "Calls for Prayer, Rallies, Boycott Mark Immigration Debate," *Catholic News Service*, April 3, 2006,1–2.

54. Mark Pattison, "Thousands Rally at Capital To Protest House-Passed Immigration Bill," *Catholic News Service*, March 8, 2006, 2; Patricia Zapor, "Hundreds of Thousands Flock to Washington to Speak up for Immigrants," *Catholic News Service*, April 11, 2006, 1–2.

55. Joe Feuerherd, "Bishops United for Immigration," *National Catholic Reporter*, April 21, 2006, 1.

56. Jerry Filteau, "Cardinals Visit White House, Hill on Immigration," *Catholic News Service*, April 28, 2006, 1.

57. "Bush's Speech on Immigration," *New York Times*, May 15, 2006; Office of Strategic Initiatives, "Broad Support for Comprehensive Immigration Reform," May 15, 2006, Todd Braunstein Files, Box 2, Folder: Immigration Files, Federalism-EO [2], GWBPP, GWBPL, 1–2; "U.S. Bishops Urge Immigration Reform," *America*, May 29, 2006, 6; "Immigration Reform," *Commonweal*, June 2, 2006, 1.

58. Feuerherd, "Bishops United for Immigration,"1.

59. Rachel Swarns, "Senate, in Bipartisan Act, Passes an Immigration Bill," *New York Times*, May 26, 2006, 1; Tom Head, "Comparing 2006 House and Senate Immigration

Bills—H.R. 4437 and S. 2611," n.d., *about.com*, at http://civilliberty.about.com/od/immigrantsrights/p/hr4437s2611.htm, 1.

60. "Catholic Bishops Applaud Senate Version of Immigration Bill; Call for Continued Pressure to Ensure Dignity for Immigrants," May 26, 2006, *Education for Justice*, n.d., at https://educationforjustice.org/node/2484, 1.

61. "Immigration," *Congress and the Nation, 2005–2008*, 694; Kathleen Arnold, *American Immigration after 1996* (University Park, Pa.: Penn State University Press, 2011), 1.

62. Karl Rove, *Courage and Consequence* (New York: Simon and Schuster, 2010), 470.

63. Mark Pattison, "Bush Touts Catholic Schools, Immigration Reform at Prayer Breakfast," *Catholic News Service*, April 13, 2007, 1.

64. Rosenblum, "U.S. Immigration Policy Since 9/11," 8.

65. "Testimony of Thomas Wenski, Bishop of Orlando, Florida, before the House Subcommittee," May 22, 2007, 1–14.

66. David Van Biema, "A Church Haven for Illegal Aliens," *Time*, July 19, 2007, 2; "Churches in Five Cities to Offer Sanctuary to Illegal Immigrants," *Fox News*, May 9, 2007.

67. "Churches in Five Cities," 1; "Churches Providing Sanctuary for Illegal Immigrants," *PBS News Hour*, June 18, 2007.

68. "Churches Providing Sanctuary," *PBS News Hour*, June 18, 2007; Brooke Levitske, "Illegal Immigration and the Church: Philanthropic Lawlessness," *Acton Institute for the Study of Religion and Liberty*, July 11, 2007, 1.

69 Angie Drobnic Holan, "John McCain Said That Barack Obama Voted Against Part of Immigration Reform," *Tampa Bay Times*, July 7, 2010, 1.

70. Ryan Lizza, "Getting to Maybe," *The New Yorker*, June 24, 2013, 53.

71 Bush, *Decision Points*, 305; "Immigration Policy," CSPAN-TV, October 1, 2013.

72. "Dreams on Hold," *America*, November 26, 2007, 1.

73. "Immigration's Dark Moments," *America*, October 13, 2008, 1; "Testimony of Most Rev. José H. Gomez, Coadjutor Archbishop of Los Angeles, Chair, United States Conference of Catholic Bishops Committee on Migration on ICE Worksite Enforcement, before the House Judiciary Committee on Immigration Policy and Enforcement," January 26, 2011, *The Migration Review*, vol. 1, January–February 2011, 9; J. D. Long-Garcia, "Fault Lines: The Immigration Debate Continues," *U.S. Catholic*, January 2009, 1–3.

74. Levitske, "Illegal Immigration and the Church," 1; "Bishops Criticize Federal Raid Policies," *America*, March 3, 2008, 7.

75. Patricia Zapor, "States Take up Immigration Bills as Congress Staying on Sidelines," *Catholic News Service*, April 21, 2008, 1, 3.

76. Daniel Wakin and Julia Preston, "Pope Speaks up for Immigrants, Touching a Nerve," *New York Times*, April 20, 2008, 1–2.

77. Wakin and Preston, "Pope Speaks up for Immigrants, Touching a Nerve," 1–2.

78. Chris Hawley and Sergio Solache, "Vatican Enters Illegal Immigration Debate," *Arizona Republic*, April 16, 2008.

79. Long-Garcia, "Fault Lines: The Immigration Debate Continues," 3–4; Karen Manges Douglas and Rogelio Saenz, "The Criminalization of Immigrants and the Immigration-Industrial Complex," *Daedalus* 142 (Summer 2013), 205; "Iowa Immigration Raid Spurs Church Response," *America*, September 8, 2008, 6.

80. "Church Works to Suspend Immigration Raids," *America*, September 8, 2008, 6.

81. Aarti Kohli, Peter L. Markowitz, and Lisa Chavez, "Secure Communities by the Numbers: An Analysis of Demographics and Due Process," October 2011, Chief Justice Earl Warren Institute on Law and Public Policy, University of California, Berkeley Law School; "Church Works," *America*, 6.

82. "Bishop Wenski Seeks Balanced, Humane Immigration Policy in 2008," *Catholic News Services*, October 20, 2008, 1–2; Long-Garcia, "Fault Lines: The Immigration Debate Continues," 13.

83. Bush, *Decision Points*, 306.

Notes to Chapter 5

1 Bill Schneider, "Skinny Kid with a Funny Name Makes Good," *CNN Politics*, July 30, 2004, at http://articles.cnn.com/2004-07-03/politics/obama; "Modes of Entry for the Unauthorized Migrant Population," *Pew Research Hispanic Trends Project*, May 22, 2006, at http://www.pewhispanic.org/2006/05/22/modes-of-e; Alan Gomez, "Panel OK's Plan to Fingerprint Foreigners," *USA Today*, May 22, 2013, sec. A, 5.

2. "Protection for Haitians," *America*, April 20–27, 2009, 5.

3. "Protection for Haitians," 5.

4. "Haiti," *New York Times*, August 26, 2012.

5. Marie Arana, "The Migrant Cash Lifeline," *International Herald Tribune*, May 17, 2013, 13; Peter Finney, "Rebuilding Haiti: An Unprecedented Challenge," *Clarion Herald*, January 22, 2011, 2–4.

6. Donald Kerwin, "The Faltering U.S. Refugee System," *Migration Policy Institute*, May 2011, 32.

7. "President Obama Signs Presidential Determination Authorizing Up to 800,000 Refugee Admissions in Fiscal Year 2010," *The White House Office of the Press Secretary*, September 30, 2009.

8. Edward Alden, "Obama Quietly Changes U.S. Immigration Policy," *New America Media*, December 28, 2009.

9. Kerwin, "The Faltering U.S. Refugee System," 1; "Refugees," *The Migration Review*, Vol.1, January–February 2011, 17; Joel Millman, "More Illegal Immigrants Ask for Asylum," *Wall Street Journal*, October 17, 2013, sec. A, 1; Mark Hetfield, "When an Asylum Claim Is the Only Way to See a Judge," Letters to the Editor, *Wall Street Journal*, October 26–27, 2013, sec. A, 12.

10. Archbishop José Gómez, "Immigration Reform after the Election," *Origins Online*, November 13, 2008, at http://orginsplus.catholicnews.com/plueb-cgi/fastweb?state_id=1336877452Eview=origi, 1.

11. David Agren, "Catholic Leaders Hopeful That Obama Will Change U.S. Immigration Policy," *Catholic News Service*, January 20, 2009, 2.

12. Barack Obama, "Interview with Regional Reporters," March 11, 2009, *Public Papers of the Presidents of the United States: Barack Obama, Book I, 2009, January 20 to June 30, 2009* (Washington, D.C.: U.S. Government Printing Office, 2010), 128.

13. Nebraska Bishops, "Immigration: A Call to Be Patient, Hospitable, and Active for Reform," *Origins Online*, March 26, 2009, at http://orginsplus.catholicnews.com/plueb-cgi/fastweb.state_id=1336956058Eveiw=origi, 1.

14. Ryan Lizza, "Getting to Maybe," *The New Yorker*, June 24, 2013, 45.

15. "Signs of the Times," *America*, August 7, 2009, 1.

16. Margaret Ramírez, "Two Nuns from Sisters of Mercy Focus on Jailed Immigrants," *Chicago Tribune*, August 9, 2009, 2.

17. Barack Obama, "Address before a Joint Session of the Congress on Health Care Reform," September 9, 2009, *Public Papers of the Presidents of the United States: Barack Obama, Book II, 2009, July 1–December 31, 2009* (Washington, D.C.: U.S. Government Printing Office, 2013), 1366.

18. Patricia Zapor, "Bishops Talk Health Care, Immigration with Members of Congress," *Catholic News Service*, September 18, 2009, 1–2.

19. "News Briefs," *America*, December 14, 2009; Nancy Frazier O' Brien, "Immigration Reform Next Up on Bishops' Wish List for Congress," *Catholic News Service*, November 25, 2009, 1–2.

20. "Reasonable Reform," *Commonweal*, May 17, 2010, 1–2.

21. Peter Wallsten, "An Uneasy Alliance," *Washington Post*, June 10, 2012, sec. A, 1.

22. Ibid., 8.

23. Ibid., 9.

24. "Widow of Slain Rancher Reflects on Border Debate," *America*, August 30–September 6, 2010, 8.

25. Bishop Joseph Galante, "Every Person Is a Neighbor," *Origins Online*, May 20, 2010, at http://orginsplus.catholicnews.com/plueb-cgi/fastueb?state_id=1336789895&veiw=origi, 1.

26. Roger Mahony, "Thank You, Arizona," *America*, June 7, 2010, 1.

27. Mahony, "Thank You, Arizona," 1; J. D. Long-Garcia, "Bishops, Other Faith Leaders Commend Ruling on Arizona Immigration Law," *Catholic News Service*, July 29, 2010, 1.

28. Archbishop Rafael Romo Muñoz and Bishop John Wester, "U.S. and Mexican President Urged to Work on Migration Issues," *Origins Online*, June 3, 2010, at http://orginsplus.catholicnews.com/plueb?state_is=1336634809&view=origi, 2.

29. Wallsten, "An Uneasy Alliance," 8–9.

30. "Dream On," *America*, July 19, 2010, 2.

31. Mark Pattison, "DREAM Act Dies in Senate: Immigration Advocates Remain Determined," *Catholic News Service*, December 10, 2010, 1.

32. Bob Woodward, *The Price of Politics* (New York: Simon and Schuster, 2012), 65.

33. "USCCB Agenda Takes Flight as Session Ends," *America*, December 20, 2010; Nancy Frazier O'Brien, "Despite Defeat, Catholic Official Sees Progress on Dream Act," *Catholic News Service*, September 27, 2010, 1.

34. Wallsten, "An Uneasy Alliance," 9; Michael Shear, "Obama's Defender of Borders Reverts to Voice for Migrants," *New York Times*, May 6, 2013, sec. A, p. 9.

35. Wallsten, "An Uneasy Alliance," 9.

36. "Immigration Advocates: Secure Communities Bring Fear, Not Trust," *America*, August 29, 2011.

37. "Guatemalan Workers in Iowa Reunite with Family Members," *America*, January 3, 2011.

38. "Testimony of Most Rev. José H. Gómez, Coadjutor Archbishop of Los Angeles, Chair, United States Conference of Catholic Bishops Committee on Migration, on ICE Worksite Enforcement, before the House Judiciary Committee on Policy and Enforcement," January 26, 2011, *The Migration Review*, 7; "Immigration Advocates: Secure Communities Brings Fear, Not Trust."

39. Aarti Kohli, Peter L. Markowitz, and Lisa Chavez, "Secure Communities by the Numbers: An Analysis of Demographics and Due Process," Chief Justice Earl Warren Institute on Law and Public Policy, University of California, Berkeley Law School, October 2011.

40. Karen Manges Douglas and Rogelio Saenz, "The Criminalization of Immigrants and the Immigration-Industrial Complex," *Daedalus* 142 (Summer 2013), 218; "Immigration Advocates: Secure Communities Brings Fear, Not Trust," 1; Susan Page, "Hispanics True Blue Again for Obama," *USA Today*, February 22, 2013, sec. A, 2.

41. Julia Preston and Helene Cooper, "After Chorus of Protest, New Tune on Deportations," *New York Times*, June 18, 2012, sec. A., 12; Julia Preston, "Agents Sue Over Deportation Suspensions," *New York Times*, August 24, 2012, sec. A, 17.

42. Mark Halperin and John Heilemann, *Double Down* (New York: Penguin, 2013), 56–58; Samuel Freedman, "Pews Tirelessly Restored, and an Immigrant Redeemed," *New York Times*, December 15, 2012, sec. A, 13.

43. Patricia Zapor, "New Policy on Deportation Reviews Could Allow Some to Stay in U.S.," *Catholic News Service*, August 22, 2012, 1–2.

44. Catholic Bishops of the United States, "Forming Consciences for Faithful Citizenship," *United States Conference of Catholic Bishops*, October 2011, at http://usccb.org/issues-and-action/faithful-citizenship/, 25.

45. "Annual Mass Unites Both Sides, Even Through a Border Fence," *America*, November 21, 2011.

46. Mark Landler, "Hispanic Adviser is Promoted at White House," *New York Times*, January 10, 2012, 2.

47. Shear, "Obama's Defender of Borders Reverts to Voice for Migrants," 1.

48. "U.S. Bishops in Fifty-State Approach to Immigration," *America*, January 2, 2012.

49. Marie Mischel, "Advocates Say Tough New State Laws Make Immigration Reform More Urgent," *Catholic News Service*, January 18, 2012, 1–3.

50. "Cardinal Urges Catholic College Leaders to Embrace Immigrant Reform," *Catholic News Service*, February 1, 2012, 1.

51. Brian Bennett, "Obama Proposes Immigration Tweak," *Chicago Tribune*, March 31, 2012, sec. 1, 3.

52. "U.S. Catholic Bishops Argue against Arizona's S.B. 1070 on Religious Liberty Grounds," *Center for Migration Studies*, New York, March 29, 2012.

53. Nancy Frazier O' Brien, "Catholics Urged to Resist Unjust Laws, Join in 'Fortnight for Freedom,'" *Catholic News Service*, April 12, 2012, 1–3; "Our First, Most Cherished Liberty: A Statement on Religious Liberty," *United States Conference of Catholic Bishops*, at http://www.usccb.org/issues-and-action/religious-liberty, 2.

54. "The Bishops and Religious Liberty," *Commonweal*, May 30, 2012.

55. "Testimony from Sister JoAnn Persch," *Connect with Mercy*, May 7, 2012, at http://mercysisters.wordpress.com/2012/05/07/testimony-from-sister-joann-persch.

56. Aracely Cruz, "Will Congress Bring My Husband Back?" *New York Times*, June 13, 2013, sec. A, 25; Halperin and Heilemann, *Double Down*, 294.

57. Christi Parsons, Brian Bennett, and Joseph Tarifani, "Obama Shifts on Immigration," *Chicago Tribune*, June 16, 2012, sec. 1, 1, 7.

58. "Dream Deferred: An Interview with Rep. Luis Gutiérrez on Immigration Reform," *U. S. Catholic*, June 2012; "Immigration Solutions?" *Commonweal*, July 13, 2012, 1.

59. "USCCB Statement on the Announcement of Deferred Action for DREAM Eligible Youth," *United States Conference of Catholic Bishops, Justice for Immigrants*, at http://www.justiceforimmigrants.org/index.shmtl, 1.

60. Georgia Pabst, "Immigrant Event Draws Hundreds," *Milwaukee Journal Sentinel*, August 20, 2012, sec. A, 7.

61. Kirk Semple, "Undocumented Life Is a Hurdle as Immigrants Seek a Reprieve," *New York Times*, October 4, 2012, sec. A, 24.

62. David Savage, "Court Draws Line on Immigration," *Chicago Tribune*, June 26, 2012, sec. 1, 1, 12.

63. "Bishops Greet Supreme Court Decision on Immigration with Hope, Caution," *National Catholic Reporter*, June 25, 2012.

64. Campbell Robertson and Julia Preston, "Appeals Court Draws Boundaries on Alabama Immigration Law," *New York Times*, August 22, 2012, sec. A, 19.

65. Ian Lovett, "Los Angeles to Cease Transferring Immigrants," *New York Times*, October 5, 2012, sec. A, 14.

66. Mosi Secret and William Rashbaum, "7-Eleven Owners and Managers Charged in Immigration Raids," *New York Times*, June 18, 2013, sec. A, 17.

67. "FY2013 ICE Immigration Removals," *U.S. Immigration and Customs Enforcement*, n.d., at http://www.ice.gov/doclib/about/offices/ero/pdf/201; Alan Gomez, Natalie DiBlasio, and Leigh Giangreco, "Thousands Rally for Immigration Bill," *USA Today*, April 12, 2013, sec. A, 3.

68. Fernanda Santos, "Shootings by Agents Increase Border Tensions," *New York Times*, June 11, 2013, sec. A, 1, 16.

69. Julia Preston, "Polled Latinos Favor Obama," *New York Times*, October 12, 2012, sec. A, 14; "A Nation of Immigrants," *Pew Research Hispanic Center*, January 29, 2013, at http://www.pewhispanic.org/2013/01/29/a-nation-of-immigrants/, 3–4; Mitchell Landberg, "Catholicism Unites, Issues Divide Rivals," *Chicago Tribune*, October 11, 2012, sec. A, 17.

70. David Lauter, "Obama, Romney Come out Swinging," *Chicago Tribune*, October 17, 2012, sec. A., 17; "A Nation of Immigrants," *Pew Research Hispanic Center*, 3; Brian Bennett, Hector Becerra, and David Lauter, "Latino Vote Puts Reform at Forefront," *Chicago Tribune*, November 8, 2012, sec. 1, 8; "President Obama's First Reelection Press Conference," November 14, 2012, at http://abcnews.go.com/Politics/POTUS/transcript-obama.

71. Brian Bennett, "Next for Obama: Immigration Bill," *Chicago Tribune*, December 7, 2012, sec. 1, 23.

72. Clarence Page, "Immigration as a New GOP Wedge Issue," *Chicago Tribune*, June 23, 2013, sec. 1, 23.

73. Michael Gerson, "The GOP's Tricky Navigation," *Washington Post*, June 18, 2013, sec. A, 15.

74. Van Le, "PICO Launches 'Separated Families Supper Table,' About Immigrant Families Torn Apart by Broken System," *America's Voice*, January 17, 2013.

75. Lizza, "Getting to Maybe," 46–48.

76. Ibid., 49.

77. Alan Gomez, "Next Fight: 'Amnesty,'" *USA Today*, January 30, 2013, sec. A, 1–2.

78. Michael Shear and Julia Preston, "Obama Plan Sees Eight-Year Wait for Illegal Immigrants," *International Herald Tribune*, February 19, 2013, 4.

79. Michael Shear and Mark Landler, "Obama Takes a Firm Hand on Immigration Overhaul," *International Herald Tribune*, February 1, 2013, 5.

80. Shear and Landler, "Obama Takes a Firm Hand on Immigration Overhaul"; Shear and Preston, "Obama Plan Sees Eight-Year Wait for Illegal Immigrants," 4.

81. Manya Brachear, "Catholics Laud Election of First Latin American, Jesuit Pontiff," *Chicago Tribune*, March 14, 2013, sec. 1, 22.

82. Lizza, "Getting to Maybe," 49–50.

83. Michael Shear and Ashley Parker, "Senate Vote Helps Illegal Immigrants Take First Step to Citizenship," *New York Times*, March 18, 2013, sec. A, 11.

84. Lizza, "Getting to Maybe," 50.

85. Kevin Clarke, "A Dolan Détente?" *America*, February 27, 2013, 2; "USCCB President Says Now is the Time to Reform Immigration System," *United States Conference of Catholic Bishops*, April 22, 2013, at http://www.usccb.org/news/2013/13-075/.cfm, 1.

86. Lizza, "Getting to Maybe," 51; Ashley Parker and Steven Greenhouse, "Deal Opens Way for U.S. Immigration Overhaul," *International Herald Tribune*, April 1, 2013, 4.

87. "Citizenship, Values, and Cultural Concerns: What Americans Want from Immigration Reform," *Public Religion Research Institute*, March 2013, at http://publicreligion.org/research/2013/03/2013-religion-v, 29, 31.

88. "Immigration Reform Efforts Funded," *America*, March 25, 2013.

89. Gomez, DiBlasio, and Giangreco, "Thousands Rally for Immigration Bill."

90. Katherine Skiba, "Hopes High on Immigration Front," *Chicago Tribune*, March 20, 2013, sec. 1, 11; Aamer Madhan, "Obama: Congress Needs to Hustle Up Immigration Bill," *USA Today*, March 27, 2013, sec. A, 5.

91. Julia Preston, "U.S. Citizens Join Immigrants in Pressing Lawmakers for Change," *New York Times*, March 14, 2013, sec. A, 22; Lolly Bowean, "Protesters Want Deportation Freeze," *Chicago Tribune*, December 25, 2012, sec. 1, 5; Brian Bennett, "High Deportation Numbers are Misleading," *Los Angeles Times*, April 1, 2014; Ginger Thompson and Sarah Cohen, "Minor Infractions Behind Most U.S. Deportations," *International New York Times*, April 8, 2014, 8; John Hicks, "ICE Chief Morton to Leave Agency," *Washington Post*, June 18, 2013, sec. B, 4.

92. Miriam Jordan, "Young Immigrants' Applications Fall," *Wall Street Journal*, March 15, 2013, sec. A, 2; "USCCB President Says," *United States Conference of Catholic Bishops*, 1.

93. Scott Clement and Sean Sullivan, "Americans Want to Have Their Cake and Eat It Too," *Washington Post*, April 17, 2013.

94. Clarke, "A Dolan Détente?"; Manya Brachear Pashman, "Immigrant Groups Face Dilemma Over Funding," *Chicago Tribune*, October 19, 2013, sec. 1, 5.

95. Michael Sean Winters, "2013: Immigration Reform," *National Catholic Reporter*, January 9, 2013, 2; "Senate Vote Helps Illegal Immigrants Take First Step to Citizenship," *South China Morning Post*, May 23, 2013, sec. A, 14.

96. Clement and Sullivan, "On Immigration Reform," 1; Alan Gomez, "Senators Trying to Find Balance in Debate Over Immigration," *USA Today*, April 24, 2013, sec. A, 2; Byron York, "Could There Be Another Wave of Illegal Immigrants?" *Washington Examiner*, April 29, 2013.

97. Susan Davis and Alan Gomez, "GOP Districts Get Less Hispanic," *USA Today*, May 30, 2013, sec. A, 4; Lisa Mascaro, "Senators Eye Compromise on Immigration Overhaul," *Chicago Tribune*, June 20, 2013, sec. 1, 15; Jonathan Weisman, "In Round Three, Immigration Bill Faces Senate Opponent Who Won Rounds One and Two," *New York Times*, June 18, 2013, sec. A, 14.

98. Ashley Parker, "Two Senators Close to a Deal on Border Security," *New York Times*, June 20, 2013, sec. A, 19; Thomas Ferraro and Richard Cowan, "Negotiations Bring Bipartisan Support for Immigration Bill," *Milwaukee Journal Sentinel*, June 20, 2013, sec. A, 5.

99. Alan Gomez, "Battle Over the Border: GOP Plan Fails in Senate," *USA Today*, June 14, 2013, sec. A, 9; Ashley Parker, "Savior or Saboteur? A Texas Senator Shakes Up the Immigration Debate," *New York Times*, June 15, 2013, sec. A, 12.

100. David Nakamura, "GOP Walking Immigration Tightrope," *Washington Post*, June 13, 2013, sec. A, 4.

101. Rich Lowry, "The Border-Enforcement Game," *New York Post*, June 18, 2013, 23.

102. Mascaro, "Senators Eye Compromise."

103. Ashley Parker, "Senate Vote on Border Gives Push to Immigration Overhaul," *New York Times*, June 25, 2013, sec. A, 16.

104. Ed O'Keefe, "Immigration Overhaul Clears Senate," *Minneapolis Star Tribune*, June 28, 2013, sec. A, 8; Sara Murray and Janet Hook, "Immigration Bill Clears Senate," *Wall Street Journal*, June 28, 2013, sec. A, 4.

105. Murray and Hook, "Immigration Bill Clears Senate."

106. Patricia Zapor, "Senate Immigration Bill Passes, Moves to Uncertain Fate in House,"*National Catholic Reporter*, June 28, 2013.

107. O'Keefe, "Immigration Overhaul Clears Senate."

108. Thompson and Cohen, "Minor Infractions behind Most U.S. Deportations," 8;"Immigration Policy," CSPAN-TV, October 1, 2013; O'Keefe, "Immigration Overhaul Clears Senate."

109. Susan Davis and Alan Gomez, "House GOP Meets Over Immigration, Plans to Go Slow," *USA Today*, July 12, 2013, sec. A, 2.

110. Ashley Parker and Jonathan Weisman, "Republicans in House Resist Overhaul for Immigration," *New York Times*, July 11, 2013, sec. A, 3–4; "Of Courage and Cantaloupes," *New York Times*, August 4, 2013, sec,. A, 10; Georgia Pabst, "Immigration Reform May Be Stalling," *Milwaukee Journal Sentinel*, October 15, 2013, sec. A, 6.

111. Nate Silver, "Five Thirty-Eight," *New York Times*, February 3, 2013.

112. Ed O'Keefe and Sean Sullivan, "The Three Paths Forward for House Republicans on Immigration," *Washington Post*, July 11, 2013; George Will, "A Need for Compromise on Immigration," *Milwaukee Journal Sentinel*, November 14, 2013, sec. A, 11; Michael Sean Winters, "USCCB Continues to Back Immigration Bill," *National Catholic Reporter*, June 25, 2013.

113. Aaron Blake, "The GOP's Best Play on Immigration: A Path to Legalization," *Washington Post*, July 11, 2013.

114. Corrie Mitchell, "Nuns on the Bus Push Congress to Pass Immigration Reform," *Washington Post*, July 25, 2013.

115. Liz Goodwin, "Catholic Colleges to Catholic Members of Congress: Pass Immigration Reform," *Yahoo! News*, July 18, 2013, at http://news.yahoo.com/religious-colleges-to-catholic-members-of-congress-pass-immigrat, 1; "Immigration Reform Letter," *Association of Catholic Colleges and Universities*, July 18, 2013, at http://www.accunet.org/i4a/pages/index.cfm?pageid=3899; Ivone Guillen, "Catholic Educators Push Immigration Reform That Includes Citizenship," *Sojourners*, July 23, 2013, 1–2.

116. "Pope Francis Visits Italy's Migrant Island of Lampedusa," *BBC News*, July 8, 2013.

117. Ashley Parker and Michael Shear, "Catholic Push to Overhaul Immigration Goes to Pews," August 22, 2013, sec. A, 12, 16; Melissa Rogers, "Catholics Mobilize for Immigration Reform," *Winning the Future: President Obama and the Hispanic Community*, September 11, 2013, at http://www.whitehouse.gov; Homily by Rev. Robert Banks, September 8, 2013, transcribed by author.

118. Sylvia Puente, "Fight for Immigration Reform Continues," *Chicago Sun-Times*, October 11, 2013, 17; "Civil Disobedience Arrests Punctuate Immigration Reform Rally, March," *Catholic Sun*, October 11, 2013; Julia Preston, "Eight Lawmakers Arrested at Immigration Protest," *New York Times*, October 9, 2013, sec. A, 16; Becca Clemons, "House Members Arrested at Rally," *Chicago Tribune*, October 9, 2013, sec. 1, 15.

119. Julia Preston and Ashley Parker, "Democrats Aim to Restore Immigration to Agenda," *New York Times*, October 19, 2013, sec. A, 13; Alan Gomez, "Immigration Bills May Still Have Legs," *USA Today*, November 15, 2013, sec. A, 8; Ashley Parker and Michael Schmidt, "Boehner Rules Out Push on Immigration," *New York Times*, November 14, 2013, sec. A, 20; Christi Parsons, "Obama: I Won't Bypass House on Immigration," *Chicago Tribune*, November 26, 2013, sec. 1, 19; Ashley Parker, "Business-Conservative Alliance Presses for Immigration Action," *New York Times*, October 30, 2013, sec. A, 16; "President Obama Press Conference," CSPAN-TV, November 14, 2013; Mary Wisniewski, "Catholic Bishops in U.S. Pick Centrists as Leaders," *Chicago Tribune*, November 13, 2013, sec. 1, 17.

120. Alan Gomez, "GOP Insists Dems Must Bend on Immigration," *USA Today*, October 18, 2013, sec. A, 5; Michael Shear, "Obama Pitches Immigration Overhaul," *New York Times*, October 25, 2013, sec. A, 16.

121. "Immigration," CSPAN-TV, October 23, 2013; David Gibson, "Catholic Bishops Challenged to Adapt to Pope Francis' Priorities," *Washington Post*, November 11, 2013; William Chip, "The Folly of Comprehensive Immigration Reform," *First Things*, May 2014, 1–2; Katherine Burgess, "Immigration Activists Gather for Prayer Vigil at the 'Fast for Families," *Religion News Service*, November 13, 2013; "Obamas Meet Fasting Protesters," *New York Times*, November 30, 2013, sec. A, 13; Preston and Parker, "Democrats Aim to Restore," 13.

122. "Meet the Press," NBC-TV, December 1, 2013; Michael Shear and Ashley Parker, "Boehner Is Said to Back Change on Immigration," *New York Times*, January 2, 2014, sec. A, 9.

Notes to Conclusion

1. "Proposed Immigration Policy," n.d., Frank Hodsoll Files, Box 9, Folder: Immigration and Refugee Policy Development [1], Ronald Reagan Presidential Papers, Ronald Reagan Presidential Library, Simi Valley, Calif., 1; Katherine Vaughns, "Restoring the Rule of Law: Reflections on Fixing the Immigration System and Exploring Failed Policy Choices," *University of Maryland Journal of Race, Gender, and Class* 151 (2005), at http://www.digitalcommons.law.umaryland.edu.facpubs/121/,1.

2. Bishop Joseph Galante, "Every Person Is a Neighbor," *Origins Online*, May 20, 2010, at http://www.originsplus.catholicnews.som/plweb-cgi/fastweb; "Citizenship, Values, and Cultural Concerns: What Americans Want from Immigration Reform," *Public Religion Research Institute*, March 2013, at http://publicreligion.org/research/2013/03/2013/2013-religion-v, 29.

3. United States Catholic Conference, "Cultural Pluralism in the United States," April 14, 1980, in *Pastoral Letters of the United States Catholic Bishops, Volume IV*,

1975–1983, Hugh Nolan, ed. (Washington, D.C.: United States Catholic Conference, 1984), 365; John Donohue, "The Uneasy Immigration Debate," *America*, March 20, 1982, 209.

4. Donald Kerwin, "Immigration Reform and the Catholic Church," *Migration Information Source, United States Conference of Catholic Bishops*, at http://www.migration. information.org/Feature/print.cfm?ID=395, 2; "Second Presidential Debate, Full Transcript," *ABC News*, October 16, 2012.

5. "Refugee Resettlement," *Select Commission on Immigration and Refugee Policy*, Box 123, Folder: SCIRP Final Report and Recommendations, 1981, March 1, 1981, Theodore Hesburgh Papers, University of Notre Dame Archives, Notre Dame, Ind., xxiii; Kerwin, "Immigration Reform and the Catholic Church," 2; Michael Foley and Dean Hoge, *Religion and the New Immigrants* (New York: Oxford University Press, 2007), 9.

6. "Presidential Memorandum—Annual Refugee Admissions Numbers," September 28, 2012, at http://whitehouse.gov/the-press-office/2002/09/28/ presidential-memorandum-annual-annual.

7. Ronald Reagan, "The President's News Conference," October 19, 1983, *Public Papers of the Presidents of the United States: Ronald Reagan, 1981* (Washington, D.C.: U.S. Government Printing Office, 1982), 1488.

8. "Text of Obama's Speech on Immigration," *Wall Street Journal*, May 10, 2011, 6.

9. "A *Newsweek* Poll on Immigration," *Newsweek*, June 1–3, 1984, n.p., Edwin Meese Files, Box 46, Folder: Immigration [2], RRPP, RRPL; Bob Smietana, "Immigration Issues Touch Denominations," *USA Today*, March 22, 2012, sec. A, 3.

10. "Talking Points," n.d., Michael Uhlmann Files, Box 3, Folder: Immigration: Talking Points [Done with C. Collins 10/1/83] OA 9445, RRPP, RRPL; Memorandum from Ryan Bounds through Karl Zinsmeister to the President, n.d., Thomas Von Der Heydt Files, Box 1, Folder: Bush Record Policy Memos, Immigration—A Timeline (2001–2008) (1), George W. Bush Presidential Papers, George W. Bush Presidential Library, Dallas, Tex., 4; Frank Keating, "Immigration is a Most Conservative Cause," *Milwaukee Journal Sentinel*, November 14, 2013, sec. A, 11.

11. Suzy Khimm, "Want Tighter Border Security? You're Already Getting It," *Washington Post*, January 29, 2013, 1; Julia Preston, "Huge Amounts Spent on Immigration, Study Finds," *New York Times*, January 8, 2013, sec. A, 11.

12. Preston, "Huge Amounts Spent on Immigration, Study Finds"; Kevin Johnson and Alan Gomez, "Mexico's Commerce Crawls Back From Drug War's Chaos," *USA Today*, February 7, 2013, sec. A, 2; Alan Gomez, "Next Fight: 'Amnesty,'" *USA Today*, January 30, 2013, sec. A, 1–2; "A Nation of Immigrants," *Pew Research Hispanic Center*, January 29, 2013, at http://www.pewhispanic.org/2013/01/29/a-nation-of -immigrants/, 3.

13. Preston, "Huge Amounts Spent on Immigration, Study Finds"; "Border Security Remains Focus of Debate," *San Francisco Chronicle*, March 22, 2013, sec. D, 5; "Mission to Central America: The Flight of Unaccompanied Minors to the United States, Report of the Commission on Migration," *United States Conference of Catholic Bishops*, November 2013, at http://www.usccb.org/migration-and-refugee-services, 2.

14. Alan Gomez, "Border Security Could Kill Bill," *USA Today*, April 4, 2013, sec. A, 1–2; David Jackson, "Obama Pushes for Immigration Bill This Year," *USA Today*, October 24, 2013, sec. A, 1.

15. Letter from Rev. Timothy Dolan and Rev. José Gómez to Rep. John Boehner, *United States Conference of Catholic Bishops*, March 22, 2012, at http://www.usccb.org/issues-and-action/human-life-and-dignity/immigration/letter, 1–2.

16. "Action Alert: Now is the Time to Pass Just and Compassionate Immigration Reform," *Justice for Immigrants: The Catholic Campaign for Immigration Reform*, United States Conference of Catholic Bishops, at http://www.capwiz.com/justiceforimmigrants/issues/alert/?alertid=62312721&type=CO.

17. José Long-Garcia, "Fault Lines: The Immigration Debate Continues," *U.S. Catholic*, January 2009, 5; Interview with Bishop John Manz by author, September 20, 2012; Alistair McDonald, "As Disparities Grow, Canada Tightens Its Immigration Rules," *Wall Street Journal*, August 31, 2013, sec. A, 1, 10; Richard Fausset, "Trouble Along Mexico's Other Border," *Los Angeles Times*, August 4, 2013, sec. A, 1, 8.

18. Kerwin, "Immigration Reform and the Catholic Church," 3.

19. "Bishops Warn against Changes in Immigration Bill That Could Kill It," *National Catholic Reporter*, June 11, 2013, 2; James Carroll, "Sealing the Border Is Part of the Problem," *Boston Globe*, August 12, 2013, sec. A, 11.

20. Peter Meilaender, "Immigration: Citizens and Strangers," *First Things*, May 2007, 1; J. D. Long-Garcia, "Fault Lines: The Immigration Debate Continues," 5; Deal Hudson and Matt Smith, "Heeding Archbishop Gómez," *American Spectator*, December 15, 2011, 1.

21. Philip Martin, "Select Commission Suggests Changes in Immigration Policy—A Review Essay," *Monthly Labor Review* 105 (February 1982), 31; Stephen Camarota, "Religious Leaders vs. Members: An Examination of Contrasting Views on Immigration," *Center for Immigration Studies*, December 2009, at http://www.cis.org/print/ReligionAndImmigrationPoll; Jeffrey Jones, "Americans' Views of Immigration Holding Steady," *Gallup Poll*, June 22, 2011, at http://www.gallup.com/poll/148154/Americans-Views-Immigration-Holding-Steady.aspx; Chester Gillis, "American Catholics: Neither Out Far Nor in Deep," in *Religion and Immigration*, ed. Yvonne Yazbeck Haddad, Jane I. Smith, and John L. Esposito (Walnut Creek, Calif.: Altamire Press, 2003), 43.

22. James Kelly, "Data and Mystery: A Decade of Study on Catholic Leadership," *America*, November 15, 1989, 345; *Flock of Shepherds: A Discussion on the National Conference of Catholic Bishops: A FADICA Symposium* (Washington, D.C.: Foundations and Donors Interested in Catholic Activities, 1992), 31, 8.

23. *Flock of Shepherds: A FADICA Symposium*, 28.

24. Russell Shorto, "Slowly, Painfully Breaking Apart 'Irish Catholic,'" *International Herald Tribune*, February 12–13, 2011, 5; Bret Schulte, "Struggling to Keep the Faith," *U.S. News and World Report*, December 19, 2004.

25. Daniel Rigney, Jerome Matz, and Armondo Abney, "Is There a Catholic Sharing Ethic?" *Sociology of Religion* 65: 2004, 163; Richard Parker, "On God and Democrats,"

The American Prospect, March 2004, 4; Ian Brumberger, "Poll Shows Catholics Ignoring Church on Election Issues," *The Humanist*, September–October 2004, 5.

26. "Few Say Religion Shapes Immigration, Environment Views: Results from the 2010 Annual Religion and Public Life Survey," *Pew Forum on Religion and Public Life*, September 17, 2010, at http://www.pewforum.org/Politics-and-Elections/Few-Say, 5.

27. "Catholic Bishops: Don't Treat Illegal Immigrants as Criminals," *Los Angeles Times*, December 12, 2011; "Cardinal Who Shielded Abusers Is Removed from Public Duties," *International Herald Tribune*, February 2–3, 2013, 5.

28. "U.S. Religious Landscape Survey: Religious Affiliation—Diverse and Dynamic," *Pew Forum on Religion and Public Life*, February 2008, at http://www.religious.pewforum.org/pdf/report-religious-landscape-study-full-pdf, 6.

29. Hope Yen, "Demographics Blur Color Lines," *Milwaukee Journal Sentinel*, March 18, 2013, sec. A, 5; "Report to the American Board of Catholic Missions on the National Catholic Rural Life Conference's Southwest Project," Gregory Cusack Subject Files, Series 1.5, Box 3, Folder: Southwest Office, 1983–1985, National Catholic Rural Life Conference Records, Marquette University Archives, Milwaukee, Wis., 1; Jim Castelli and George Gallup, *The American Catholic People* (Garden City, N.Y.: Doubleday, 1987), 143; Kerwin, "Immigration Reform and the Catholic Church," 2.

30. Memorandum from Richard Wirthlin to Edwin Meese, James Baker, and Michael Deaver, May 28, 1981, Edwin Meese Files, Box 22, Folder: Immigration and Refugee Matters [1], OA 6518, RRPP, RRPL, 1; Memorandum from Henry Zuñiga to Elizabeth Dole through Diana Lozano, March 31, 1982, Elizabeth Dole Files, Box 5, Folder: Hispanics, January–June 1982 (4 of 5), RRPP, RRPL, 1, 7.

31. Ronald Reagan, "The President's News Conference," June 14, 1984, *American Presidency Project*, at http://www.presidency.ucsb.edu/ws/?pid=40049.

32. Rubén Rosario Rodríguez, "Symposium Review," *U.S. Catholic Historian* 30 (Fall 2012), 108; "Survey Highlights Struggles of Young Hispanic Catholics," *National Catholic Reporter*, October 24, 2011, 2.

33. Archbishop José Gómez, "Remarks on Immigration Policy," *Knights of Columbus*, August 3, 2011, at http://www.kofc.org/un/en/conv/2011/addresses/gomez.html; Liz Goodwin, "Catholic Colleges to Catholic Members of Congress: Pass Immigration Reform," *Yahoo! News*, July 18, 2013, at http://news.yahoo.com/religious-colleges-to-catholic-members-of-congress-pass-immigrat, 1; Dave Gibson, "Catholic Church Encourages Illegal Immigration after Losses from Molestation Scandal," *Examiner.com*, at http://www.examiner.com/article/catholic-church-encou.

34. Mark Hugo Lopez, "How Hispanics Voted in the 2008 Election," November 5, 2008, at http://pewresearch.org/pubs/1024/exit-poll-analysis-hispanics, 1.

35. Timothy Matovina, "Hispanic Catholics in the U.S.: No Melting Pot in Sight," *America*, March 16, 1991, 289–90.

36. Catherine Wilson, *The Politics of Latino Faith* (New York: New York University Press, 2008), 19–25; Richard Alba, Albert Raboteau, and Josh DeWind, eds., *Immigration and Religion in America* (New York: New York University Press, 2009), 15.

37. David Badillo, "Latino/ Hispanic History Since 1965: The Collective Transformation of Regional Minorities," in *Hispanic Catholic Culture in the United States*, ed. Jay Dolan and Allan Figueroa Deck (Notre Dame, Ind.: University of Notre Dame Press, 1994), 65, 68.

38. Arthur Jones, "Lobbying Game," *National Catholic Reporter*, June 3, 2005, 3; "Master Calendar: 2013 Advocacy/Education Actions for Comprehensive Immigration Reform," Office for Immigrant Affairs and Immigration Education, Archdiocese of Chicago, at http://www.archchicago.org/immigration.

39. "Law Briefs," *United States Catholic Conference*, May 1990, 1–2; "CREW Asks IRS to Investigate U.S. Conference of Catholic Bishops," *Citizens for Responsibility and Ethics in Washington*, November 2, 2012, at http://www.citizensforethics.org/legal-filings/entry/crew-asks-irs-investigate-cat, 2.

40. "Vatican Declaration on Abortion," *Origins*, December 12, 1974, 385; "Response of Cardinal Bernardin to Lt. Gen. Abrahamson," *Origins Online*, July 7, 1988, at http://originsplus.catholicnews.com/plweb/egi/fastweb?state.

41. "'Faithful Citizenship' Reissued without Major Changes," *America*, October 17, 2011, 1–2; "Forming Consciences for Faithful Citizenship," *United States Conference of Catholic Bishops*, October 17, 2011, at http://www.usccb.org/issues-and-action/faithful-citizenship/up, 3, 9.

42. Paul Baumann, "Rome's Cassandra: On George Weigel," *The Nation*, June 3, 2013, 3.

43. Susan Bibler Coutin, *The Culture of Protest: Religious Activism and the United States Sanctuary Movement* (Boulder, Colo.: Westview Press, 1993), 109–10; Philip Lawler, "Clarity, Please, on Illegal Immigration," *Catholic Culture.Org*, December 13, 2011, at http://www.catholicculture.org/commentary/oth.cfm?id=876.

44. Gómez, "The Immigration Crisis and the Duty of Christian Witness"; "Few Say Religion Shapes Immigration," *Pew Forum*, 5; Antonio Spadaro, "A Big Heart Open to God," *America*, September 30, 2013, 8; "Immigration Policy," CSPAN-TV, October 1, 2013.

45. Philip Lawler, "How Catholics Might Advance the Debate on Immigration," *Catholic Culture.Org*, December 6, 2011, at http://www.catholicculture.org/oth.cfm?id=875.

46. Michael Sean Winters, "USCCB All-In on Immigration Reform," *National Catholic Reporter*, April 23, 2013, at http://ncronline.org/print/blogs/distinctly-catholic/uscc.

47. "Catholic Nun and DNC Speaker Simone Campbell on Abortion: 'That's Beyond My Pay Grade," *The Weekly Standard*, September 5, 2012, at http://www.weeklystandard.com/blogs/catholic-nun-dr; David Gibson, "'Nuns on the Bus' Will Hit the Road for Immigration Reform," *Huffington Post*, May 1, 2013, at http://www.huffingtonpost.com/2013/05/01/nuns-on-the-bus-will-hit-the-road-for-immigra.

48. Alan Simpson, *Right in the Old Gazoo: What I Learned in a Lifetime of Meeting the Press* (New York: William Morrow, 1997), 68–69; Philip Schrag, *A Well-Founded Fear: The Congressional Battle to Save Political Asylum in America* (New York: Routledge, 2000), 251; Michael Chertoff, Carlos Gutierrez, and Joel Kaplan, "Press Briefing on Immigration Reform," n.d., Thomas Von Der Heyt Files, Box 2, Folder: Immigration—A Timeline," GWBPP, GWBPL, 9.

49. David Iaconangelo, "Immigration Reform 2013: Ten Activists Arrested for Blocking New York City Street," *Latin Times*, August 22, 2013; "Immigration Policy," CSPAN-TV.

50. Marc Rosenblum, "U.S. Immigration Policy Since 9/11: Understanding the Stalemate Over Comprehensive Immigration Reform," *Migration Policy Institute*, 2011, 12.

51. Schrag, *A Well-Founded Fear: The Congressional Battle*, 82.

52. Laura Sheahen, "When Did We See You a Stranger? Cardinal Theodore McCarrick on Immigration," *Beliefnet*, April 2006, at http://www.beliefnet.com/Faiths/Christianity/2006/04/When-Did-We-See-You-A-Stranger-Cardinal-Theodore-McCarrick-On-Immigration,aspx?p=1, 2; Hudson and Smith, "Heeding Archbishop Gómez," 1.

53. "Newsmakers," CSPAN-TV, August 30, 2013; Ross K. Baker, "Lobbyists Can't Win on Immigration," *USA Today*, October 1, 2013, sec. A, 8.

54. Esther Cepeda, "Immigration Reform's Long Odds," *Milwaukee Journal Sentinel*, August 22, 2013, sec. A, 9; Julia Preston, "Illegal Immigrants Are Divided Over Importance of Citizenship," *New York Times*, November 21, 2013, sec. A, 1.

55. Ana Gonzalez-Barrera, Mark Hugo Lopez, Jeffrey S. Passel, and Paul Taylor, "The Path Not Taken," *Pew Research Center*, February 4, 2013, at http://www.pewhispanic.org/2013/02/04/the-path-not-taken, 1; Mark Hugo Lopez, Paul Taylor, Cary Funk, and Ana Gonzalez-Barrera, "On Immigration Policy, Deportation Relief Seen as More Important Than Citizenship," *Pew Research Center*, December 19, 2013, at http://www.pewhispanic.org/2013/12/19/on-immigration-policy-deportation-relief-seen-a, 1; Peter Skerry, "No Kidding," *The Weekly Standard*, August 12, 2013, 15; Preston, "Illegal Immigrants are Divided," 3.

56. Michael Novak, "Defining Social Justice," *First Things*, December 2000, 1.

57. E. J. Dionne, *Souled Out: Reclaiming Faith and Politics after the Religious Right* (Princeton: Princeton University Press, 2008), 176, 178.

58. "By the Comptroller General: Report to the Congress of the United States," 1980, Box 122, Folder: [SCIRP—Immigration], Draft Options &Recommendations, 1980, THP, UNDA, 16; "U.S. Immigration Organizations: Advocacy, Legal, Lobbying," n.d., at http://www.husterman.com/immigrationorganizations.html; Kathleen Arnold, *American Immigration After 1996* (University Park, Pa.: Penn State University Press, 2011), 17.

59. Gary Gerstle, "Minorities, Multiculturalism, and the Presidency of George W. Bush," in *The Presidency of George W. Bush*, Julian Zelizer, ed. (Princeton, N.J.: Princeton University Press, 2010), 275.

60. Jose Antonio Vargas, "Not Legal, Not Leaving," *Time*, June 25, 2012, 29.

61. "Jose Antonio Vargas: Immigrant Hero," *New York Post*, February 15, 2013; "Comprehensive Immigration Reform," Senate Judiciary Committee, February 13, 2013, available at http://www.judiciary.senate.gov/hearings/hearing.cfm?i ,1.

62. "Catholic Bishops: Don't Treat Illegal Immigrants as Criminals," *Los Angeles Times*.

63. Raúl Reyes, "Immigration Reform Hopes for 2014," *USA Today*, December 26, 2013; Julia Preston and Rebekah Zemansky, "Demonstration at Arizona Border

Divides Supporters of Immigration Overhaul," *New York Times*, August 5, 2013, sec. A, 10; Alan Gomez, "Undocumented Migrants Fight Deportations," *USA Today*, September 19, 2013, sec. A, 7; Marc Rosenblum, "U.S. Immigration Policy Since 9/11: Understanding the Stalemate Over Comprehensive Immigration Reform," 8, 1.

64. "Immigration Reform," *Congress and the Nation, Vol. VII, 1985–1988* (Washington, D.C.: Congressional Quarterly, 1990), 717; Romano Mazzoli and Alan Simpson, "Enacting Immigration Reform Again," *Washington Post*, September 15, 2006, 1; Letter from Sen. Alan Simpson to Rep. Romano Mazzoli, February 5, 1984, Series VI, Box 362, Folder: 98th Congress, 1983–84 Immigration Subcommittee, Romano Mazzoli Papers, University of Louisville Archives, Louisville, Ky.

65. Interview with Bishop Manz by author.

66. Christopher Foreman, "Ambition, Necessity, and Polarization: The Obama Domestic Agenda," in *The Obama Presidency: Appraisals and Prospects*, ed. Bert Rockman, Andrew Rudalevige, and Colin Campbell (Los Angeles: Sage, 2012), 33.

67. Foreman, "Ambition, Necessity, and Polarization," 33; "GOP's Harsh Immigration Stances Repel a Natural Constituency," *USA Today*, August 28, 2012, sec. A, 6.

68. "Presidential Approval Ratings—George W. Bush," *Gallup*, at http://www.gallup .com/poll/116500/presidential-approval-rati; "Presidential Approval Ratings— Barack Obama, *Gallup*, at http://www.gallup.com/poll/116479/barack-obama -presidenti; "Job Performance Ratings for President Reagan," *Roper Center*, at http:// www.ropercenter.uconn.edu/roper/presidential/w.

69. Todd Purdum, "The Big Flip," *Vanity Fair*, June 2012, 2; Susan Davis, "Moderate Dems' Ranks Slip in House," *USA Today*, February 8, 2012, sec. A, 4; Clarence Page, "Republicans Divided by Immigration Debate," *Chicago Tribune*, October 30, 2013, sec. 1, 25.

70. Robert Schmuhl, "Going to Extremes," *Notre Dame Magazine*, Spring 2013, 53; Mary Jo Bane, "A House Divided," *Commonweal*, November 4, 2013; "Catholic Support for Immigration Reform Called a 'Moral Imperative'," *Catholic News Service*, July 16, 2013.

71. "Statement of the Most Rev. Robert Sanchez, Archbishop of Santa Fe, In Behalf of the United States Catholic Conference before the Subcommittee on Immigration and Naturalization of the Senate Committee on the Judiciary Concerning S. 3074, To Amend the Immigration and Nationality Act," March 17, 1976, 4; Ronald Reagan, "The President's News Conference," June 14, 1984.

72. "Press Conference of the Honorable William French Smith, Attorney General of the United States with Members of the Press," July 30, 1981, Frank Hodsoll Files, Box 1, Folder: Immigration [5], RRPP, RRPL, 9–10.

73. *Special Commission on Immigration and Refugee Policy, Second Semi-annual Report to Congress*, Box 123, Folder: [SCIRP—Imm], Second Semiannual Report to Congress, 1980, THP, UNDA, 145.

74. Otis Graham, *Immigration Reform and America's Unchosen Future* (Bloomington, Ind.: Author House, 2008), 325; "Amnesty Plus," 2006, Todd Braunstein Files, Box 3, Folder: Immigration Files [Immigration Reform], GWPP, GWBPL.

75. Interview with Bishop Manz by author; Barack Obama, "Remarks by the President on Immigration," June 15, 2012, at http://www.whitehouse.gov/the-press-office/2012/06/15/remarks-president-immigration, 1.

76. Christian Schneider, "Ryan Teaches Conservatives How to Talk," *Milwaukee Journal Sentinel*, June 19, 2013, sec. A, 13; Genevieve Wood, "Sorry, But It's Still Amnesty," *Milwaukee Journal Sentinel*, June 18, 2013, sec. A, 9.

77. Ronald Reagan, "Apples," November 29, 1977, in *Reagan in His Own Hand*, ed. Kiron Skinner, Annelise Anderson, and Martin Anderson (New York: The Free Press, 2001), 302.

78. Otis Graham, *Immigration Reform and America's Unchosen Future*, 387.

79. "President Obama's Second Inaugural Address," *Washington Post*, January 21, 2013.

80. Patricia Zapor, "Senate Immigration Bill Passes, Moves to Uncertain Fate in House," *National Catholic Reporter*, June 28, 2013, 1; Letter from Catholic Charities Maine Refugee and Immigration Services, Catholic Community Services Family Immigration Services, Catholic Legal Immigration Network, Inc., et al. to President Barack Obama, n.d., *National Immigration Forum*, at http://www.immigrationforum.org/images/uploads/ForgingCo,3.

81. Coutin, *The Culture of Protest*, 95.

82. Otis Graham, *Unguarded Gates: A History of America's Immigration Crisis* (New York: Rowman and Littlefield, 2004), 106.

83. Fernanda Santos, "Along with Dolls and Stuffed Animals, Making Time for Immigration Activism," *New York Times*, July 17, 2013; Esther Cepeda, "A Reality Check on Immigration," *Milwaukee Journal Sentinel*, August 29, 2013, sec. A, 9.

84. Marisa Gerber, "Gomez Takes Strong Stand on Immigration Bill," *Los Angeles Times*, August 3, 2013, sec. A, 11; Long-Garcia, "Fault Lines: The Immigration Debate Continues," 7; Joshua McElwee, "On Immigration Reform, Catholics Need Pulpit Speak," *National Catholic Reporter*, July 25, 2013, 3; Joshua McElwee, "Obama Issues Rallying Cry for Immigration Reform," *National Catholic Reporter*, October 24, 2013.

85. Jeff Sessions, "Migrants' Benefits Burden Taxpayers," *USA Today*, June 24, 2013, sec. A, 8; Manuel Roig-Franzia, "The Provocateur at the Border," *Washington Post*, June 18, 2013, sec. C, 1, 4; Susan Page, "Americans Conflicted on Immigration," *USA Today*, June 24, 2013, sec. A, 1–2.

86. Tom Krattenmaker, "Christian Left Can Learn From Right," *USA Today*, August 27, 2013, sec. A, 6.

87. V. Lance Tarrance and Associates and Peter D. Hart Research Associates, "Hispanic and Black Attitudes Toward Immigration Policy: A Nationwide Survey Conducted for Federation for American Immigration Reform," Executive Summary, June–July 1983, RRPP, RRPL, 5–6; Andrew Wroe, *The Republican Party and Immigration Politics* (New York: Palgrave MacMillan, 2008), 92.

88. James Davidson, Andrea Williams, Richard Lamanna, Jan Stenftenagel, Kathleen Maas Weigert, William Whalen, and Patricia Wittberg, *The Search for Common Ground* (Huntington, Ind.: Visitor Press, 1997), 166; "A Demographic Portrait of

Mexican-Origin Hispanics in the United States," *Pew Hispanic Center*, May 1, 2013, at www.pewhispanic.org, 7; "Survey Highlights Struggles of Young Hispanic Catholics," *National Catholic Reporter*, 2.

89. Elizabeth Dias, "Evangélicos!" *Time*, April 15, 2013, 20–22, 25; Frank Newport, "U.S. Catholic Hispanic Population Less Religious, Shrinking," *Gallup Poll*, February 25, 2013, at *http://www.gallup.com/poll/16091/catholic-hispanic-population-religions-shrinking*, 1.

90. Betsy Cooper and Kevin O'Neill, "Lessons from the Immigration Reform and Control Act," *Migration Policy Institute Policy Analysis* 3 (August 2005), 8; Marie Arana, "The Migrant Cash Lifeline," *International Herald Tribune*, May 17, 2013, 13.

91. Alan Gomez, "Improved Economy Draws Migrants," *USA Today*, October 26–28, 2012, sec. A, 1; "A Nation of Immigrants," *Pew Research Hispanic Center*, 1; Ted Fishman, "Immigrants Help Grow Our Economy," *USA Today*, February 5, 2013, sec. A, 9; Alan Gomez, "Illegal Immigration May Be Rising," *USA Today*, September 24, 2013, sec. A, 1; Damien Cave, "For Migrants, New Land of Opportunity Is Mexico," *New York Times*, September 22, 2013, sec. A, 1; Thomas Friedman, "How Mexico Got Back in the Game," *International Herald Tribune*, February 25, 2013, 8.

92. Mario Cuomo, "In the American Catholic Tradition of Realism," in *One Electorate under God? A Dialogue on Religion and American Politics*, ed. E. J. Dionne, Jean Bethke Elshtain, and Kayla Drogosz (Washington, D.C.: Brookings Institution Press, 2004), 15.

93. "America's Politics," *Commonweal*, September 13, 2013, 6.

94. Manya Brachear, "A Priest, a Scholar, and a Friend," *Chicago Tribune*, June 6, 2013, sec. 1, 12.

95. Vaughns, "Restoring the Rule of Law," 18; "Legalization and the Common Good," *Justice for Immigrants*, n.d., at http://www.justiceforimmigrants.org/documents/legalizatio.

Index

immigration reform, 53–74, 219; Immigration Reform and Control Act of 1986, 7, 35, 53; national identification cards, 58–59; riots by Cuban detainees, 33–34; Task Force on Immigration and Refugee Policy, 23, 25, 58–59

Reed, Bruce, 104, 117–18

Reese, Thomas, 128, 202

Refugee Act of 1980, 20, 24, 26, 53, 97, 209

Refugee Educational Assistance Act, 22

Refugee Relief Act, 6

refugees: asylum, 83–84, 101–6; Bush (George H. W.) administration policies and actions, 76–84; Bush (George W.) administration policies and actions, 125–31; Carter administration policies and actions, 20–22; Clinton administration policies and actions, 95–106; Cold War concerns and policy, 20; Cuban and Haitian under Reagan, 29–35; definitions of, 5, 6, 20–21; Hesburgh Commission, 19, 23–25; Obama administration policies and actions, 151–54; Reagan administration policies and actions, 22–53, 74; Reagan administration task force, 23; United Nations mandate, 19–20

Reid, Harry, 139, 144, 160, 185

Reilly, Robert, 40–41

Reim, Dan, 172, 180

"Relieving Third World Debt" (United States Catholic bishops), 89

religious liberty, 167–68

Rendón, Paula, 123

Reno, Donald, 42–43

Reno, Janet, 100, 102, 111

Rerum Novarum (Of New Things; Leo XIII), 9

"Resolution on Immigration Reform" (American bishops), 67

"Resolution on the Pastoral Concern of the Church for People on the Move" (American bishops), 21

Reyes, Raul, 216

Ricard, John (auxiliary bishop of Baltimore), 115

Riley, Francis, 55

Rising, Mark, 45

Rivera y Damas, Arturo (archbishop of San Salvador), 51–52

Roach, John (archbishop of St. Paul), 31, 39, 43–44

Roberts, Craig, 58

Robinson, James, 62

Robinson, Randall, 98–99

Rodi, Sharon, 23–24

Rodino, Peter, 67

Rodríguez, Juan, 159–60

Rodriguez, Mike, 45

Roe v. Wade, 209

Rolph, Elizabeth, 1

Román, Augustin (bishop of Miami), 33–34

Romero, Oscar (archbishop of San Salvador), 37

Romney, Mitt, 173, 218

Roosevelt, Franklin, 5–6

Rosazza, Peter (auxiliary bishop of Hartford), 44

Rosenblum, Marc, 2, 212, 216

Rove, Karl, 124, 139

Rozental, Andrés, 124

Rubio, Marco, 174–75, 177, 183, 190

Ruiz, Lorenzo, 41

Rumbaut, Rubén, 215

Ryan, Paul, 220

Ryscavage, Richard, 103

Saile, Kathy, 161

Salas, Angelica, 172

Sanchez, Robert (archbishop of Santa Fe), 20, 219

Sanctuary movement: dissension within, 45–48; internal memo on, 49; John Paul II and, 49–50; origins of, 35–37; prosecution of, 42–45; Reagan administration policy, 38–42, 45, 48–49

Sandoval, Moisés, 13

Sandweg, John, 166

San Pedro, Enrique (bishop of Galveston-Houston), 33

Santana, Olga, 133

Santos, Fernanda, 223

Refuge in the Lord: Catholics, Presidents, and the Politics of Immigration, 1981–2013 was designed in Quadraat with Quadraat Sans display type and composed by Kachergis Book Design of Pittsboro, North Carolina. It was printed on 60-pound Natures Book Natural and bound by Thomson-Shore of Dexter, Michigan.